Separated spouses

Separated spouses

A study of the matrimonial jurisdiction of magistrates' courts

O. R. McGREGOR
LOUIS BLOM-COOPER
COLIN GIBSON
LEGAL RESEARCH UNIT, DEPARTMENT OF SOCIOLOGY,
BEDFORD COLLEGE, UNIVERSITY OF LONDON

GERALD DUCKWORTH & CO LTD
3 HENRIETTA STREET LONDON WC2

First published in 1970 by
Gerald Duckworth & Company Ltd
3 Henrietta Street, London WC2

© *O. R. McGregor, Louis Blom-Cooper*
and Colin Gibson

Printed in Great Britain by
The Garden City Press Limited
Letchworth, Hertfordshire

ISBN 0 7156 0549 6

Contents

APPENDIXES

List of tables

List of figures

Preface

Little or nothing has been known about the family jurisdiction of magistrates' courts. We undertook this study to provide knowledge of a legal institution which handles annually thousands of broken marriages. We planned to investigate the legal and social characteristics of the jurisdiction so that we might compare the law in the text-books with the law in practice. We wished also to portray the wives and husbands who appear in these courts, to discover their opinions about the working of the jurisdiction, to evaluate their experiences, and to find out how many of them go on from the magistrates' court to the divorce court.

The main study was financed by the Nuffield Foundation. We are grateful both to the Trustees for their support and to Mr. Brian Young and Dr. K.W. Blyth for their help. For the preliminary work, we received a small grant from the Miriam Sacher Trust. At the request of the National Council for the Unmarried Mother and her Child, we included affiliation orders in our survey and the Council obtained for us a grant for the purpose from the Hilden Trust. At the request of the Committee on the Enforcement of Judgment Debts (the Payne Committee), we carried out a survey of attachment of earnings orders, which was financed by the Treasury.

At the outset, two of us (L.J.B-C. and O.R.M.) spent one summer examining the records of Croydon Magistrates' Court in order to test the feasibility of extracting data from court records. The then Clerk to the Croydon justices, Mr. A. J. Chislett, a past President of the Justices' Clerks' Society, hospitably accommodated us at his court and gave us much of his time and expert advice. At a later stage, we made a similar study of a court collecting office. One of us (C.S.G.) was fortunate to be invited by Mr. L. H. Crossley, Clerk to the Uxbridge justices and a past President of the Justices' Clerks' Society, to spend some months in his court. Mr. Chislett and Mr. Crossley were extremely helpful and we benefited from their unrivalled knowledge of the administration of this branch of magisterial jurisdiction. But in one respect we were unexpectedly misled. Much later, when we were immersed in the research, we discovered that the records kept by the courts administered by Mr. Chislett and Mr. Crossley were among the best in the country, and that our experience in their courts had raised expectations which were not always fulfilled elsewhere.

We could not even have begun to design our survey without the help of the Association of Municipal Corporations which allowed us to use its unpublished *Report* on the work-load of magistrates' courts throughout the country outside the London area. We were also fortunate that Miss J. Davison of the Organisation and Methods Division of the Treasury taught us how to interpret the information collected by the Association. When we reached the stage of asking courts in different parts of the country for their co-operation, we received indispensable help from Mr. G. I. de Deney, of the Home Office, who put himself to much trouble on our behalf. Later still, when we came to examine records in the Principal Registry in Somerset House and in District Registries throughout the country, we were entirely dependent upon the good offices of Sir John Compton Miller, Senior Registrar, Principal Probate and Divorce Registry, and of Mr. J. D. Kewish of the Lord Chancellor's Office.

We cannot here mention by name the large number of Justices' Clerks and their staffs who opened their records to us and who also assisted in the task of extracting data from them and helping us to understand them. We received similar help in respect of divorce records from Mr. B. Slater, of the County Courts Branch of the Lord Chancellor's Office, from Mr. B. P. Tickle, of the Principal Probate and Divorce Registry at Somerset House, and from District Registry staffs all over the country. As our work progressed, we came to appreciate that we were completely dependent upon court staffs. Their friendliness and cheerful willingness to add to their labours by helping us made it possible to complete the task of extracting data.

We held that it was essential to obtain information about the feelings and opinions of those who had experienced the jurisdiction, and we wished to learn particularly what these wives and husbands thought of the way they were treated by magistrates' courts. This part of our study could not have been undertaken without the help of Mr. Graham Stanford and of the *News of the World*. We thank the *News of the World* for its willing contribution to academic research.

Research in this field requires the active assistance of the legal authorities, of government departments, and of such bodies as the Magistrates' Association and the Justices' Clerks' Society. We were especially fortunate to receive such help through an Advisory Committee under the chairmanship of Sir Jocelyn Simon, President of the Probate, Divorce and Admiralty Division of the High Court, and having as members Professor J. N. D. Anderson, Director of the Institute of Advanced Legal Studies, University of London, Mr. L. H. Crossley, a past President of the Justices' Clerks' Society, Sir Charles Cunningham, formerly Permanent Under-Secretary of State, Home Office, Mr. Morris Finer, Q.C., Mr. W. R. Gowers, Solicitor, Mr. F. B. Hindmarsh (who succeeded Mr. F. Jackson), both of the Supplementary

Benefits Commission of the Department of Health and Social Security, Lord Merthyr, Chairman of Council of the Magistrates' Association, Lord Runcorn, who died in 1968, the last Chairman of the National Assistance Board, Sir Leslie Scarman, Chairman of the Law Commission, and Lady Summerskill. Members of the Advisory Committee made a major contribution to the research by giving their knowledge, advice and time. We are very sensible of our debt to their generosity. Needless to say, none of them is responsible for any statement or opinion in this book, and none can be held to have approved any part of it.

We are very grateful to our colleague, Professor A. R. Ilersic, who gave us statistical advice and guidance at all stages of the work. We are also indebted for statistical help to Dr. John Spring of Punch Card Services Ltd.

We have indicated briefly in our final chapter some of the conclusions which may follow from our findings. But we wish to emphasize that it is not our intention in this book to urge this or that scheme for the modification or reconstruction or abolition of the present jurisdiction. In particular, it may be thought that we have dealt (page 214) too cursorily with the proposal to substitute administrative action by the social security authorities for the jurisdiction of magistrates which the Committee on Statutory Maintenance Limits (the Graham Hall Committee) raised for discussion at the end of its *Report*. We make no apology. Informed discussion of this proposal would require a further investigation as well as separate and extensive treatment.

Finally, we thank Sir Jocelyn Simon who has done more than anyone else to promote this study. Indeed, we are so much in his debt that we are unable to make an adequate acknowledgement. Not only did he act as chairman of the Advisory Committee but he also gave us continuous support and encouragement. We shall always remember his unstinting aid and kindness.

O. R. MCGREGOR
LOUIS BLOM-COOPER
COLIN GIBSON

September, 1970

CHAPTER 1

The duty to maintain

After the Reformation, England maintained the jurisdiction of ecclesiastical courts over marriage and divorce, and their law of a formless and uncertain marriage contract combined with the rigorous theory of indissolubility of marriage prevalent in medieval times. Indeed, a principal effect of the Reformation on marriage in England was the abolition of the very evasions, fictions and loopholes which had made the medieval system tolerable in practice.

A cumbersome and expensive escape from the inconveniences of indissoluble marriage was provided from the end of the seventeenth century for a small number of husbands[1] wealthy enough to proceed by Private Act of Parliament. In the earliest cases Parliament provided by express enactment that the wife should not be left destitute. Later, the House of Commons came to have a functionary known as the "Ladies' Friend", an office usually filled by some member interested in the private business of Parliament, who undertook to see to it that any husband petitioning for divorce made suitable provision for his wife. Although clauses relating to the maintenance of the wife were not inserted in the Bills[2], it was well understood that they would not pass through Committee in the Commons unless husbands had entered into bonds to secure moderate incomes for their wives. This practice continued until the Private Act procedure was abolished in 1857, and it survived the objections of such members of the House of Lords as Lord Thurlow who denounced a principle which "is an encouragement to immorality and a gross injustice. It enables the woman who has injured her husband to carry part of that husband's fortune into the arms of her paramour, which is both an

---

[1] Between the end of the seventeenth century and 1857 there were some 330 Divorce Acts, only four of which were passed at the suit of a wife, the first being obtained by a Mrs. Addison in 1801. In 1798 the Parliamentary divorce procedure was regularized by standing orders of the House of Lords which required that all applications for Private Acts should be supported by a sentence of divorce *a mensa et thoro* from the ecclesiastical court, and by a verdict of damages for criminal conversation secured against the wife's seducer in the Common Law courts. In practice a husband could proceed against a merely adulterous wife but the four successful wives all proved adultery aggravated by some enormity such as incest.

[2] In 1811, the House of Commons neglected this precaution and required one husband to allow his wife £400 a year; when the Bill came back to the House of Lords, the Commons' clauses were rejected and the Bill abandoned.

incitement to the crime and a reward for it."[1] For the rest of the population, the only remedy for matrimonial difficulties was the divorce *a mensa et thoro* (the equivalent of a modern judicial separation) which could be granted only by the ecclesiastical courts on the grounds of the respondent's adultery or cruelty[2].

If the wife was the successful petitioner, the general rule seems to have been to award her one-third of the husband's income. If the husband's conduct had been particularly bad or if his income came largely from his wife's property which he had acquired on marriage, the court might award as much as one-half. The only sanction available to the ecclesiastical courts had been excommunication. After 1813 imprisonment by a writ *de contumace capiendo* was substituted but there is no record that it was ever successfully utilized. It may be doubted if wilfully defaulting husbands went in fear of the enforcement procedures of the ecclesiastical courts, at least after people ceased to believe in hell and damnation. This jurisdiction was transferred to the secular courts in 1857 when Private Act divorces were abolished for England[3]. The path had been cleared when the state intervened in 1753 by Lord Hardwicke's Marriage Act whereby for the first time public formalities were required to constitute a valid marriage. The provisions of the 1753 Act forced many papists and protestant dissenters to flout either the law or their consciences and led finally to the Marriage Act 1836 which broke the Church of England's exclusive control[4] over marriage by establishing an alternative and wholly secular rite.

The canon law and the common law obligation

In this state of affairs, it might have been expected that the common law courts, with more effective enforcement procedures at their disposal, would have entertained a method by which wives could obtain their maintenance. But the exclusive jurisdiction of the ecclesiastical courts over marriage and divorce led the common law courts after the middle of the seventeenth century to tend to avoid any intrusion upon the canon law's preserve. But, through a cluster of cases involving claims by tradesmen suing the husbands of wives to whom credit had been given, the common law courts found themselves willy-nilly involved in matrimonial law. Could a wife contractually bind her

---

[1] Quoted by Frederick Clifford, *A History of Private Bill Legislation* (1885), Vol. 1, p.413. This paragraph follows Clifford's account, pp. 387–422.

[2] If the wife were the petitioner, a decree of divorce *a mensa et thoro* could also be pronounced on the grounds that the husband had committed rape or an unnatural offence. The Matrimonial Causes Act 1857 preserved the existing grounds but added two years' desertion which was extended by the Matrimonial Causes Act 1884 to include failure to comply with a decree for restitution of conjugal rights. (P. M. Bromley, *Family Law* (3rd ed. 1966) p. 200.)

[3] They continued for Ireland.

[4] A submission along these lines failed to convince Sir Jocelyn Simon P. in *Padolecchia v. Padolecchia* [1968] P. 314, 316–17, 335[E].

husband when purchasing on credit, food and clothing for the matrimonial household? Was there any duty at common law on a husband to support and maintain his wife by virtue of their married state? If so, how far did this duty give the wife any claim in a common law court to enforce that obligation?

In the earliest reported case, of *Manby v. Scott*[1] in 1660, the policy of the common law courts was established after the case had been argued on at least seven separate occasions. It was finally decided in the Exchequer Chamber in 1663 by all the Common Law judges, namely the Justices of the King's Bench and the Barons of the Exchequer. We discuss it at length because the respective judgments of the majority and minority of the judges clarify the grounds upon which it was held that the common law declined any jurisdiction in matrimonial affairs but provided a partial remedy by way of the law of agency which permitted a wife to pledge her husband's credit for necessaries.

The case arose out of an action by a mercer who sold some yards of silk and velvet to the value of £40 on credit to Dame Scott, the wife of Sir Edward Scott. She had left her husband against his will and lived for twelve years separate from him, although she then entreated him to renew cohabitation; but he refused to have her back. While she lived apart from her husband, Sir Edward Scott had prohibited several persons from supplying her with goods or necessaries of any kind, and declared he would not pay for them if they were supplied. Although he had prohibited the mercer specifically from giving credit to Dame Scott, the mercer nevertheless sold on credit the silk and velvet in question, and sued Sir Edward Scott for the price. A jury found that these were necessary for Dame Scott having regard to the standard of living of her husband. It was held that the right to pledge his credit arose from the fact of cohabitation rather than from the status of marriage[2]. A wife who left her husband without justification and without his consent could not bind him by her contracts, even for necessaries. Judgment was entered for Sir Edward Scott on the ground that the Dame could not bind him as she lived separate from him.

The case was first referred by the trial judge, Mr. Justice Mallet, to four judges in the King's Bench. They were equally divided, Chief Justice Foster and Mr. Justice Windham giving judgment for the mercer. The differentiation of jurisdiction between the ecclesiastical and common law courts was prominent in the judges' minds. Mr. Justice Twisden observed that "though alimony be recoverable in the spiritual court, yet if the husband be obstinate, and will not obey their sentence, yet how shall the woman live? And if he will obey it, yet how shall she live in the meantime?"[3] to which Chief Justice

---

[1] (1663) 1 Lev. (K.B.) 4; 1 Sid. 109; 1 Mod. Rep 124; Vol. 2, Smith's Leading Cases, 13 ed., P. 417; Keble 69, 80, 87, 206, 337, 361, 383, 429, 441, and 482.
[2] See also *Jolly v. Rees* (1864) 15 C.B. (N.S.) 628, 640.
[3] *Manby v. Scott*, Smith's Leading Cases, Vol. 2, p. 418.

Foster and Mr. Justice Windham rejoined that the "laws of England have provided for wives more reasonably than to make them their own carvers[1]; (viz.) to go to the Ordinary (the judge in the ecclesiastical court) for alimony, the costs of which suit the husband shall pay, if the wife hath just cause of complaint"[2].

This controversy was reproduced throughout the proceedings in the Exchequer Chamber, which ultimately decided that, unless the wife could be held to be the husband's agent (in a commercial sense) to buy goods for him, the common law gave her no remedy or independent right to maintenance but left her to the remedies of the ecclesiastical jurisdiction. Mr. Justice Tyrell, Mr. Justice Twisden and Mr. Justice Mallet dissented.

The main argument of the majority was that the canon law formed an integral part of the English law[3] and the common law courts had from an early date conceded supervision of all matrimonial matters[4]: Mr. Justice Windham observed: "Debates between the husband and wife are not to be brought to the common law but are left to the Ordinary to whom it belongeth by the ancient common law. That *placitum de matrimonio* with testamentary causes appertain to his jurisdiction, though when these jurisdictions were taken away, men did endeavour to have remedy at law, the Ordinary did allow by paternal care fitting maintenance to the wife, which we cannot do now[5] . . . alimony is with them in the proper jurisdiction in the Spiritual Court."[6]

Counsel for the plaintiff had urged upon the judges the inadequacy of the ecclesiastical remedy. He complained that the common law would be gravely deficient if provision were made to maintain the wife only pending a decree of restitution of conjugal rights. Even after the decree all that the ecclesiastical court could do in the event of non-compliance was to excommunicate the husband and if he remained obdurate there was no jurisdiction over his estate to compel obedience[7]. Defendant's counsel replied, in anticipation, that this action was "but a device to let in alimony to the common law"[8]. Mr. Justice Twisden's dissenting judgment distinguished between maintenance during marriage without judicial separation and alimony on a decree of judicial separation. He agreed that rights of matrimony were matters for the ecclesiastical courts, but argued that "alimony is not properly a matrimonial cause, by reason it depends not on separation . . . and by the course of the Spiritual Court they do not allow alimony till separation; and no case hath been cited

---

[1] "He may not, as unvalued persons do, carve for himself", Hamlet, 1.3.20.

[2] *Manby v. Scott*, Smith's Leading Cases, Vol. 2, p. 419.

[3] Canon Law was only accepted as custom, and therefore operated only to the extent that it was not in conflict with common law or statute.

[4] See *Caudrey's Case* [of the King's Ecclesiastical Law] (1592) 5 Co. Rep. 1: 77 E.R.1.

[5] 1 Keble 80; 83 E.R. 832. Chief Justice Foster specifically concurred in this view.

[6] 1 Keble 80; 83; 83 E.R. 823, 825, Hyde, J., 1 Keble 429, 430; 83 E.R. 1035; Bridgeman C.B., ditto, pp. 448 and 1046 and Hyde, J., 1 Mod. Rep 124, 131; 86 E.R. 781, 785.

[7] 1 Keble 206–7; 83 E.R. 902.

[8] 1 Keble 69, 70: 83 E.R. 816, 817.

where alimony alone originally was sued for there"[1]. The answer of the majority was pithily expressed by Chief Justice Foster: " . . . yet when she doth assent to marriage, she inclusive agrees to all the incidents thereof" being determined in the ecclesiastical court[2].

The minority further argued that since, by common consent, a husband at common law was bound to maintain his wife, and since the spiritual sanctions of the ecclesiastical courts were clearly insufficient, "that the Ordinary will give remedy in these cases is more specious than satisfactory"[3]. They argued that the common law should not take away all the wife's property on her marriage and then send her to another court for relief when she needed maintenance. Mr. Justice Twisden later reiterated the deficiencies of the ecclesiastical courts and added: "For the very reasons given by those who have argued for the defendant of disobedience being encouraged, if the remedy for wives shall be at the common law and not in the spiritual court, lead us to adjudge that their remedy shall be exclusively at common law." The evil consequences of leaving the wife with her remedy in the ecclesiastical courts would be that wives will become refractory and disobedient because alimony is grantable only after separation; and, if maintenance is compellable only in the spiritual courts, husbands will be cruel to their wives when they know that punishment at the worst will mean excommunication and "what little regard the men of this age have for that is too well known; and then the entangling of the body and soul of the husband in the meshes of excommunication will neither feed nor clothe the wife."[4] To which Mr. Justice Hyde gave a spirited reply: "It is not sending the wife to another law, but leaving the case to its proper jurisdiction; the case being of ecclesiastical conusance (cognisance)[5] . . . and it is no more strange to send women to Spiritual Courts for alimony than for C.B. [Common Bench] to send cutpurse into B.R. [King's Bench] or B.R. to send feme for dower into C.B. or into Chancery for equity. . . .[6] Are the censure of the Holy Mother the Church grown of so little account with us, or the separation *a communione fidelium* become so contemptible as to be shifted with but excommunication? Hath our law provided any remedy, so penal, or can it give any judgment so fearful as this?"[7]—an early argument in favour of deterrent sanctions to effect enforcement of maintenance obligations.

The conclusive argument for rejecting any common law remedy for maintenance was the supposed inconvenience of developing any such rule. Baron Turner made no bones about the evil consequences of a wife's right to maintenance: "It's better that she have no power than if she had, however it will be exceeding mischievous to the husband, who hereby shall be forced to pay every strangers demand of money for wares sold to her, so she might take up necessary apparel of one, then of another, and the last man brings the

[1] 1 Keble 384; 83 E.R. 1008.   [2] 1 Keble 483; 83 E.R. 1066.
[3] 1 Keble 364; 83 E.R. 997 per Tyrell, J.   [4] Smith's Leading Cases, Vol 2, pp. 431–2.
[5] 1 Mod. 132; 86 E.R. 786.   [6] 1 Keble 430; 83 E.R. 1035.
[7] See also Hyde J., 1 Mod. 127; 86 E.R. 783.

action first, and recovers, so may everyone after by combination. The law hath provided for her better than to be expected out of the general rule, viz. the Ordinary: also the law of God, and of nature, hath made a better provision."[1]

Behind all this rationalization lay the basic notion that "by marriage, the husband and wife are one person in law, the very being or legal existence of the woman is suspended during the marriage or at least is incorporated and consolidated into that of the husband; under whose wing, protection and cover she performs everything . . ."[2] A woman could not herself enter into a contractual obligation; "the contract of a woman binds not herself, ergo not the husband"[3]. Only to the extent that the wife was impliedly the husband's agent for her necessaries, unless negatived by the husband, could the tradesman who supplied the goods on credit sue the husband for his wife's purchases. The law of England, however, did not leave the wife entirely at her husband's mercy. So long as the wife was "helpful to him and liveth with him"[4] the husband was bound to provide for her. The husband had a duty to keep himself and not be a charge on the community, and keeping himself involved keeping his wife because they were one person and the person was indisputably at law the husband[5]. The law recognized the wife was "bone of his bone, flesh of his flesh, and no man did ever hate his own flesh so far as not to preserve it"[6]. The common law courts would compel a husband not to let his wife become destitute, but they never "made a decree to compel him to pay a separate maintenance to his wife"[7]. Although his duty to keep his wife was an incident of the state of matrimony and was not contractual in nature[8], the wife on marriage could contract for maintenance to be paid during the subsistence of her marriage in such a way as to be perhaps enforceable in the courts of equity rather than in the common law courts which would have held that marriage dissolved any contract made between the spouses[9].

Manby v. Scott was an overwhelming and longstanding precedent for the proposition that a wife's right to maintenance as such was enforceable exclusively in the ecclesiastical courts, limited as that right was. The remedy of spiritual censure was in harmony with the notion of moral, rather than practical, enforcement of marital obligations. From 1663 until Parliament

[1] 1 Keble 362; 83 E.R. 995. See also Hyde J., 1 Mod. 86 E.R. 783.
[2] Sir W. Blackstone *Commentaries on the Laws of England*, Vol. 1. Of the Rights of Persons, p. 442.
[3] Baron Turner in *Manby v. Scott* 1 Keble 362; 83 E.R. 996.
[4] Hyde J. in *Manby v. Scott* 1 Keble 430; 83 E.R. 1035.
[5] A later commentator put this doctrine of henosis in an anatomically graphic way; "the Creator took from Adam a rib and made it Eve; the common law of England sought to reverse the process, to replace the rib and to remerge the personalities", de Montmorency, "The Changing Status of Married Women", (1897) 13 L.Q.R. 187. 192; see also Glanville Williams, "The Unity of Husband and Wife", (1947) 10 M.L.R.16.
[6] Hyde J. In *Manby v. Scott* 1 Mod. Rep. 128; 86 E.R. 784.
[7] Lord Hardwicke, L.C. in *Head v. Head* (1747) 3 Atk. 550; 26 E.R. 1116.
[8] *Dewe v. Dewe* [1928] P. 113, 119.
[9] *Watkyns v. Watkyns* (1740) 2 Atk. 96; 26 E.R. 460; *Head v. Head, supra.*

intervened two centuries later, the common law courts never entertained a claim to maintenance as such. When faced with claims by tradesmen against husbands to whose wives they had given credit, the courts applied the rules of mercantile law which bound a principal for the acts of his agents. The common law courts were careful not to go beyond the application of the doctrine of agency and so to trespass on the jurisdiction of the ecclesiastical courts[1]. The germ of this commercial approach, based on the concept of agency, lay in *Manby v. Scott* itself. In consequence, the wife was enabled to feed, clothe and sustain her mode of life, but only to the extent that her husband had not denied her the right to be provided with the wherewithal commensurate with his former standard of living and to the extent that he had credit. Consistent with this principle, the common law courts developed two basic rules. First, that the wife could never be provided, by order of the court, with money; and secondly that her claim to maintenance was never enforceable directly against her husband or against his property but only in kind by pledging whatever credit he had.

In *Manby v. Scott* itself the judges (with only one dissentient voice on this point) resolved "that the marriage does not give the wife any innate and uncontrollable power to render the husband liable". The husband's duty to pay the debts incurred by his wife with tradesmen stemmed from his expressed or implied authority to her to act as his agent. But the husband could always control the existence or extent of his wife's agency; he could deny, withdraw or limit the scope of that authority effectively to prevent the tradesman granting any credit; and reluctant tradesmen could refuse to give credit.

The principle of agency was necessarily modified to meet the marital situation. While husband and wife were living together there was a presumption that the husband assented to his credit being pledged by his wife for the necessaries of this life; the presumption arose from cohabitation and not from matrimony[2]. But an explicit revocation of this authority terminated the agency even if the tradesman concerned had no notice of the revocation. Thus the apparent authority arising from the circumstance of cohabitation was often in effect nullified because the courts, applying strictly the ordinary law of agency, founded the authority on principles of contract and not on rights peculiar to the conjugal relations. As Erle C.J. put it in *Jolly and another v. Rees*, "it is a solecism in reasoning to say that she derives her authority from his will [wish], and at the same time to say that the relation of wife creates the authority against his will"[3].

---

[1] *Dyer v. East* (1669) 2 Keble 554; *James v. Warren* (1702) Holt K.B. 104; *Etherington v. Parrot* (1703) Holt K.B. 102; *Montague v. Benedict* (1825) 3 B. & C. 631; *Seaton v. Benedict* (1828) 5 Bing. 28; *Jolly and another v. Rees* (1864) 15 C.B. (N.S.) 628; 143 E.R. 931; *Debenham v. Mellon* (1886) 6 App. Cas. 24; see generally Smith's Leading Cases, 13th ed. Vol. 2, p. 417 ff and 456–477.

[2] A mistress could equally pledge her "husband's" credit, but in such a case no presumption of authority continued after separation, and an actual authority must be proved: *Munro v. de Chamant* (1815) 4 Camp, 215; *Ryan v. Sams* (1848) 12 Q.B. 460.

[3] (1864) 15 C.B. (N.S.) 641, 143 E.R. 936.

Where the wife was living apart from her husband the presumption was against any agency of authority to pledge his credit unless he had deserted his wife or by his conduct (such as adultery or cruelty) compelled her to live apart from him without his having properly provided for her. In such cases the law gave her an irrevocable authority to pledge his credit ("an authority of necessity to pledge his credit for her necessary maintenance, unless she has adequate means for that purpose")[1]. This was important because desertion by itself gave her no right to an ecclesiastical decree of judicial separation, with its ancillary relief of alimony. On the other hand she was not entitled to pledge her husband's credit if she separated from him without cause, or even in consequence of mutual agreement to live separately.

The agency extended only to the pledging of credit for "necessaries"; these were defined by Mr. Justice Willes in 1860[2] as "articles necessary and suitable to the style in which the husband chooses to live in so far as they fall within the domestic department which is ordinarily confided to the management of the wife", a formula akin to "standard of living". If the goods were not needed to sustain the spouses' appropriate standard of living the tradesmen could not recover the price, unless the husband specifically affirmed the particular contract. And the husband could always claim either that the goods purchased went beyond his wife's needs or that he had provided her with a personal allowance sufficient to enable her to purchase the goods without resort to credit.

A wife, separated from her husband in consequence of his matrimonial misconduct sufficient to found a decree of judicial separation, was in a more favourable position than her married sister who, when her marriage failed, either tolerated her husband's behaviour or separated by agreement, stipulating first for some kind of financial support (often out of her property which the husband acquired on marriage). This was necessary because until the mid-nineteenth century the courts declined to enforce separation agreements. In addition to the wife's qualified right to pledge her husband's credit, the husband had a statutory obligation to reimburse the poor law authority for the cost of maintaining his wife if she fell upon the authority. This obligation persists in the National Assistance Act 1948[3], and in its successor the Ministry of Social Security Act 1966[4].

The wife's right to necessaries may have been a limited right. It was nevertheless valuable to a class of women to whom tradesmen would be prepared to give credit. No tradesman would have dreamed of granting credit to the mass of married women for fear that their husbands themselves were not credit-worthy.

The following reported cases illustrate some of the preceding rules. In

[1] *Debenham v. Mellon* (1880) 6 App. Cas. 24, 31, 35: *Smith's Leading Cases*, Vol. 2, pp. 468–469. See also *Ellerington v. Parrot* (1703) Holt K.B. 90 E.R. 955.
[2] *Phillipson v. Hayter* (1860) L.R. 6 C.P. 38.
[3] National Assistance Act, 1948, s. 42 and s. 43.
[4] Ministry of Social Security Act 1966, s. 22 and s. 23.

Bentley v. Griffin[1] an attorney "not in very extensive practice" was sued at Westminster for £813 for articles of fashionable goods supplied to his wife. The jury's verdict in favour of the tradesman was set aside on the ground that there was overwhelming evidence that the credit had been to the wife and not to the husband. In such cases the husband cannot be liable even though the husband and wife are living together and he sees her in possession of the goods. At Devon Assizes in 1821 a ship's surgeon's wife was supplied by a butcher with meat to the value of £15. The surgeon was held not liable since he was held to have made his wife an adequate allowance of £100 a year[2]. At the Middlesex sittings in 1844 Chief Baron Pollock said in a case involving £5,287: "How can you distinguish between clothes and rings, which are both ornamental? Jewelry may be just as fit to be ordered by a lady as lace or any other article of dress."[3] In *Jolly and another v. Rees*[4] Messrs. Jolly, hosiers and drapers at Bath, supplied goods to the wife of a magistrate, a "gentleman of small fortune". He had allowed his wife £115 a year (£65 of which was settled for her separate use) but he had forbidden her to pledge his credit; the suing tradesman failed in his action. In *Seaton v. Benedict* a fashionable milliner in Richmond supplied the wife of "a gentleman in the profession of the law", living together with her husband with "kid glove, ribbands muslins, lace and silks and silk stockings, 13 pairs of which were of a very expensive description". In dismissing the claim, Chief Justice Best said that the court must "lay down a rule that shall protect the husband from the extravagances of the wife"[5]. In the later case of *Paquin Ltd. v. Beauclerk*[6], decided after the Married Women's Property Act 1893, the House of Lords were divided as to whether knowledge on the part of a tradesman that a woman was married and acting as agent for her husband made good his claim against her for the price of goods received. Lord Macnaghten remarked in that case that " . . . it is not required by the Act of 1893 that she should communicate to the person with whom she is dealing the fact that she is her husband's agent or state that she is not acting on her own behalf . . . it can hardly be expected", he continued, "that such domestic confidences should be whispered across the counter or imparted to some forewoman in the comparative privacy of an inner appartment". Further, he said, "there is really no hardship on the tradesman who deals with a married woman. He is under no obligation to give credit at all, or to continue or extend the credit, if credit is given. He may make any inquiries he pleases of the customer or of anybody else. If he chooses to trust a lady with unlimited credit, when he is not sure of his ground, he has only himself to blame if anything should go wrong."[7] The House of Lords affirmed the decision of the Court of Appeal that it was immaterial

---

[1] (1814) 5 Taunton 356; 128 E.R. 727.
[2] *Holt v. Brien* (1821) 4 B & Ald. 252; 106 E.R. 930.
[3] *Lane v. Ironmonger* (1844) 13 M. & W. 369–370; 153 E.R. 153; See also *Montague v. Benedict* (1825) 3 B. & C. 631.   [4] (1864) 15 C.B. (N.S.) 628; 143 E.R. 931.
[5] (1828) 5 Bing. 31, 130 E.R. 971.   [6] [1906] A.C. 148.
[7] [1906] A.C. 163–164.

whether the appellants did or did not know that the respondent was a married woman, she having as a matter of fact contracted as agent for her husband.

If the financial position of a married woman was parlous, children were much worse off. With the important exception of his obligations under the Poor Law, a father had no legal duty unless he specifically contracted with the children's mother to maintain his children. Only if he criminally neglected a child was the father under any liability to pay maintenance to the child's mother. The absence of any financial responsibility of a father towards the offspring he sired was mitigated to some extent by the courts. Parliament in the Custody of Infants Act 1839 had conceded to the mother custody rights (which the common law had given exclusively to the father) over her children up to the age of seven. The judges held that the reasonable expenses of providing for the child's maintenance where she had custody of them were part of the reasonable expenses for which she had authority to pledge her husband's credit[1]. Here again the husband could limit or extinguish his liability to the child just as he could to the child's mother by withdrawing his agency of authority. But by the mid-nineteenth century it was possible to enforce the duty of the father to maintain his children through proceedings before the justices at the suit of the local Poor Law Authority.

The statutory obligation

The transfer of the ecclesiastical and parliamentary jurisdiction over marriage and divorce to the Court for Divorce and Matrimonial Causes in 1857 affected no direct change in the substantive law relating to the maintenance of wives and children. It retained the principle that maintenance of the wife was only ancillary to the main matrimonial relief of annulment or dissolution of marriage or judicial separation. In the case of judicial separation, alimony could be awarded in the same manner as before. The court obtained powers to provide for the custody of the children of the marriage, and could order maintenance for them to be paid to the wife in addition to alimony. It was also provided that an order of alimony had the effect of removing the wife's right to pledge her husband's credit so long as the payments under the award were kept up. The other major change was that alimony became a legal debt enforceable by the common law courts. But this was an indirect and unintended reform brought about by the application of the High Court practice in relation to the enforcement of judgment debts.

The introduction of the legal dissolution of marriage brought entirely new problems for maintenance. The wife's right to alimony was based on the fact that, notwithstanding separation, the wife remained the wife and the husband retained his duty to maintain. But, on dissolution of a marriage, the liabilities flowing from the marital status ceased. The 1857 Act, therefore, gave to the

[1] *Bazeley v. Forder* (1868) L.R. 3 Q.B. 559; *Clarke v. Wright* (1861) 6 H. & N. 849. 860.

courts the power which Parliament had exercised pre-1857, namely of grant-ing a decree only on the husband settling upon the wife sufficient property to produce an income for her basic support[1]. In fact, the Act declared that "the court may in such case, if it sees fit, suspend the pronouncing of its decree until such deed shall have been executed" (that is, for payment of money to the wife) "and upon any petition for dissolution of marriage the court shall have the same power to make interim orders for payment of money, by way of alimony or otherwise to the wife as it would have in a suit instituted for judicial separation[2]".

The Court for Divorce and Matrimonial Causes, which was absorbed into the Supreme Court of Judicature in 1873, had to feel its way through the complexities of a novel jurisdiction of maintenance on and after a decree of divorce. Initially, after the passing of the Act of 1857 maintenance could only be granted to the wife in exceptional circumstances or if she were the peti-tioner because it was then (in marked contrast to the Private Act period) held to be contrary to public policy that a husband should be obliged to provide out of his earnings for an adulterous wife[3]. The first Judge Ordinary of the new court, Sir Cresswell Cresswell, still subscribed to the view that the sanc-tity of marriage should be upheld. The Court of Appeal later expressed surprise that the wife had to show exceptional circumstances before being granted maintenance[4]. Since 1902 it has been accepted as a general principle that even a guilty wife is not to be left to starve. Adultery on the part of a petitioner in a divorce case remained a discretionary bar to relief until the Divorce Reform Act 1969 came into force. Whereas the court today is generally in other than exceptional cases willing to exercise discretion in favour of a petitioner who has been guilty, nevertheless when it turns to finance it has been enjoined to "look at the whole conduct of the spouses during the marriage and award the wife maintenance according to her deserts"[5] The financial protection provided for divorce on the grounds of separation under the Divorce Reform Act 1969[6] has not only given specific power to the courts to enforce proper maintenance but has also confirmed the judicial opinion under which the economic well-being of dependant wives generally safeguarded.

On the other hand, separation did not cause so many problems. Ecclesiasti-cal practice was reasonably well established for the granting of separation decrees and the allotment of alimony. There was never any doubt that alimony

[1] The subject is fully developed by J. L. Barton in *The Enforcement of Financial Provisions*, pp. 352, 357 ff. in *A Century of Family Law* (1957) by R. H. Graveson and F. R. Crane.
[2] Matrimonial Causes Act (1857), section 32.
[3] Barton J. L., *op. cit.*, p. 358.   [4] *Robinson v. Robinson* (1883) 8 P.D. 94.
[5] *Sydenham v. Sydenham and Illingworth* (1949) 65 T.L.R. 489; *Iverson v. Iverson* [1967] P. 134. An adulterous wife was normally deprived of a claim to maintenance, although a husband could be required to provide a small amount of maintenance, "so that she may not be turned out destitute on the streets", see *Ashcroft v. Ashcroft* [1902] P. 270, 273; *Trestain v. Trestain* [1950] P. 198. This by no means represents current practice; c.f. s.2(3), Matrimonial Proceed-ings (Magistrates' Courts) Act 1960.
[6] Section 6.

could not be granted to an adulterous wife. This is still the case today with alimony after judicial separation. Again, the actual amount remained the same as under the ecclesiastical rule. However, the court increasingly awarded amounts in excess of one-third of the husband's income.

The ancillary power of the High Court to award alimony was available in practice only to a fraction of the population of married women, that is, those who themselves, or as implied agents for their husbands, could afford litigation in the High Court, although some wronged wives proceeded *in forma pauperis*. There was no jurisdiction in the courts for a claim to maintenance during marriage. Until the summary courts were given fuller matrimonial jurisdiction in 1878, magistrates could only make "protection orders" to prevent deserting husbands laying their hands on their wives' earned income[1]. The jurisdiction acquired by magistrates in the Matrimonial Causes Act 1878 had no counterpart in the procedure of the ecclesiastical courts.

It was not until the case of *R. v. Jackson*[2] in 1891 that it was decided that a husband was not legally entitled to chastise or to imprison his wife. Before then, it had been very difficult to protect a wife whose husband abused his power over her. John Stuart Mill observed that "in no other case (except that of a child) is the person who has been proved judicially to have suffered an injury, replaced under the physical power of the culprit who inflicted it. Accordingly wives, even in the most extreme and protracted cases of bodily ill-usage, hardly ever dare avail themselves of the laws made for their protection: and if, in a moment of irrepressible indignation, or by the interference of neighbours, they are induced to do so, their whole effort afterwards is to disclose as little as they can, and to beg off their tyrant from his merited chastisement."[3] By the early 1870s physical violence of all kinds had become a public and political issue. The earlier outbreak of garrotting had forced a discussion of the deterrent efficacy of flogging and the Home Office published in 1875 *Reports on the State of the Law relating to Brutal Assaults*[4]. The year before, Colonel Egerton Leigh made an appeal in the House of Commons for intervention to relieve the sufferings of working class wives. The Prime Minister, Disraeli, replied with the hope that the House would allow "the Secretary of State for the Home Department, whose mind is now occupied with this and similar subjects, time to reflect as to the practical mode in which the feeling of the country upon this subject can be carried into effect. . . ."[5]

Indignation that the law was ineffective was reinforced by lurid newspaper reports and by the campaigns of such reformers as Serjeant Pulling and Frances Power Cobbe. The annual meeting of the National Association for the Promotion of Social Science in 1876 was held in Liverpool, a city which provided Serjeant Pulling with much material for his discourse on the repression of crimes of violence. He found that

[1] Matrimonial Causes Act 1857 s.21.   [2] [1891] 1 Q.B. 671.
[3] *The Subjection of Women*, Everyman edition, p. 232. The essay was written in 1861 but not published until 1869.   [4] C. 1138.
[5] Hansard, House of Commons, Vol. 219, col. 396.

among the inhabitants of this large and prosperous town there is an amount of savage brutality certainly not exceeded in any part of her Majesty's dominions, and that nowhere is the ill-usage of women so systematic and so little hindered by the strong arm of the law; making the lot of a married woman whose locality is the "kicking district" of Liverpool simply a duration of suffering and subjection to injury and savage treatment, far worse than that to which the wives of mere savages are used.

He argued that defects in procedure and the lack of a public prosecutor seemed designed not to repress violence against wives but merely to discourage complaints.

the lesson taught to the ruffian is, that if he ill-uses his dog or his donkey, he stands a fair chance (thanks to the Society for Preventing Cruelty to Dumb Animals) of being duly prosecuted, convicted, and punished; but that if the ill-usage is merely practised on his wife the odds are in favour of his entire immunity, and of his victim getting worse treatment if she dare appear against him[1].

Serjeant Pulling saw the solution in terms of procedural changes and of making flogging part of the sentence imposed on a husband convicted more than once of aggravated assault. A striking feature of Pulling's paper, and of the extended discussion which followed it, was that the maintenance of the wife whose husband had been flogged and imprisoned was never considered. Frances Power Cobbe was more realistic.

After much reflection I came to the conclusion that in spite of all the authority in favour of flogging the delinquents, it was *not* expedient on the women's behalf that they should be so punished, since after they had undergone such chastisement, however well merited, the ruffians would inevitably return more brutalised and infuriated than ever; and again have their wives at their mercy. The only thing really effective, I considered, was to give the wife the power of separating herself and her children from her tyrant. Of course, in the upper ranks, where people could afford to pay for a suit in the Divorce Court, the law had for some years opened to the assaulted wife this door of escape. But among the working classes, where the assaults were ten-fold as numerous and twenty times more cruel, no legal means whatever existed of escaping from the husband returning after punishment to beat and torture his wife again. I thought the thing to be desired was the extension of the privilege of rich women to their poorer sisters, to be effected by an Act of Parliament

[1] *Transactions of the National Association for the Promotion of Social Science* (1876) pp. 345–6.

which should give a wife whose husband had been convicted of an aggravated assault upon her, the power to obtain a Separation Order under Summary Jurisdiction[1].

Miss Power Cobbe wrote articles on the subject for the reviews, published a pamphlet, *The Truth on Wife Torture*, and canvassed the help of members of parliament, including Alfred Hill[2], Russell Gurney, Mr. (later Lord) Herschell and Sir Henry (later Lord) Holland, to introduce a Bill which she had drafted. This was read for the first time in the House of Commons in the same month that Lord Penzance who, as Sir James Wilde, had been Judge Ordinary from 1863 until 1872, was bringing a Bill into the House of Lords to remedy defects concerning the costs of intervention by the Queen's Proctor in matrimonial causes. He immediately added to his Bill a clause giving assaulted wives the relief which had been proposed by Miss Power Cobbe[3]. It passed without opposition and provided that a husband convicted of aggravated assault upon his wife should

> pay to his wife such weekly sum as the Court or magistrate may consider to be in accordance with his means, and with any means that the wife may have, for her support, and the payment of any sum of money so ordered shall be enforceable and enforced against the husband in the same manner as . . . under an order of affiliation; and the Court or magistrate . . . shall have power from time to time to vary the same on the application of either the husband or the wife, upon proof that the means of the husband or wife have been altered in amount since the original order. . . .[4]

The Act also enabled the court to give legal custody of any children of the marriage under the age of ten to the mother.

In this way working class wives acquired a statutory right to maintenance against their husbands. Little attention was given to maintenance in the discussions which preceded the legislation and it is significant that the Act itself imposed no limit on the amount that the court could award. In 1878, the High Court declined to interfere with a decision to award £3 a week to a wife on the ground that it had not been plainly shown that this amount was excessive[5]. The maximum limit of £2 was however imposed by the Married Women (Maintenance in Cases of Desertion) Act 1886, when a wife could complain on the ground that her husband had wilfully neglected to maintain her, although the unlimited amount awardable under the sole ground of com-

---

[1] *Life of Frances Power Cobbe*, Vol. 2, (1894) pp. 220–1.

[2] The son of Matthew Davenport Hill, who, as Recorder of Birmingham, had exercised great influence on penal reform.

[3] It is not known why Lord Penzance acted in this manner. Miss Power Cobbe says that "I have taken as probable" that he "had seen our Bill" and "had had his attention called to the subject, either by it, or by my article in the Contemporary Review" . . . "I went at once to call on him . . . (he) received me with the utmost kindness. . . ." *op. cit.* pp. 222–3.

[4] Section 4(1).   [5] *Grove v. Grove* (1878) 39 L.T. 546; 27 W.R. 324.

plaint in the 1878 Act remained unaffected by the new provisions. Maximum maintenance limits for all grounds from 1895 onwards persisted (though increased from time to time) until the recommendation of the Committee on Statutory Maintenance Limits (The Graham Hall Committee) to remove all limitations on the amount of maintenance which can be awarded to a wife or child, was enacted in the Maintenance Orders Act 1968. Proved adultery on the wife's part, unless there had been condonation, conducement or connivance, deprived her of the right to maintenance. This was later statutorily enacted[1]; but has not, under the 1960 Act, prevented justices awarding to an adulterous wife the custody or maintenance of her child[2].

Lord Penzance's modest legislative contribution sparked off more sweeping reforms in 1886 and in 1895. The Married Women (Maintenance in Case of Desertion) Act 1886 gave a more direct and economically useful remedy to wives. Where a married woman could establish that her husband was able to support her and his children but had refused or neglected to do so and had deserted her, it enabled the magistrates' court to award her maintenance up to the limit of £2 a week. Unlike the 1878 Act, it did not provide for the wife's protection by way of a non-cohabitation order; indeed, the 1886 Act by implication reinforced the wife's duty to live with her husband by declaring that she was bound to give her husband consortium if he wished to re-establish cohabitation.[3] It was not until 1891 that the courts held that a husband could not physically enforce his right to cohabitation. But she could still proceed under the terms of the 1878 Act if she needed protection.

A crucial stage in endowing married women with rights to maintenance came with the Summary Jurisdiction (Married Women) Act 1895. Its promoter, Mr. E. W. Byrne, modestly described the intention of his Bill as getting rid of "some of the anomalies which existed in the civil law and the criminal law in cases of aggravated assaults on wives by husbands, and further to give similar relief in cases of persistent cruelty by a husband towards a wife, as now existed in cases of aggravated assault"[4]. The new Act was significant in conferring a general matrimonial jurisdiction on magistrates' courts. They were given extensive powers which in certain respects were wider than those of the High Court. Apart from consolidating the provisions of the 1878 and 1886 Acts, magistrates were enabled to make orders for separation[5] and maintenance where husbands had wilfully neglected to maintain their wives and families. This power was denied to the High Court until 1949 when it was empowered to award maintenance on the ground that the husband had wilfully neglected to maintain his family.

The 1895 Act contained the nucleus of grounds for complaint that now appear compendiously in the 1960 Act. A wife could complain to the magistrates' courts (a) when her husband had been convicted of an aggravated

---

[1] Now s.2(3)(b), 1960 Act.   [2] Section 4, 1960 Act.
[3] *R. v. Jackson* [1891] 1 Q.B. 671.   [4] Hansard, House of Commons, Vol. 34, col. 62.
[5] *Harriman v. Harriman* [1909] P. 123.

assault; (*b*) when her husband had been convicted on indictment of an assault upon her and had been sentenced to pay a fine of more than £5 or to a term of imprisonment exceeding two months; (*c*) when her husband deserted her; (*d*) when her husband had been guilty of persistent cruelty to her, causing her to leave the home and live separately from him; and (*e*) when her husband was guilty of wilfully neglecting to provide reasonable maintenance for her or her infant children whom he was bound to maintain, such as to cause her to live separate from him. The powers of the justices on finding a complaint proved were similarly expanded. They could make a separation order; order payment of maintenance not exceeding £2 a week; and grant the wife custody of a child under the age of sixteen, a power which had been available under the Guardianship of Infants Act 1886. An adulterous wife was once again deprived of the right to maintenance, unless the adultery had been connived at, condoned, or the husband had conduced to it by wilful neglect or misconduct. Any adultery, or resumption of cohabitation for a period of six weeks, subsequent to the making of the order was a ground for revoking the order. Separate maintenance for a child was not available until the Married Women (Maintenance) Act, 1920 by which a wife could be awarded up to ten shillings from the husband for the maintenance of each child up to the age of sixteen.

For the rest, change was piecemeal and sporadic, stemming sometimes from unlikely sources: Britain must be unique in altering its matrimonial law in the course of regulating the liquor trade. The Licensing Act 1902 filled a gap in the protective net devised by the legislature for ill-used wives. Ever since 1878 wives had had a remedy against husbands who assulted them, but none against the husbands who were habitual drunkards assaulting their wives occasionally but insufficiently to merit a separation order. The Act added habitual drunkenness, as defined in the Habitual Drunkards Act 1879, as a ground for complaint; and it was at that time the only ground on which a husband could obtain a separation order against his wife, though he was then usually ordered to pay maintenance to her[1]. This provision drew the tart comment from Eleanor Rathbone that "in this matter legislation has been inspired less by tenderness for the wife than by the reflection that a drunken or worthless woman is likely to become chargeable to the rate payers"[2].

Thus, by the early twentieth century, there were two systems of legal remedy for matrimonial difficulties in England. Working class women went to the magistrates' courts and there obtained some 8,000 matrimonial orders every year; their financial betters went to a centralized divorce court and obtained annually some 600 divorces, that is, licences to marry again, and some 80 judicial separations. Domestic brutality was less evident and less talked about than thirty years before. But it was never far below the surface. Young Somerset Maugham drew on his experience as a medical student at

---

[1] In the years immediately after 1902, there was an upsurge in the number of orders but this ground of complaint soon fell into disuse.
[2] *The Disinherited Family* (1924), p. 96.

St. Thomas's Hospital for the harsh picture of slum life in his first novel, *Liza of Lambeth*, published in 1897. When Thomas Holmes, a police court missionary, surveyed the matrimonial work of the London courts in 1900, he wrote of the "number of women who followed each other in quick succession, each bearing an outward and visible sign of the fact that she had been cruelly ill-used. Each woman was a wife, and each one wanted a 'protection order' against her husband, until the experienced magistrate, rising from his seat, declared that he could stand it no longer. Every magistrate in London has the same experience."[1] In Middlesbrough in 1907 among the ironworkers described by Lady Bell, "wife-beating is not so entirely a thing of the past as some of us would like to think"[2]. Nevertheless upper class opinion was shifting to a concern with the reported imperfections of working class sexual behaviour and to a recognition that environmental and social influences were obstacles to the acceptance of the approved familial code. A famous pamphlet, *The Bitter Cry of Outcast London*, described housing conditions in parts of London in 1883. It was read by Queen Victoria with the result that the Prince of Wales was required to become a member of the Royal Commission on the Housing of the Working Classes appointed in 1884. *The Bitter Cry* wrote of the immorality of the submerged poor.

> Marriage, it has been said, "as an institution is not fashionable in these districts". And this is only the bare truth. Ask if the men and women living together in these rookeries are married, and your simplicity will cause a smile. Nobody knows. Nobody cares. Nobody expects that they are. In exceptional cases only could your question be answered in the affirmative. Incest is common; and no form of vice and sensuality causes surprise or attracts attention. Those who appear to be married are often separated by a mere quarrel, and they do not hesitate to form similar companionships immediately[3].

Charles Booth thus commented on attitudes in parts of East London at the end of the 1890s.

> With the lowest classes pre-marital relations are very common, perhaps even usual. Amongst the girls themselves nothing is thought of it if no consequences result; and very little even if they do, should marriage follow, and more pity than reprobation if it does not. As a rule the young people, after a few experiments, pair off and then are faithful, and usually end by marrying. It is noted by the clergy who marry them, how often both the addresses given are from the same house. . . . More licence is granted by public opinion to the evasion of the bonds of marriage by

---

[1] *Pictures and Problems from London Police Courts* (1900), p. 72.
[2] *At the Works* (rev. ed. 1911), p. 331. The 1st ed. was published in 1907.
[3] p. 7.

those who have found it a failure, than is allowed to those whose relations to each other have not yet assumed a permanent form. This peculiar
code of morality is independent of recognized law, and an embarrassment to religion, but it is intelligible enough and not unpractical in its
way . . . I do not know exactly how far upwards in the social scale this
view of sexual morality extends, but I believe it to constitute one of the
clearest lines of demarcation between upper and lower in the working
class[1].

Such assessments helped to shape the early twentieth century recognition of
the moral as well as the physical consequences of the disamenities of urban
working class life. Military considerations also reinforced social anxieties. An
Inter-Departmental Committee on Physical Deterioration was set up in 1903
to inquire into "allegations concerning the deterioration of certain classes of
the population as shown by the large percentage of rejections for physical
causes of recruits for the Army (at the time of the Boer War)"[2]. From this
Committee's *Report* came statutory provision for school meals and for the
school medical service. Awareness of a declining birth rate among the higher
income groups was turned by exponents of the new "eugenics" into gloomy
prediction of a reduction in "the best stocks" of the nation and a fast increase
in the incompetent and unsound[3]. These influences lay behind the insistence
of Winston Churchill in 1909 that the object of the Liberal Party's social
policy was "to buttress and fortify the homes of the people"[4]. They also help
to explain why Sir Gorell Barnes, President of the Probate, Divorce and
Admiralty Division of the High Court, contrived his judgment in the case of
Dodd v. Dodd in 1906 as a call to reform.

That the present state of the English law of divorce and separation is not
satisfactory can hardly be doubted. The law is full of inconsistencies,
anomalies, and inequalities amounting almost to absurdities; and it does
not produce desirable results in certain important respects. Whether any,
and what, remedy should be applied raises extremely difficult questions,
the importance of which can hardly be overestimated, for they touch the
basis upon which society rests, the principle of marriage being the fundamental basis upon which . . . civilised nations have built up their social
systems . . . This judgment brings prominently forward the question
whether . . . any reform would be effective and adequate which did not
abolish permanent separation, as distinguished from divorce, place the
sexes on equality as regards offence and relief. . . .[5]

---

[1] *Life and Labour of the People in London: Religious Influences* (Third series) (1902) vol. 1,
pp. 55–56.
[2] [Cd. 2175] 1904, p. v.
[3] As in, for example, W. C. D. and C. D. Whetham, *The Family and the Nation: A study in
Natural Inheritance and Social Responsibility* (1909).
[4] *The People's Rights* (1910), p. 120.   [5] [1906] P. 207–208.

Sir Gorell Barnes persuaded the Asquith Government to set up a Roya
Commission on Divorce and Matrimonial Causes in 1909 with himself as
chairman. The *Report* reflected the chairman's conviction that "permanent
separation without divorce has a distinct tendency to encourage immorality
and is an unsatisfactory remedy to apply to the evils which it is supposed to
prevent"[1], and proposed to restrict the powers of magistrates to make separation orders of unlimited duration. The inadequacy of the lay magistracy was
a recurrent theme of the deliberations of the Gorell Commission. Lay magistrates had little knowledge or training. The Stipendiary Magistrate for Hull,
one of only nineteen stipendiary magistrates then outside the metropolitan
area, told the Commission that "the reason why the Act has an unsettling
influence is that it is not understood by, I am afraid, many of the justices
of the peace in the country to be permissive—that the court may, but it is
not necessarily obliged to separate people"[2]. Since the jurisdiction was more a
question of deciding who hit whom than of engaging in a fine calculation of
familial economics, the lay justices before the Kaiser's war found the work
more akin to their criminal jurisdiction than it has since become. There were
also many objections that this essentially civil jurisdiction affecting women and
children should be handled in a criminal court. Surprisingly, nobody suggested linking this jurisdiction with that of the juvenile courts established
in 1908.

Some evidence was given about the difficulties of enforcing maintenance.
The Metropolitan Police Magistrate for West London, Mr. E. W. Garrett,
explained that "Even if (the magistrate) leaves the man only the barest
necessities of existence, in which case he will not comply with the order,
there is insufficient to maintain the wife and children in the home. In my
experience the result of the majority of cases is that the wife has no
alternative but either to return to her husband, in which case her position is
worse than before, or go with her children into the work house."[3] Many witnesses pointed to the futility of the situation in which the wife had no means
of tracing her husband, the police lent little assistance, and even if he was
traced, the hopes of enforcing maintenance were slender. Magistrates had
only the power to issue a summons against a husband calling upon him to
attend the hearing of his wife's application for maintenance. A warrant which
gave the police authority to bring the husband before the court, was issuable
only on behalf of the poor law guardians if the wife obtained outdoor or
workhouse relief with its "very strong feeling that going into the workhouse
carries with it a sort of stigma which attaches permanently"[4].

Arrears in payment of maintenance were widespread. Failure to receive
maintenance led many wives to find another man who could provide for

[1] *Dodd v. Dodd* [1906] P. 207.
[2] *Minutes of Evidence*, (Cd. 6479), 1912, Vol. 1, q. 7234.
[3] *Minutes of Evidence*, (Cd. 6480), 1912, Vol. 2, q. 12952.
[4] *Op. cit.* (Cd. 6479), q. 7784, the evidence of Mr. B. C. Brough, the Stipendiary Magistrate
for the Potteries District.

them. The ensuing adulterous relationship could then be seized on by the husband to absolve him from any maintenance obligation. Those wives who managed to maintain themselves and who pursued their husbands were not much more successful at enforcing the financial obligation. If the husband decided to leave the district and to stop payment, it was hard to enforce the order. Imprisonment gave the wife no advantage because it operated to cancel the arrears. Where husbands were amenable to maintenance orders, there were complaints that awards were totally inadequate. Witnesses asserted that magistrates dealt leniently with the husband when it came to deciding maintenance, on the basis that a man had to keep himself respectable, and if he was to be at work, he must live well[1].

The main recommendations of the Gorell Commission concerning the summary jurisdiction were that:

(a) The power of magistrates' courts to make orders having the permanent effect of a decree of judicial separation should be abolished.
(b) The jurisdiction to grant separation and maintenance orders should be kept but limited "so that orders should only be granted where they are necessary for the reasonable immediate protection of the wife or husband or the support of the wife and the children with her".
(c) If permanent separation were desirable, it should be obtainable in the High Court by a simplified process.
(d) The list of grounds for complaint under the 1895 Act and under the Licensing Act 1902 should be extended.

Three private members' Bills which made fleeting appearances in parliament in this period are worthy of note. Mr. Philip Snowden introduced a Summary Jurisdiction Bill in 1911 to give the wife a claim for maintenance without the intervention of the Poor Law Guardians, by enabling her to obtain a magistrates' order enforceable through the husband's employer, when necessary by deducting the amount awarded from the husband's wages. But wives had to wait nearly half a century for the legislative sanction of attachment of the wages of their defaulting husbands. The second, significant Bill, The Summary Jurisdiction (Matrimonial Causes) Bill, to make "further and better provisions with respect to the hearing and determination of matrimonial causes by courts of summary jurisdiction", was introduced both in 1913 and in 1914. It failed however to reach the stage of second reading. It provided that a wife could obtain an order if the husband had been guilty of adultery since the marriage or had wilfully deserted without reasonable cause or had infected her with venereal disease. This Bill would also have given wider discretion in the cases of adulterous wives. A third legislative essay, the Assaults on Wives (Outdoor Relief) Bill, was introduced by Mr. J. C. Wedgwood in 1910. He sought to provide outdoor relief at a rate not

[1] *Op. cit.* (Cd. 6480), q. 20277.

exceeding ten shillings a week to a wife whose husband was sentenced to more than one month's imprisonment for an aggravated assault upon her.

The Criminal Justice Administration Act 1914, an oddly titled statute to assist separated wives, implemented one of the significant recommendations of the Gorell Commission. It relieved wives from having to take steps to enforce a maintenance order, and instead allowed a magistrates' court to order that payments could be made through an officer of the court. This procedural device transformed the situation of separated wives attempting to enforce their declared rights to be maintained by their husbands. War in 1914 postponed any further parliamentary action but the immediate post-war years brought two acts. The Married Women (Maintenance) Act 1920 introduced maintenance orders for children under sixteen up to ten shillings a week[1], and the Maintenance Orders (Facilities for Enforcement) Act 1920 introduced a system of registration for maintenance orders made by the Courts in the Commonwealth.

With the passing of the Summary Jurisdiction (Separation and Maintenance) Act 1925, the emphasis in social and legislative action shifts away from physical protection of the wife in favour of providing her with financial security. By then, the separation order had ceased either to be a social necessity or even the prime legal remedy awarded to married women. The chief reforms made in 1925 were: (a) additional grounds for which wives and husbands could claim orders; hitherto nearly all the grounds of complaint had been exclusively available to wives; (b) power in the courts to grant maintenance whether the parties were in fact living together or separate; and (c) increased powers to enforce maintenance orders, and wider powers conferring custody and access rights over children of the marriage.

The 1925 Act was primarily concerned with extending the grounds on which a married woman could issue a complaint. The new grounds were that a husband (a) was guilty of persistent cruelty to the wife's children; (b) insisted on sexual intercourse while knowingly suffering from a venereal disease; or (c) was forcing his wife to engage in prostitution. The right to discharge an order on the ground of the wife's adultery was modified by permitting continuance of the order if the wife's adulterous behaviour was due to the unreasonable failure of the husband to maintain his wife. The second main concern of the Act was to relieve a wife from the necessity of leaving her husband before complaining of cruelty or wilful neglect to maintain, thus bringing these grounds of complaint into line with the others available; though if she was still living with him three months after the order was made, the order lapsed. (The former law had forced a woman who sought financial support to leave her home, and thus deprived her of one right in order that she might gain another right.) It was not yet fully recognized that a

---

[1] Strictly it is more accurate to say that the award is for the wife in respect of any child for whom she is legally responsible, and is not directly support for the child: *Kinnane v. Kinnane* [1954] P. 41, approved in *Northrop v. Northrop* [1968] P. 74.

wife's complaint to the magistrates' court was perhaps the most eloquent testimony that a marriage had collapsed whether or not the spouses had physically separated[1].

Enforcement of maintenance orders became an increasing public concern. Following the 1895 Act the average annual number of awards was about 6,500. By the 1920s the number had doubled, and the extent of non-payment was reflected in the increasing number of men committed to prison. While the number of maintenance orders made annually nearly doubled within three decades, the number imprisoned annually multiplied by three and a half times:

Year	Number of Applications	Number of Orders made	Numbers imprisoned
1900	9,553	6,583	1,288
1910	9,891	6,723	2,265
1920	16,545	11,602	2,403
1930	15,991	11,296	4,274

The silting up of local prisons with maintenance defaulters and with ordinary debt defaulters prompted the government in 1934 to set up a Departmental Committee on Imprisonment by Courts of Summary Jurisdiction in Default of Payment of Fines and Other Sums of Money (the Fischer Williams Committee). A large part of that report dealt with the problem of non-payment of maintenance orders. The Committee quoted figures demonstrating that in 1932, out of 53,150 imprisonments for all causes, 38% (20,416) fell within the scope of the Committee's enquiry. Of this latter figure, 3,648 (7%) were maintenance defaulters. The Committee also estimated that in that year 52,114 live maintenance orders were in force.

The Committee thought that it was not possible to generalize about the reasons for non-payment. Some husbands made no effort, or showed little desire, to pay. Others were genuinely unable to pay, often for unforeseen circumstances. At that time, a husband who was two weeks in arrears with payments could be arrested. Imprisonment wiped out all arrears up to the time of committal to prison, but the magistrates could, but rarely did, order that the arrears should accrue during the period of sentence, which averaged a month. The Committee strongly deprecated the fact that there was no legal requirement to consider the husband's ability to pay the sum ordered before imprisoning the defaulter; it recognized however, the difficulty of obtaining reliable information about the man's earnings. It concluded unhappily that a

[1] There were some perceptive commentators. In 1925, a London magistrate, Cecil Chapman, *The Poor Man's Court of Justice* (1925), p. 58, wrote that wives were prepared to put up with much bad treatment before coming to the court, but by then the trouble was beyond hope of reconciliation. Matrimonial disharmony often meant that the dependant wife and children were economically vulnerable, if not destitute.

situation where "a court dispensing justice should have to act on less information than a society dispensing charity is an indication of one of the defects of the present system"[1].

Among the Committee's recommendations on this aspect of the report were that magistrates' courts should have power to make independent enquiries into the parties' means; it should be made obligatory (and not merely permissive as under the Criminal Justice Administration Act 1914) to order maintenance payments to be made through a collecting officer of the court, and that the latter should have statutory power to take proceedings, with the wife's consent, for the recovery of arrears of maintenance. Arrears accumulated over more than two years should be irrecoverable and, most important, the court should invariably investigate a defaulter's financial and social circumstances before committing him to prison[2]. The Committee wound up its radical proposals with a suggestion for attachment of earnings: defaulter's employers should be ordered to make deductions from wages or salary. If the defaulter had left the district, then the order should be transferable from court to court, with power to enforce, vary, or even revoke the order. The enforcing court should have at its disposal the services of an investigation officer. The Committee concluded that, given the necessary changes to make enforcement more effective, it was practicable to reduce considerably the number of imprisonments.

A notable omission from the Money Payments (Justices' Procedure) Act 1935, which substantially enacted many of Fischer Williams Committee's proposals, was the proposal for the attachment of wages: only in other minor respects did the Act otherwise depart from the report's recommendations. Section 8(1)(b) provided that the court was obliged to determine whether non-payment of the maintenance order resulted from wilful refusal or from culpable neglect; if due to neither, an order committing the defaulter to prison ought not to be made.

The ensuing reduction in the numbers imprisoned was marked but short-lived. In 1935, 2,271 maintenance defaulters went to prison; in 1936 it was 1,828, a 20% reduction. More significantly, the proportion of prison committals to maintenance orders dropped from 25% to 19%. (This drop was, however, part of the steady decline over a number of years; the proportion in 1923 had been 46% and in 1932 40%.) Peaks of numbers imprisoned for debt—both civil and maintenance obligation debts—coincided with the periods of greatest industrial depression. Until the last war, the proportion of defaulters going to prison remained constant around 18%. During the war, it dropped to around 12%, but picked up in the post-war years with a return to the 1935 percentage of 24, the numbers actually imprisoned running at well over 3,000. The Maintenance Orders Act 1958, introducing

[1] Cmd. 4649, 1934 p. 41, para 125.
[2] Similarly the report of the Morton Commission on Marriage & Divorce, Cmd. 9678, paras 1099–1107.

attachment of earnings, brought a reduction both in total numbers and in the proportion of orders.

Parallel with this trend in the enforcement procedure, reconciliation became once more a dominant theme in public comment. The 1930s, in particular, witnessed a growing concern that the judicial process and the atmosphere of magistrates' courts were not conducive to resolving the problems of matrimonial discord. Many commentators felt strongly that much more attention should be devoted to attempts at reconciliation. Reliance upon matrimonial relief in the courts, they claimed, induced separation, thereby acknowledging the rift in the family without attempting to repair the breach. Ideas about how the law could contribute to reconciliation, however, remained vague. What ideas there were concentrated on the physical environs of the courts rather than on any social work for spouses in matrimonial conflict. Bills in Parliament reflecting this limited approach received cursory treatment. A Courts of Domestic Relations Bill appeared in the House of Commons on three occasions from 1928 to 1930. Each succeeding Bill provided that a magistrates' court exercising matrimonial jurisdiction "shall sit either in a different building or room from that in which the ordinary courts are held, or on different days or at different times from those at which the ordinary sittings are held". And the court was to be given the title of a "court of domestic relations". There were ancillary provisions limiting the persons who could be present when the court sat and providing for maintenance orders in respect of children to be paid through the court.

The insistence on procedural reform was nevertheless maintained. In 1934 Lord Listowel introduced a Summary Jurisdiction (Domestic Procedure) Bill designed to produce a "special technique" for dealing with domestic cases. One of the Bill's clauses introduced the "special conciliation" summons under which either spouse could summons the other to appear before a court which would then assist the parties to resolve their matrimonial difficulties. The premise of the Bill was that the law should move away from the technique of the accusatorial system, in which the court adjudicates on issues presented to it by the parties, in favour of a social work approach. While no one was willing to decry this attempt at providing the right forum for matrimonial disputes, many (mostly lawyers) had a hearty dislike of any alteration of the basic common law principles vindicated in the Stuart constitutional struggles. This doctrinal conflict was shelved by setting up a government inquiry, the departmental committee on the *Social Services in Courts of Summary Jurisdiction*[1].

The Committee's report in 1936 observed that the law, in providing for separation and maintenance orders, had no thought of reconciling the spouses, although some courts and individual magistrates exercising the jurisdiction had long recognized the need for a conciliation procedure. The

[1] Cmd. 5122 (1936).

Committee conducted a limited enquiry into the types of cases currently brought to the courts. This showed great diversity of practice. In London, where 79% of the prospective complainants were first seen by a probation officer, only 9% of these cases were eventually adjudicated upon. In the County Borough and County Divisional Courts, where only 28% of prospective complainants first saw a court official other than a probation officer, 22% and 40% respectively later came before the magistrates for a decision. Of the 6,222 persons interviewed, the report concluded that 2,989 cases showed an apparently successful reconciliation[1]. In 914 cases an order was made, and in the remaining 2,319 cases the inquiry made no attempt to analyse the results of the conciliation procedure.

The Committee's conclusions were tentative. It felt on unsure ground when it observed that "it would be obviously unsound to assume that matrimonial differences have been successfully and permanently adjusted merely because the parties do not appear before the court within a limited period"[2]. Even more significant was the Committee's warning that attempts at conciliation could easily be taken too far. The interposing of a court official between the complainant and the court ready to adjudicate carried a real danger that the conciliator (usually the probation officer) might easily, and not unnaturally, misjudge his role in regard to the court proceedings, thus denying justice to the complainant.

The Committee's recommendations reflected its circumspection. Conciliation was not to be excluded; indeed it was to be encouraged. But it was not to be formalized, and should be left to the discretion of the courts. All complainants should be seen by the court before issuing the complaint, and at any stage of the proceedings, attempts at conciliation could be effected, but not by the court itself. Probation officers should be used for conciliation purposes. In an endeavour to promote conciliation, a greater use should be made of interim orders, but the complainants should always have direct access to the court, and the conciliation procedure conducted by probation officers should be supervised by the court itself.

The other proposals were all designed to minimize the formality of the procedure. Cases should be heard at special sessions; the experiment of evening sessions was also to be considered. The Bench was to be composed as far as possible of three people, one of whom should be a woman. Applications for a summons should be heard in private and the court be empowered to sit *in camera*. Although legal formalism was to be discouraged by ensuring, for example, that the court should help in cross-examining witnesses where there was no legal representative, there should be greater provision for legal representation of those who could not afford it. The Summary Procedure (Domestic

[1] 6,222 persons, covered by the study's questionnaire, were seen by the following court officials: Warrant officer (or the Bench itself): 1,704; Justices' Clerk (or his assistant): 1,335; Probation Officer or Missionary: 3,152; Magistrate sitting otherwise than in court: 31.
[2] *Op. cit.*, p. 10.

Proceedings) Act 1937 largely enacted the report's recommendations[1]. It stripped domestic proceedings in magistrates' courts of their rigorously imposed judicial atmosphere[2]. The law had, to some extent, come to recognize that in this jurisdiction the courts were engaged as much in securing the social well-being of separated wives and their dependant children as in conducting judicial business.

The change in 1937 in the divorce law brought incidental change in the magistrates' courts. By Section 11 of the Matrimonial Causes Act of that year the grounds of complaint in magistrates' courts were extended to include adultery by either the husband or the wife. (In the original Bill there was even a provision for a petition of divorce to be presented to a magistrates' court for consideration and, if the court thought proper, for reference to the High Court. In the meantime, the court itself could make an interim order of maintenance. Another sub-section of the clause would have raised the financial limits for a wife from £2 to £5, and £2, instead of fifteen shillings, for a child. This clause was dropped from the Bill at committee stage.)

Whereas reconciliation had been the preoccupation of family law reformers in the immediate pre-war years, the aftermath of Hitler's war brought the fresh thinking in social policy evidenced by the Beveridge *Report*. The *Report* said: " . . . loss of her maintenance as a housewife without her consent and not through her fault is one of the risks of marriage against which she should be insured: she should not depend on assistance"[3]. This view was reflected in the Finance Act 1944[4], in the Family Allowance Act 1945, and in the National Assistance Act 1948[5]. Reconciliation went temporarily by the board. The emphasis was on providing the family with a basic minimum income.

The first line of attack in the area of maintenance orders was the upper limit of the magistrates' courts' power to award maintenance[6]. The limit for a wife had remained at £2 since 1886; since 1920, ten shillings had been the upper limit for a child. The Married Women (Maintenance) Act 1949 substituted £5 as the wife's maximum weekly maintenance and thirty shillings for a child. Two years later, in the Guardianship of Infants Act 1951, the rate of maintenance for a child on a guardianship order was similarly raised to

[1] In the same year (1937) the Departmental Committee on courts of Summary Jurisdiction in the metropolitan area under the chairmanship of Sir Alexander Maxwell, recommended that metropolitan magistrates should have the assistance of lay justices, including women, in hearing domestic cases, and that an informal court should be available for such sittings.

[2] The provisions of the 1937 Act were repealed and re-enacted in the Magistrates' Courts Act 1952.

[3] *Social Insurances and Allied Services*, 1942, Cmd. 6404, p. 134, para 347.

[4] Section 25 allowed certain payments for maintenance of married women, or for benefit, maintenance or education of a person under sixteen which did not exceed £2 or £1 a week respectively should be made without deduction of tax from the taxable income of the husband.

[5] Sections 42 and 43; see L. Neville Brown, 'National Assistance and the Liability to Maintain one's Family' (1955) 18 *M.L.R.* 112–116.

[6] The history of the statutory maintenance limits is usefully set out in the *Report* of the Graham Hall Committee, Cmnd. 3587 (1968), pp. 84-8. We have printed the Graham Hall Committee's tabular history as Appendix A, Part 2.

thirty shillings from £1. During the Bill's passage through Parliament, members were reminded of a suggestion made in 1920 that there should be no upper limit. Mr. Newbould asked whether maintenance orders for separated wives were still limited to £2; whether this limit was irrespective of the means of the husband and father and the size of the family; and whether in view of the rise in the cost of living and the hardship consequently inflicted on separated wives and their children, the Home Secretary would consider the desirability "of entirely removing the limit of £2 to be paid under these orders and substituting an arrangement whereby the sum granted should be such as the court, having regard to the means both of the husband and of the wife, considers reasonable"[1]. The Home Secretary replied that such matters were under review.

In that same year, 1949, when Parliament raised the limits of awards in respect of maintenance orders in magistrates' courts, the Law Reform (Miscellaneous Provisions) Act, by section 5[2] gave a wife the right to apply to the High Court for an order of maintenance, unlimited in amount, on the grounds of her husband's wilful neglect to maintain his family.

If limits of maintenance loomed large in legislation of this period, enforcement of maintenance orders was recognized as a continually pressing problem for court administrators. During the debate on the 1949 Bill, Mr. Asterley Jones concentrated his attention on the problems posed by persistent defaulters. He suggested that courts should have the power to order the National Assistance Board to pay part of the amount awarded and then to take action against the husband to recover any amount up to the maximum amount of the Order. (An underwriting by the National Assistance Board of a maintenance order featured in a Bill introduced in the House of Lords by Lady Summerskill in 1965, to which the Government replied that it awaited the results of the present study[3].)

Throughout the post-war years much of the disquiet about the matrimonial jurisdiction of magistrates' courts was aggravated by the lack of knowledge of its social effects. Yet in spite of the lack of anything more than the most rudimentary information, successive governments did not hesitate to legislate along familiar lines. The Matrimonial Proceedings (Magistrates' Courts) Act 1960[4] was largely a consolidating statute, but it did more than just bring together all the disparate provisions relating to the matrimonial jurisdiction of magistrates' courts. It incorporated some of the recommendations made in 1956 by the Royal Commission on Marriage and Divorce (The Morton Commission) and was modelled on a Bill prepared by the Departmental Committee under the chairmanship of Mr. Justice (now Lord Justice)

---

[1] Hansard, House of Commons, Vol. 133, col. 1935–6.

[2] Later section 23, Matrimonial Causes Act 1950, now section 22, Matrimonial Causes Act 1965.

[3] Lord Mitchison said that this research was preferable to a departmental committee, but "ultimately they will have to be dealt with as part of the general review of the social services". H. L., Hansard, Vol. 263, 1965, col. 648.   [4] See Appendix A, Part 1.

Arthian Davies. The Act completed the move towards equality of the sexes by permitting husbands to be complainants for all the applicable grounds of complaint. The main practical change was to raise the financial limits of the jurisdiction from £5 to £7 10s a week for a spouse, and from £1 10s. to £2 10s. for a child. These amounts were arbitrarily chosen, since there was no statistical or other evidence available to indicate the amounts in fact awarded by the courts.

In the 1960s the pendulum began once again to swing away from consideration of methods of enforcement towards discussion of the amounts of maintenance.

In 1967, Mr. Quintin Hogg introduced a private members' Bill to provide for an increase in the maximum weekly payment for a child, the subject of affiliation proceedings, from fifty shillings to £5. A further provision delegated to the Home Secretary powers to increase, by statutory instrument, the limit for wife maintenance. On the Bill's second reading, Mr. Dick Taverne, Under-Secretary of State for the Home Office, welcomed its aims and explained that the Government was waiting for the report of the Graham Hall Committee. If the Committee[1] recommended abolition of the statutory limits, the Government might wish to act on the recommendations[2]. The Committee so reported, and the Maintenance Orders Act 1968 had written into it, at committee stage in the Lords, the necessary provision to abolish the limits.

Professor Kahn-Freund has observed that "ever since the Elizabethan Poor Relief Act, 1601, the English law of family maintenance has been closely linked with what may broadly be called the law of social welfare"[3]. In its concluding chapter, the Graham Hall Committee stepped outside its terms of reference to discuss whether and how far decisions about maintenance should be based on court proceedings. "One incidental result of the recent development of social security has been to set new standards for maintenance. As it is most often families with the least resources that are involved in maintenance proceedings, it is inevitable that unfavourable comparisons are drawn between uncertain, irregular and meagre payments obtained through a court and the assured support of supplementary benefit provided as of right by the Ministry of Social Security."[4] For centuries, a wife left destitute by her husband could only fall back upon her kin or on the poor law. Since 1948, she has acquired a right of support without stigma in her capacity as a citizen[5]. Thus, family law and the law of social security have become entwined and "it may be that the

---

[1] It was set up as a result of a recommendation contained in the first report of the Law Commission, and did not owe its existence to any discernible public pressure.

[2] Hansard, House of Commons, Vol. 755, col. 1866-7.

[3] In W. Friedmann (ed.), *Matrimonial Property Law* (1955), p. 304.

[4] Cmnd. 3587, 1968, *op. cit.*, p. 76.

[5] The poor law imposed a stigma as a matter of policy on those who applied for relief. As a matter of policy, it was intended that no stigma should attach to applicants for national assistance or supplementary benefit. But for many citizens with memories running back to the poor law, there is still a stigma attaching to the receipt of "public assistance".

needs of deserted wives for whom maintenance is ordered by a court are so similar to those of fatherless families generally that separate provision for the former would be unrealistic"[1]. The Law Commission has recommended the abolition of the wife's agency of necessity "which today achieves no useful purpose; it has long been an anachronism and, in the light of social security legislation, of the right to obtain maintenance without limitation of amount in the magistrates' court, and of the Legal Aid Scheme, it fulfils no social purpose"[2]. Clearly, the stage is now set for that "further and far-reaching evolution of the maintenance system" which the Graham Hall Committee expected "within the next decade or so"[3]. It is hoped that this study will promote that evolution by providing knowledge of the working of one part of the system.

[1] *Ibid* p. 77. A Departmental Committee on One-Parent Families (the Finer Committee) was set up in 1969 with terms of reference so wide that they must include the social aspects of the matrimonial jurisdiction of the summary courts.

[2] (No. 25) *Family Law: Report on Financial Provision in Matrimonial Proceedings* (1969), para 109. It was statutorily abolished in 1970, sec. s.41, Matrimonial Proceedings and Property Act 1970.

[3] *Op. cit.*, p. 79.

CHAPTER 2

The official statistics

When Sir John Macdonell became editor in 1894, the *Civil Judicial Statistics* entered what the Adams Committee has recently described as their "Golden Age"[1]. One of his many innovations was the tabulation of much useful information about the divorcing population derived from petitions and the marriage certificates attached to them. In particular, the revised statistics showed the duration and number of children of the marriage at the time of the decree, and the occupations of husbands[2]. Official enthusiasm for enlightened judicial statistics did not survive Macdonell's death in 1921 and, when their compilation was transferred shortly afterwards from the Home Office to the newly formed County Courts Branch of the Lord Chancellor's Office, "their content was rigorously reduced very much to what it is today"[3]. Nevertheless, demographic interest in divorce ensured that the Registrar General's annual publications made good some of the deficiencies of the *Civil Judicial Statistics*, and today's information includes the duration of the marriage at the time of the decree, the ages of the spouses, the number of their children, the proportion of divorced people who marry again, an indication of the length of time which men and women of different ages wait before embarking on their next marriage, and their chances of failing again. In addition, the Law Society's annual *Reports on Legal Aid and Advice* clarify the extent to which petitioning since 1950 has become dependent upon legal aid[4].

Until recent decades, petitioners for divorce constituted a minority of those seeking remedies from the courts for their matrimonial troubles. In the early years of this century, divorce petitions made up less than one-tenth of all matrimonial proceedings; by the eve of Hitler's war they amounted to less than half; today they have risen to nearly two-thirds. Figure 1 shows the

---

[1] *Report of the Committee on Civil Judicial Statistics*, Cmnd. 3684, 1968, p. 3.

[2] *The Civil Judicial Statistics* contained this occupational information in a rather crude form from 1896 until 1921; it has not since been available in official sources but data about the occupational composition of the divorcing populations of 1871 and 1951 were published by Griselda Rowntree and N. H. Carrier, The Resort to Divorce in England and Wales, 1858–1957, Population Studies, Vol. XI, No. 3, 1958.

[3] Cmnd. 3684, *op. cit.*, p. 3.

[4] This is neatly demonstrated in Appendix B of The Law Commission's Report on *Reform of the Grounds of Divorce: The Field of Choice* Cmnd. 3123, 1966, pp. 58 and 59.

relationship of divorce petitions and complaints to magistrates for matrimonial guardianship, and poor law orders since 1900.

FIGURE 1   Divorce petitions and complaints to magistrates for matrimonial orders, 1900–1968.

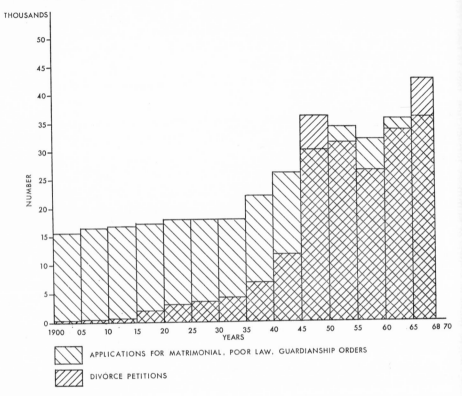

Statistics of the numbers of matrimonial proceedings in the summary courts did not become available until 1893. Table 1 shows the extent since then of the intervention by magistrates in familial relationships.

Throughout the period covered by Table 1, magistrates have been empowered to enforce their orders for maintenance by imprisoning defaulters. Table 2 shows the numbers against whom this sanction has been used.

Tables 1 and 2 disclose all that can be learned from official statistical sources about the past results of the matrimonial jurisdiction of the summary courts Table 3 presents the most recently available data.

Since these statistics were first published in 1893, there have been no significant changes in their compilation or presentation. Under the County and Borough Police Act, 1856, police forces throughout the country make separate returns to the Home Office of information supplied by the Clerks of some 1,000 Magistrates' Courts. These returns are aggregated and published

TABLE 1 Matrimonial Orders and certain other Orders made in Courts of Summary Jurisdiction, 1893 to 1968 (Yearly averages except where otherwise stated).

Period	Matrimonial orders No. of applications	% successful	Poor Law, Nat. assistance and social security orders No. of applications	% successful	Bastardy and affiliation orders No. of applications	% successful	Children and young persons orders[1] No. of applications	% successful	Guardianship of infants orders[2] No. of applications	% successful
1893	3,482	74	3,540	86	8,566	74				
1894	3,618	72	3,659	84	8,749	75				
1895/9	7,355	72	4,098	88	8,415	77				
1900/04	10,736	69	4,754	90	7,895	78				
1905/09	11,067	68	4,958	91	8,404	80				
1910/13	10,765	69	4,022	91	8,491	80				
1914/18	Not available									
1919	14,911	71	2,182	91	11,862	82				
1920/24	13,603	70	4,022[3]	94	9,157	80				
1925/29	14,475	72	3,357	92	7,923	82			454	82
1930/34	14,382	70	3,452	90	6,992	79			831	79
1935/39	10,340[4b]		4,448[4a]		4,363[4a]		656[4a]		1,068[4a]	
1940/44	12,355[4c]		Not available							
1945/49	19,138[4d]	55	1,362[4e]	87	4,430[4e]	83	1,231[4e]	91	6,120[4e]	69
1950/54	26,835	55	365	92	4,855	83	4,001	86	6,960	69
1955/59	24,089	55	172	79	4,543	84	4,382	89	7,763	73
1960/64[5]	28,306	59	340	94	6,659	86	3,789	91	7,095	80
1965/68	30,208	66	268		9,596		2,519		5,423	

[1] Orders for payment of maintenance under the Children and Young Persons Act 1933, ss. 87 and 88.
[2] Orders under The Guardianship of Infants Acts 1886 and 1925 and The Administration of Justice Acts 1886 and 1925 and The Administration of Justice Acts 1928, s.16; Children and Young Persons Act 1932, s.79; and Childrens Act 1948. These figures are only shown from the year 1925.
[3] Figures available only for 3 years 1922/24.
[4] From 1936 up to and including 1949, the number of applications are not given.
[4a] The average number of orders made during the 4 years 1935/38.
[4b] The average number of orders made during the 5 years 1935/39.
[4c] The average numbers of orders made during the 5 years 1940/44.
[4d] The average number of orders made during the 5 years 1945/49.
[4e] The average number of orders made during the 4 years 1946/49.
[5] The numbers of all orders made after 1959 are inflated by the inclusion of attachment of earnings orders. This is discussed on p. 35.

TABLE 2 Numbers committed by Magistrates' Courts for non-payment of wife's and children's maintenance, of bastardy arrears, and of Poor Law, National Assistance or Social Security Orders, 1893–1968. (Yearly averages except where otherwise stated).

Year	Matrimonial Orders			Poor Law, National assistance and social Security Orders			Bastardy and Affiliation Orders		
	No. of Orders	No. of Imprisonments	% Imprisonments to Orders*	No. of Orders	No. of Imprisonments	% Imprisonments to Orders*	No. of Orders	No. of Imprisonments	% Imprisonments to Orders*
1893	2,591	587	23	3,029	1,697	56	6,375	909	14
1894	2,588	767	30	3,056	1,652	54	6,577	979	15
1895/99	5,063	962	19	3,617	1,729	48	6,482	936	14
1900/04	7,375	1,662	23	4,244	2,039	48	6,182	1,081	17
1905/09	7,500	2,114	28	4,506	2,202	49	6,699	1,693	25
1910/13	7,408	2,145	29	3,661	2,015	55	6,767	1,683	25
1914/18	Figures not available				(877)[4]				
1919	10,572	1,288	12	1,980	546	28	9,771	530	5
1920/24	9,510	3,560	37	3,759[1]	1,557[1]	41	7,350[1]	3,100[1]	42
1925/29	10,467	3,905	37	3,071	1,170	38	6,473	2,741	42
1930/34	10,022	3,576	36	3,102	893	29	5,551	2,217	40
1935/39	10,340	2,029	20	4,448[2]	643[2]	14	4,363[2]	906	21
1940/44	12,355	1,627	13	Figures not available			Figures not available	325	
1945/49	19,138	2,859	15	1,362[3]			4,430[3]	351	8
1950/54	14,799	3,430	23	317			4,024	503	12
1955/59	13,333	2,828	21	158			3,766	466	12
1960/64	17,635	2,177	12	270			5,571	262	5
1965/68	19,818			252			8,267	408[5]	5

* Imprisonments are shown as percentages of orders made; $\left(\dfrac{\text{Imprisonments}}{\text{Orders}} \times 100\right)$

[1] Figures for 1922/24 only (others are not available).
[2] Figures for 1935/38 only (others are not available).
[3] Figures for 1946/49 only (others are not available).
[4] Figures for 1914, 17, 18 only.
[5] Figures for 1965, 66, 67 only.

TABLE 3[1] **Magistrates' courts 1969: maintenance, separation and children**

Type of order	Numbers of Applications	Numbers of Orders made
Affiliation Orders	9,601	8,481
Matrimonial Orders	29,408	20,045[a]
Guardianship of Infants Orders	5,909	4,883
Social Security: Orders for maintenance of wife, family or relatives	123	115
Children and Young Persons: Orders for the payment of maintenance under the Children and Young Persons Act, 1933, ss.87 and 88	1,619	1,459
Total	46,660	34,983

(*a*) In addition to these Orders, 50 and 133 Orders were received from overseas for registration and confirmation respectively under the Maintenance Orders (Facilities for Enforcement) Act, 1920. Under the same Act, 177 and 121 Orders were sent overseas for registration and confirmation respectively.

in the annual *Criminal Statistics*[2]. This seventy-year-old anomaly has been noticed in the *Reports* of several recent committees. The Latey Committee on the Age of Majority recommended that "the statistics of domestic proceedings should be separated from the Criminal Statistics"[3]. The Perks Committee on Criminal Statistics endorsed the Latey Committee's recommendation, stated that "the present inclusion of a table relating to non-criminal proceedings in magistrates' courts is an anomaly which should be discontinued", and urged that the statistics should be published in the *Civil Judicial Statistics*[4]. The Adams Committee on the Civil Judicial Statistics approved this suggestion[5] and, as a result, the *Civil Judicial Statistics* for 1968 contained, for the first time, tables relating to maintenance proceedings in magistrates' courts[6].

A statistical appendix to the *Report* of the Graham Hall Committee on Statutory Maintenance Limits revealed that "since 1959 the figures for each category of order published (in the *Criminal Statistics*) have included the number of attachment of earnings orders made during the year to enforce substantive orders in that category"[7]. Despite this, the *Criminal Statistics* carry no warning or explanation of the resulting distortion, although the 1969 volume of the *Civil Judicial Statistics* prints corrected tables which appear below as Tables 4 and 5.

The report of an examination of the *Criminal Judicial Statistics* was published with the annual volume for 1893. It pointed to the inescapable defects

[1] Extracted from *Criminal Statistics*, Cmnd. 4398, 1970, Table VI.
[2] From 1893–1921 they appeared as Table XIV, from 1922–1923 as Table IX, from 1924–1931 as Table XI, from 1932–1934 as Table XII, from 1935–1937 as Table XI, and in 1938 as Table XXI. They were not published during the war. They appeared again as Table X from 1946–1948, became Table XII from 1949–1963, and have been Table VI since 1964.
[3] Cmnd. 3342, 1966, para 185.   [4] Cmnd. 3448, 1967, para 34.
[5] Cmnd. 3684, 1968, para 38.   [6] Cmnd. 4112, 1969, para 44 and Tables K and L.
[7] Cmnd. 3587, 1968, Appendix G, p. 102.

TABLE 4[1] Magistrates' court maintenance proceedings 1958–1969.

Year	Affiliation orders		Married women maintenance orders		Guardianship of Infant orders		National Assistance/Social Security		Children and Young Persons Act—maintenance	
	Applied for	Granted	Applied for	Granted	Applied for	Granted	Applied for	Granted	Applied for	Granted
1958	4,663	3,868	24,655	13,795	7,949	5,438	195	183	4,604	4,003
1959	4,996	4,160	24,520	13,358	8,527	5,670	186	172	4,044	3,483
1960	5,690	4,754	27,793	16,539	10,691	7,373	195	177	3,861	3,440
1961	5,697	4,715	25,471	14,621	7,065	5,023	298	259	3,793	3,343
1962	6,507	5,389	26,128	15,497	5,988	4,437	381	313	4,057	3,544
1963	6,994	5,832	25,717	15,516	5,440	4,216	530	327	3,421	3,030
1964	7,760	6,429	26,069	15,764	5,825	4,429	274	254	3,373	3,024
1965	8,181	6,951	27,262	16,442	5,202	3,994	249	233	3,024	2,711
1966	8,664	7,458	27,586	17,353	4,727	3,800	205	193	2,568	2,315
1967	8,764	7,643	27,146	17,630	4,949	4,004	247	238	1,769	1,596
1968	9,334	8,096	28,004	17,428	5,436	4,287	307	280	1,485	1,329
1969	8,718	7,611	26,753	17,424	5,680	4,656	111	103	1,420	1,269

[1] Cmnd. 4416, 1970, Table L, p. 19.

TABLE 5[1] Attachment of Earnings Orders, 1959–1969.

Year	Affiliation	Married Women Maintenance	Guardianship of Infants	National Assistance	Children and Young Persons	Total
1959*	268	1,054	212	11	212	1,757
1960	656	2,872	821	22	501	4,872
1961	737	2,873	648	34	637	4,929
1962	661	2,585	558	27	575	4,406
1963	626	2,301	383	20	415	3,745
1964	638	2,476	463	21	435	4,033
1965	788	2,989	404	26	402	4,609
1966	934	2,874	360	13	357	4,538
1967	834	2,344	301	16	260	3,785
1968	785	2,483	295	9	204	3,776
1969	870	2,621	227	12	190	3,920

* For this year, only the total number of orders is known. The distribution by type of order has been calculated in accordance with the distribution for 1960–1964.

[1] Ibid., Table M, p. 20.

in tables compiled from returns made by 191 independent police forces which had not been given sufficient instructions to ensure their preparation on a uniform basis. "It would have been better that they should all be wrong, provided that they all made the same mistake, than that some should be right and others wrong..."[1] Little has changed since late-Victorian days. In October 1967, Miss Jean Graham Hall, Chairman of the Committee on Statutory Maintenance Limits, complained in a letter to Chief Master Adams, Chairman of the Committee on Civil Judicial Statistics, that the work of her committee was being hindered by the unreliability of official statistics.

> The only information published about maintenance orders made by Magistrates' Courts is contained in Table VI of the annual volume of the criminal statistics. This information is confined to the number of applications made and the number of orders resulting from these. Even this information, limited as it is, must be regarded as unreliable ... There appear to be no instructions (to police forces) about the definition of an application and it would seem that the variations between the information provided in respect of different courts are very considerable. The number of applications may in some areas relate to separate summonses (where there are several grounds for complaint in one case, a separate summons may be issued in respect of each ground) and in other areas applications for variation orders may be included as well as those for original orders. You will appreciate, therefore, that such published figures as there are provide no reliable guide for any further studies[2].

The statistical consequences of the failure to impose uniform definitions of "applications" and "orders" upon Clerks of Court when they make returns to the police of their district are shown in detail in Table 6 which lists the proportion of matrimonial orders made to applications by police districts arranged by the Registrar General's Standard Regions[3].

The variation from place to place in the proportion of successful applications illustrates and reinforces Miss Graham Hall's criticism of the published statistics. The extreme instances are set out in Table 7.

Thus, the national totals of applications and orders displayed in the present Table VI of the *Criminal Statistics*, the sole source of statistical data about the exercise of matrimonial jurisdiction by magistrates' courts, conceal local variations which range from a success rate for applications of 97% in Liverpool to one of 34% in Birmingham. Clearly, the figures in Table VI must be used with caution.

Summary proceedings are socially and quantitively a main element in the legal regulation of marriage breakdown but even the most elementary

---

[1] C. 7725, 1895, p. 18.
[2] *Report* of the Committee on Civil Judicial Statistics, Cmnd. 3684, 1968, p. 60.
[3] We are greatly indebted to the Home Office which gave us this unpublished information.

TABLE 6 Proportion of successful matrimonial applications, by police district and Registrar General's standard region 1966. Police reports for England and Wales.

Registrar General's Standard Regions	Police district code number	Applications	Orders made	% Orders made to applications
1. Northern	24	94	76	81
	25	64	37	58
	35	826	644	78
	36	97	90	93
	38	194	104	54
	39	240	143	60
	64	34	33	97
	105	192	159	83
	106	264	123	47
	107	33	28	85
	108	—	—	—
	146	19	17	89
	156	178	178	100
	157	173	113	65
		2,408	1,745	72
2. East and West Riding	154	53	49	92
	155	130	125	96
	159	191	153	80
	160	1,061	941	89
	161	51	49	96
	162	620	365	59
	163	34	29	85
	164	68	45	66
	165	106	101	95
	166	64	49	77
	167	1,680	847	50
	168	73	69	95
	169	438	363	83
	170	79	73	92
		4,648	3,258	70
3. North Western	12	382	353	92
	13	142	107	75
	19	188	123	65
	20	62	50	81
	60	2,143	1,486	69
	65	143	91	64
	66	171	104	64
	67	186	186	100
	68	50	50	100
	69	83	63	76
	72	399	387	97
	73	1,622	671	41
	74	153	111	73
	75	115	98	85
	76	94	88	94
	77	68	66	97
	78	339	150	44
	79	46	42	91
	80	69	44	64
	81	45	40	89
		6,500	4,310	66

Registrar General's standard regions	Police district code number	Applications	Orders made	% Orders made to applications
4. North Midland	26	293	246	84
	28	64	49	77
	82	175	121	69
	83	168	153	91
	84	25	25	100
	86	15	15	100
	88	46	37	80
	89	72	51	71
	90	21	21	100
	101	139	135	97
	102	87	74	85
	109	308	292	95
	111	312	193	62
		1,725	1,412	82
5. Midland	45	29	20	69
	115	49	44	90
	125	802	572	71
	127	133	119	89
	128	50	27	54
	129	466	383	82
	142	283	226	80
	143	2,480	855	34
	144	164	124	76
	150	145	143	99
	151	7	6	86
	153	9	9	100
		4,617	2,528	55
6. Eastern	1	59	47	80
	3	67	56	84
	40	530	408	77
	42	114	107	94
	47	103	101	98
	49	75	63	84
	97	85	78	92
	99	97	77	79
	100	48	40	83
	130	58	55	95
	131	70	58	83
	132	20	18	90
		1,326	1,108	84
7. London and South Eastern	50	216	204	94
	999	5,789	3,104	54
	133	67	61	91
	136	124	106	85
	137	9	8	89
	138	34	33	97
	139	24	20	83
	141	136	106	78
		6,399	3,642	57

Registrar General's standard regions	Police district code number	Applications	Orders made	% orders made to applications
8. Southern	4	85	82	96
	5	45	42	93
	7	108	98	91
	113	30	24	80
	120	216	173	80
	122	97	95	98
	123	197	123	62
		778	637	82
9. South Western	21	41	33	80
	30	3	2	67
	31	50	44	88
	32	33	21	64
	34	99	76	77
	43	283	192	68
	44	117	85	73
	117	123	111	90
	118	31	31	100
	121	76	59	78
	148	51	41	80
		907	695	77
10. Wales	95	105	82	78
	96	44	32	73
	175	58	34	59
	177	27	16	59
	178	42	39	93
	179	192	186	97
	180	336	241	72
	181	73	30	41
	183	226	154	68
	184	40	35	88
	185	10	6	60
	186	39	37	95
		1,192	892	75
Regional areas: Total		30,500*	20,227*	66

* These being the two figures shown in Table VI of the *Criminal Statistics* for 1966.

knowledge about them is lacking. The known characteristics of spouses petitioning for divorce cannot usefully be compared with those of the population passing through the magistrates' courts because, in the case of the latter, nothing is known about their age, the duration of their marriages or the numbers of their children at the time of their complaints. It is not known on what grounds orders are made or for how long they last or what amounts of maintenance are ordered to be paid to wives and children or by what amounts and how frequently payments fall into arrears[1]. The total number of "live" orders has

[1] A study was undertaken by the Home Office on behalf of the Committee on Statutory Maintenance Limits which produced much information about amounts of maintenance ordered by the courts. The findings are discussed in Chapter 6.

TABLE 7   **Analysis of police divisions with over 200 matrimonial applications in 1966.**

Police district	Number of applications	% successful applications
These four police divisions granted orders in 90% or more of the cases:		
72 Liverpool City	399	97
109 Nottinghamshire	308	95
50 Kent Co.	216	94
12 Chester Co.	382	92
These four police divisions granted orders in fewer than 50% of the cases:		
143 Birmingham City	2,480	34
73 Manchester City	1,622	41
78 Salford City	399	44
106 Newcastle-upon-Tyne	264	47
These five police divisions granted orders in between half and two-thirds of the cases:		
167 Leeds City	1,680	50
999 Metropolitan	5,789	54
162 Bradford City	620	59
39 Nottingham City	312	62
111 Sunderland Boro.	240	60

always been estimated by crude guesswork.[1] However, our data have per-mitted a calculation which suggests that there were some 165,000 matri-monial orders and some 41,000 affiliation orders live on the 1st January 1966[2].

The growth of an awareness of the significant role of these summary matrimonial proceedings can be measured by comparing the views of the Morton Commission on Marriage and Divorce in 1956 with those of the Adams Committee on Civil Judicial Statistics in 1968. The Morton Com-mission reported that

> Our attention was drawn to certain gaps in the statistical information in respect of matrimonial proceedings in magistrates' courts . . . there would be some advantage in having fuller statistical information . . . if this could be readily provided. But we were informed that to collect and tabulate this information would involve a good deal of extra work, additional

[1] The Fischer Williams Committee on Imprisonment by Courts of Summary Jurisdiction in Default of Payment of Fines and Other Sums of Money (Cmd. 4649, 1934) is an example.
"We have tried to make an estimate by taking for five Courts in different parts of the country the number of orders in force and the number of imprisonments in default, and assuming that the ratio of imprisonments to orders given by the experience of these Courts, holds good for the rest of the country. The figures for these five courts show that with 2,464 orders in force, there were 173 imprisonments in default, i.e. 7 imprisonments for every 100 orders in force. If this ratio holds true for the rest of the country, the 3,648 imprisonments recorded for 1932 give a figure of 52,114 as the number of maintenance orders then in force in the whole country". (p. 37.)
Another example is the statement made by the Justices' Clerks' Society to the Committee on the Enforcement of Judgment Debts in 1966 that "we estimate that not less than 300,000 maintenance orders are currently being collected by Magistrates' Courts". The Society did not explain how its estimate was made.
[2] The details of the method of calculation are set out in Appendix B, Part 2.

clerical help in many courts and considerable expense. Our conclusion is that, in present circumstances, the value of the additional information would not be sufficient to justify the work and expense of obtaining it[1].

Although weighing "the restricting factors of limited manpower and finance"[2], the Adams Committee recommended wide-ranging changes in the compilation and content of these statistics. If their detailed recommendations which are reproduced in Appendix C are adopted, the official statistics will show *inter alia*, by type of order the grounds on which orders are made, the duration and number of children of the marriage at the time of the complaint and the amount of maintenance ordered to be paid.

[1] Cmnd. 9678, 1956, para 1152 and 1153.
[2] Cmnd. 3684, 1968, p. 37 and pp. 38–40.

CHAPTER 3

The design of the survey

The object of this study is to discover how the matrimonial jurisdiction of magistrates is exercised, and to make a preliminary exploration of its social results. As official information is so meagre, only a national survey could produce reliable findings. A national survey required a sample of magistrates' courts, representative of all magistrates' courts in the country, from which a number of matrimonial, affiliation and attachment of earnings orders could be extracted for examination sufficiently large to permit valid conclusions about the working of the system and the social characteristics of the wives and husbands who use it. At the outset we recognized that a national sample would impose limitations on the survey. From his experience in charge of research at the Department of Health and Social Security, Mr. G. Beltram has pointed out that "because the numbers in such a sample have to be limited, interest in regional and local variations may have to be subordinated to the need for a national coverage"[1]. We have concentrated on the national picture and our survey was not designed to show regional variations or comparisons. Our preparatory investigations showed that courts throughout the country keep accessible files[2] only of those complaints which result in orders; for the remainder the court record shows simply "complaint dismissed". Table 1 (page 33) shows the proportion of successful applications for the different types of order since 1893, and it is only these which can be studied from court records.

There has been no previous attempt to draw a random sample of case files from all courts in the country and many difficulties had to be faced. Chief of these was the impossibility of using Home Office statistics to distribute matrimonial applications among the magistrates' courts of England and Wales because each court's statistical return is made first to its Police Division and there scrambled with returns from other courts before the Division's aggregate return is passed on to the Home Office. But without knowledge of the number of applications made in different courts, it would have been impos-

---

[1] "Methods of surveying categories of people presenting special problems or needs", *Statistical News*, February 1970, Vol. 8, p. 18.

[2] In some, perhaps many, courts there is no record of proceedings which resulted in the refusal of orders.

sible to construct a sample of courts. This obstacle was overcome by using unpublished data[1] obtained by a Working Party appointed by the County Councils' Association, the Association of Municipal Corporations and the Central Council of Magistrates' Courts' Committees at the instance of the Home Secretary in 1957 "to work out and report on the details of a work measurement system which might be recommended to Magistrates' Courts' Committees and County and County Borough Councils"[2].

In 1964, in collaboration with the Organization and Methods Division of the Treasury, the Working Party invited all Justices' Clerks employing full-time staff (except the Clerks to the Metropolitan Magistrates' Courts) to complete a questionnaire about the work-load of their courts. The replies showed in particular the orders, including orders for variation, revocation and discharge, made in matrimonial, guardianship and affiliation cases during the year ending on the 30th September 1964 and also the number of maintenance orders under which payments had been made during the same period. Thus, it was possible to learn both the distribution of new orders made and the number of live orders being enforced in those courts administered by Clerks who replied to the Working Party's questionnaire. At that time, there were 901 Petty Sessional areas in England and Wales with 1,080 courts administered by some 530 Justices' Clerks serving full-time or part-time. The Working Party obtained information from 341 Clerks. The Home Office wrote on our behalf to the full-time Clerks who had no full-time staff and to the part-time Clerks who were not consulted by the Working Party; and we dealt directly with the Clerks to the Metropolitan Courts excluded from the Working Party's study. We also wrote, sometimes several times, to those Clerks who did not reply to the letter from the Home Office. As a result, our sample was constructed on the basis of answers from more than three-quarters of all Justices' Clerks in the country whose courts held 90% of all live orders. After the courts to be sampled had been selected, we continued to follow up the Clerks who had not responded to the original questionnaire from the Working Party in 1964 or to the letter from the Home Office. In the end, we had full information from 500 of the 520 Justices' Clerks administering 96% of the country's summary courts and holding 99% of all the live orders. The remainder of the Clerks from whom we failed to obtain replies were chiefly part-timers running small courts.

It was decided to stratify the sampling frame so that large courts would be sampled in proportion to their size and smaller courts in accordance with their regional distribution. The sample contained 46 courts of which 9 were drawn from the large County Borough and Borough Courts, 34 from the Petty Sessional Division courts and 3 from the Metropolitan Magistrates'

[1] We are very grateful to the Organization and Methods Division of the Treasury which made this material available to us and especially to Miss J. Davison who gave us indispensable help in interpreting it.

[2] *Working Party on Work Measurement in Justices' Clerks' Offices, Interim Report* (1963), unpublished, p. 1.

Courts. We concluded that an examination of some 1,200 matrimonial orders would yield statistically reliable conclusions. A draft questionnaire framed after preliminary study of the data available in the records of a number of courts was sent, with a covering letter from the Home Office explaining the purpose of the study, to the Clerks of the 45 courts constituting the sample of courts[1]. The Clerks were asked to help in three ways

(i) by reporting the number of live orders held in their courts on 1st January 1966;

(ii) by completing a small number of pilot questionnaires and by commenting on the questions and the layout; and

(iii) by encouraging members of their staffs to volunteer to complete the required number of questionnaires which would be calculated after the total number of live orders held by their courts had been reported.

A small fee was offered to the court staff for each completed questionnaire. In the event only two courts in the large court sample and eight in the small court sample failed to provide volunteers. In these courts and in the Metropolitan Magistrates' Courts, the work was carried out by our own research staff.

The forty-five courts were asked to complete questionnaires in proportion to the number of live orders they had reported. Completed questionnaires were twice checked by research staff. The reliability of a sample of court officials' work in extracting data from court records and in completing the questionnaires was tested tactfully by visiting research staff. Complete returns were secured from all courts in the sample. By similar means, a sample of some 550 affiliation orders live on 1st January 1966, was also obtained. Further, on behalf of the Committee on the Enforcement of Judgment Debts (the Payne Committee) we undertook a separate but related study of some 950 attachment of earnings orders made under the Maintenance Orders Act 1958 drawn from a further sample of forty-three courts[2].

Throughout the period of the study, research staff were visiting courts in the sample and were consulting Justices' Clerks and their staffs. In this way, additional information not available in court records about such administrative matters as the opening hours of court collecting offices and their regulations for the receipt and payment of maintenance, was collected. Court records and staffs could not provide us with systematic information about the attitudes and feelings of wives and husbands who had experienced the matrimonial

---

[1] Appendix B, Part 1, sets out the method by which the sample of courts was selected. The matrimonial order, the affiliation order and the attachment of earnings questionnaires are printed in Appendix B, Part 4.

[2] "Court" may be an ambiguous term because one Clerk may administer several courts. If a questonnaire is sent to a Clerk, several courts may be treated as one in his return, as was the case with several courts in our sample. A list of the sample courts is given in Appendix B, Part 3.

jurisdiction of magistrates' courts; and our resources did not permit a survey designed for this purpose, even if we could have overcome the formidable technical and other obstacles[1]. Nevertheless, we were convinced that the opinions of spouses whose marriage breakdowns had been scrutinised by the courts were indispensable to a realistic assessment of this jurisdiction. We therefore approached Mr. Graham Stanford of the *News of the World*, and he very generously helped us by inviting his readers to write to us. In the event, we received 1,300 letters from which we eventually obtained 281 wives and 263 husbands who gave us detailed accounts of their experience of the jurisdiction[2].

The different types of live matrimonial and affiliation orders in the survey and the categories of summary court at which they were held on 1st January 1966 are shown in Table 8. These orders are defined in Appendix G.

TABLE 8   **Type of order and category of summary court at which orders were held on 1st January 1966.**

(a) Matrimonial Orders

| Type of order | Category of Summary Court | | | | | | | |
| | Stipendiary | | County Borough or Borough | | Petty Sessional Division | | Total | |
	No.	%	No.	%	No.	%	No.	%
Guardianship of Infants and children only	15	15	101	22	132	20	248	20
Married Women	49	43	120	26	186	28	355	29
Married Women and Children	48	43	236	52	343	52	627	51
Total	112	100	457	100	661	100	1,230	100
% of Total		9		37		54		

(b) Affiliation orders

Affiliation	57	10	187	34	306	56	550	100

The different types of attachment of earnings orders in the special study undertaken for the Committee on the Enforcement of Judgment Debts are shown in Table 9.

It is difficult to validate the sample of orders on which the survey is based because it cannot easily be compared with the known characteristics of relevant populations. Only in the case of the attachment of earnings sample is a

[1] For example, any direct study which relied upon interviews would have to discover means of (a) obtaining the names and addresses of wives and their husbands at the time of the first complaint, and (b) of following up the parties after the order has been made. Even if the legal authorities were willing to give the necessary information, it is unlikely that a research project could succeed in maintaining contact with husbands as this task baffles many of their wives as well as the Supplementary Benefits Commission.

[2] The source and analyses of the data are explained in Chapter 8.

TABLE 9 Type of attachment order and category of originating court[1].

Type of attachment order	Stipendiary No.	Stipendiary %	County Borough or Borough No.	County Borough or Borough %	Petty Sessional No.	Petty Sessional %	Total No.	Total %
Affiliation	1		51	13	79	14	131	14
Married Women	2		221	58	351	64	574	61
Guardianship	1		58	15	87	16	146	16
National Assistance	—		1	1	4	1	5	1
Children and Young Persons	—		49	13	28	5	77	8
Total	4		380	100	549	100	933	100
% of Total		1		41		58		100

direct comparison possible of the types of order in the sample with those made in the same period for England and Wales as a whole. Table 10 shows the comparison.

TABLE 10 Distribution of Bedford College sample of attachment orders among different types of attachable orders compared with that of all attachment orders made in England and Wales, 1960–1965[2].

Type of order	England and Wales All orders	England and Wales %	Bedford College sample Sample	Bedford College sample %
Affiliation	4,106	15·4	131	13·8
Married women	16,096	60·5	585	61·5
Guardianship	3,277	12·3	152	16·0
National Assistance ..	150	0·6	5	0·5
Children and Young Persons	2,965	11·2	78	8·2
Total	26,594	100·0	951	100·0

On behalf of the Committee on Statutory Maintenance Limits (the Graham Hall Committee), the Home Office analysed "the amounts of maintenance ordered by magistrates' courts in England and Wales as a result of maintenance proceedings of various kinds during the months of September and October 1966"[3]. The data were derived from the returns which courts are required to make to the Board of Inland Revenue under provisions which apply to orders for "small maintenance payments" for income tax purposes, and consisted of all orders made by all courts in the country in the two months. As our sample contains orders made over a long period of time and the Home Office sample

[1] The Table excludes four orders of unknown origin and fourteen orders which had originated in the High Court and which were registered in magistrates' courts.
[2] Orders made in 1959 have been excluded from the national total because the Home Office cannot provide a breakdown by type of order for that year.
[3] Cmnd. 3587 (1968) p. 105.

contains orders made in the autumn of 1966, the only characteristics by which their composition may be compared directly are by the number of children per order at the time the order was made both for guardianship orders and for matrimonial orders with provision only for children, and by the distribution of matrimonial orders of different type. Tables 11 and 12 show the comparisons.

TABLE 11   Comparison of guardianship orders and matrimonial orders with provision only for children in Bedford College and Home Office samples by number of children per order.

Number of children per order, guardianship orders and matrimonial orders with provision only for children	Bedford College Number of orders	%	Home Office Number of orders	%
1 child	127	51	417	49
2 children	69	28	276	32
3 children	33	13	114	13
4 or more children	19	8	53	6
Total number of orders	248	100	860	100

The difference between the distributions by the number of children per order in the two samples is not statistically significant, and it is therefore reasonable to conclude that the two samples were drawn from the same population. The comparison in Table 12 of the distribution of matrimonial orders by type suggests a similar conclusion. As all the Home Office orders were made in 1966, the comparison has been restricted to the orders in the Bedford College sample which were made in 1964 and 1965.

TABLE 12   Number and distribution of original maintenance orders by type made in 1964 and 1965 in the Bedford College and those made in 1966 in Home Office samples.

Matrimonial orders making provision for	Sample			
	Bedford College orders made in 1964 and 1965		Home Office orders made in 1966	
	No.	%	No.	%
Wives only	58	21	635	18
Wives and children	157	57	1,977	57
Children only and Guardianship of Infants	62	22	859	25
Total	277	100	3,471	100

One further comparison can be made. In 1966, the Ministry of Social Security surveyed a sample of 2,500 families (families with only one child were excluded) in the course of an enquiry into the *Circumstances of Families*[1]. Table 13 compares the distribution by family size of the two survey populations.

[1] Published under this title in 1967.

TABLE 13 Comparison of family size of families with two or more children in the Bedford College sample with the size of fatherless families in the Ministry of Social Security enquiry into the circumstances of families.

	Sample	
	Bedford College	Ministry of Social Security
Family Size	%	%
2 children	65	62
3 children	22	21
4 children	8	10
5 children	3	4
6 or more children	2	3
Total	100	100

The reliability of sample data may be adversely affected by the deficiencies of the sampling frame and the failure to adhere to strict statistical processes in drawing the sample, together with the inevitable non-response. The sample on which the present study is based seems to meet these tests satisfactorily. The sampling frame of courts was simple to define, the checks on the work of the Clerks in selection of case files and the extraction of data were verified, while the extent of non-response was remarkably low. Finally, the validation tests with such national data as are available strengthen confidence in the representativeness of the sample.

CHAPTER 4

The applicant and the court

The application

The first, formal step for a wife or a husband who wishes to obtain a maintenance order is to make a complaint under section 1 of the Matrimonial Proceedings (Magistrates' Courts) Act 1960.[1] The complainant must appear before the court. In most courts applications are heard by a single magistrate, who may issue the summons which requires the respondent to appear before the court to answer the complaint[2].

What the magistrate must be told before a summons is granted varies from court to court, and the law regulating the practice is ambiguous. The central issue is whether at this preliminary stage the court may delay the summons in order to attempt to reconcile husband and wife, or whether a complainant who has formally demonstrated the court's jurisdiction is entitled as of right to proceed forthwith without being compelled to accept an offer of conciliation. Reconciliation has been a distinctive feature of this branch of family law since the Summary Procedure (Domestic Proceedings) Act 1937, although little use is made of the power once the courts have begun to hear the complaint. Magistrates are empowered at any stage of the proceedings to ask a probation officer or any other person to attempt to reconcile the parties and to report to the court if such attempts are unsuccessful[3]. If reconciliation is an important function of magistrates' courts, the earlier it starts the greater the chance of success. Mr. L. M. Pugh, the Stipendiary Magistrate for Liverpool, observes that "it is generally recognized that magistrates are acting wisely and in the interests of the parties and particularly the children by offering

[1] Where the ground of complaint is adultery the complaint must be made within six months of the time when the complainant first knew of the adultery, s.12, Matrimonial Proceedings (Magistrates' Courts) Act 1960. Complaints based on any other ground must be made within six months from the time when the ground of complaint arose, section 104, Magistrates' Courts Act 1952; this period of limitation has no significance in cases of desertion and wilful neglect to maintain, since these are continuing matrimonial offences.

[2] From 1st April 1970 a complaint may be made to, and a summons issued by, a justices' clerk, Justices' Clerks Rules 1970, S.I. 231 (L.12)/1970.

[3] Section 59, Magistrates' Courts Act 1952. Section 60 provides that the court may employ a probation officer to ascertain more precisely the financial state of the parties: *Kershaw v. Kershaw* [1966] P. 13.

the service of a probation officer with a view to reconciliation. Clearly the earlier in the proceedings that such an offer is made the better. . . ."[1] In its practice guide, the Magistrates' Association endorses this approach. It recognizes that lay magistrates may even decide to defer the grant of a summons until the probation officer has seen the parties. But the guide adds that the complainant has the right to a summons if a legal cause for complaint is shown, and to refuse any attempt at reconciliation.[2]

In exercising criminal jurisdiction under Section 1(1) of the Magistrates' Courts Act 1952, a single magistrate must be satisfied that an applicant asking for the issuance of a summons has a prima facie case. The section provides that a summons may be issued "upon information being laid before a justice of the peace . . . that any person has committed an offence". Section 43 of the Magistrates' Courts Act 1952 gives the magistrate a discretionary power to issue a summons on receipt of a complaint. But the issue of a summons in matrimonial proceedings is not to be equated with that in a criminal charge. If Parliament had intended to put the "complaint" process of matrimonial proceedings on the same footing as the "information" process applicable to criminal proceedings, it could have re-phrased Section 1 to read: "upon information *or complaint* being laid before a justice of the peace . . . that any person either has, or is suspected of having, committed an offence, or has *incurred a legal obligation*. . . ." By declining to amalgamate the two procedures the legislature has contemplated different rules for the criminal and for the matrimonial jurisdictions[3]. The power to order maintenance has always been treated as a civil jurisdiction[4]. Moreover, a wife who proceeds in the High Court for maintenance on the grounds of wilful neglect to maintain by way of originating summons automatically, and without judicial interposition, invokes the court's jurisdiction[5]. Thus, there is no reason why complainants before magistrates should be differently treated from applicants to the High Court; and no ground for holding that a magistrate has to be satisfied that a complainant has a *prima facie* case. It is clearly not the duty of a magistrate to make his own inquiries into the facts upon which an application for a summons is based before deciding to grant it[6]. But it would be difficult in practice to suggest that a summons ought to be issued merely because a complaint has been made. This is why, naturally, magistrates depart from the strict letter of the law. Few complainants have legal advice at this stage, and experience shows that many have no clear objectives in mind when invoking the assistance of the court. Many wives are numbed by personal and financial

[1] L. M. Pugh, *Matrimonial Proceedings before Magistrates* (2nd ed. 1966) p. 31.

[2] Pugh, *op. cit.*, p. 31, states that "the first point to be borne in mind is that the parties are under no obligation to accept the offer of conciliation. If they prefer to pursue their remedies they are entitled to and have the right to ask the court to hear the complaint and to adjudicate without reference to such refusal, and the court must then proceed".

[3] The point has never been tested in the courts.

[4] S.54(4), Magistrates' Courts Act 1952.

[5] *Caras v. Caras* [1955] 1 W.L.R. 254; *Dyson v. Dyson* [1954] P. 198.

[6] *Sammy-Joe v. G.P.O. Mount Pleasant Office* [1967] 1 W.L.R. 370, 374 H.

difficulties; they seek financial support but have no knowledge of the legal procedures through which they must substantiate their right to weekly maintenance. Some have been given advice by the Supplementary Benefits Commission, or the Citizens' Advice Bureau (or other social advice agency), which has directed them to the Justices' Clerk's office. The social agencies are not at present adequately equipped to provide legal advice.

In attempting to discover what complainants really want and whether they have a case at all, most courts turn to the probation officer[1]. Indeed, it is frequent practice for a probation officer to attend with the applicant before the magistrate. This may be intended as a means both of eliciting sufficient information to warrant the issue of a summons and of attempting reconciliation. Nevertheless neither object seems to have been contemplated in the legislative provisions relating to the issue of a summons. Section 59 of the 1952 Act envisages that the services of a conciliator may be invoked only when both spouses are before the court after the summons has been issued. Even then, the magistrates themselves must never attempt to reconcile the parties. A magistrate is, therefore, obliged legally to confine his enquiries to ensuring (a) that the complainant is lawfully married (he need not investigate at all to discover whether the marriage is polygamous or bigamous); (b) that the complainant has come to the right court and within the time-limit prescribed for bringing the complaint; and (c) that the complaint relates to a matrimonial offence which falls within one of the nine categories listed in Section 1(1) of the 1960 Act.

In view of the lack of clarity of the legislation and in the absence of judicial guidance, magistrates' courts interpret their powers in diverse ways. All the Justices' Clerks whose courts constituted the sample for this study were asked to complete a questionnaire about the procedure used in their courts, and forty-two replied. Their general view was that conciliation is a permissible function for court officials from the moment that a complainant approaches the court. Only two clerks said that no conciliation procedure was available in their courts at the stage prior to the issue of the summons. In all the other courts, probation officers are always at hand if there is any hope of reconciliation. Few courts deliberately hold up the application for a summons in order to promote conciliation, although some do. Of the forty-two replies, thirty-two indicated that magistrates act on the basis of having no discretion to refuse a valid application for a summons. The remainder think that magistrates possess such a discretion but rarely use it in the interests of

---

[1] The annual probation statistics prepared by the Home Office show the great importance of the conciliation work undertaken by the probation service. In 1966, probation officers dealt with 39,000 broken marriages. Some 6,000 of these were referred to them by the courts, over 2,000 being before a summons was issued and almost 4,000 after; over 1,100 were referred by Justices' Clerks; over 5,300 were referred by social agencies, the police and others; and over 26,000 resulted from direct application by the spouses. The result of this conciliation work was that the spouses were believed to be living together again in about 19,500 cases. Reconciliation failed in almost 13,000 cases and the outcome of the remainder is unknown.

reconciliation. Thus, although magistrates throughout the country interpret their powers in different ways, their actual procedure is well standardized.

The pattern is that the complainant calls personally at the Justices' Clerk's office. If no solicitor has been instructed to act for her, she will be told that it is advisable and that legal aid is available. Even when a solicitor has been advising the complainant, it is unusual for the complainant to be accompanied by anyone from the solicitor's office on her first visit to the court office, mainly because the solicitor has not then been instructed to act but only to advise. At this stage some courts make an appointment for the complainant to attend on another day for the particulars of the complaint to be taken; others arrange for a single magistrate to participate in the pre-application procedure, almost always with a view to interviewing the complainant about the prospects of keeping the marriage together and thus obviating maintenance proceedings. Some courts use a probation officer, a senior court official or even the warrant officer to perform the same function. Most courts, however, either immediately or at a later appointed day, take down the particulars through the justices' clerk or one of his assistants. A small number of courts complete a form on which the necessary details about the marriage, family circumstances and income are filled in. A good example is the form used by the Justices' Clerk to the City of Leicester Justices which is printed in Appendix D.

After the complainant has given the requisite particulars either orally or in writing, she is told to attend before the magistrates for the application to issue the summons. Some courts arrange for this application to be heard at a special time in the magistrates' private room with the hope of effecting reconciliation, the procedure adopted is akin to counselling. But most courts deal with the application at the hearing of ordinary business at the beginning of the day's work and in open court. Whether the application is heard privately or in public, the Justices' Clerk or his deputy and often a probation officer are in attendance.

Most courts report that at this stage magistrates are concerned only to see if the prerequisites for issuance of the summons are complied with. On the other hand, those which sit in private discuss the family circumstances, the necessity for court proceedings and a possible adjournment. Only if the complainant is willing to accept help will the court instruct the probation officer to intervene. If the complainant insists on going ahead with her application and the magistrate is satisfied that she has established grounds for the issuance of the summons, the summons will automatically be issued. But most complainants are reluctant to spurn the court's offer of help towards reconciliation, however little they may be disposed towards it.

Those courts which have built up an elaborate procedure before issuing a summons are quite clear about their motives. They feel that early intervention by a probation officer offers the best, if not the only hope of reconciliation. Once the husband is confronted with the summons for maintenance, their experience shows that the marital antagonism is further exacerbated. Certainly the widely held view is that the best chance of reconciliation is lost once the parties confront each other in court with allegations and counter-allegations of matrimonial offences. One cynic observed that all hope of reconciliation disappears, at least when the wife's mother hears her daughter's evidence in court. These courts are well satisfied with the effectiveness of their reconciliation machinery; but, as they cannot follow up their cases and do not keep records, it is not possible to assess their rate of success.

Time spent awaiting hearing

One of the major problems facing a wife left with dependant children without sufficient financial assistance is the speed with which she can obtain an order from the court and enforce it against her husband. Where the need is urgent, the wife must turn to the Supplementary Benefits Commission. But there are many cases where wives, who have some money to tide them over the period immediately after a husband's desertion, require a maintenance order within a reasonably short period of time.

Each type of order in the survey was sorted according to the length of time it took for the complaint to be heard from the moment the complaint was lodged. This information was available for those cases in which the delay was more than eight weeks (15% of the total of 791). These were analysed to ascertain the reason for the delay.

Three-quarters of the wife complainants obtained their orders within six weeks. 6% of the complainants had to wait more than twelve weeks. The longest delays occurred in Guardianship of Infant cases, but this is possibly explicable on the grounds that there is less urgency where maintenance for a child only is sought, although delay may often be occasioned by the necessity to obtain a welfare report, involving an adjournment. Delays of more than eight weeks usually resulted from a request of the parties, or of one of them. In 60% of these cases, hearings scheduled to be heard within 6 weeks were adjourned on the application of either or both of the parties. It is noticeable that the average time spent awaiting a hearing increased after 1961. Prior to 1961, 82% of all hearings took place within six weeks; thereafter only 68% were heard within six weeks. In 1965 the figure further dropped to 64%. The probable explanation is the increased use of legal aid, which results in delays while the complainant or respondent obtains it, or while solicitors are gathering evidence and preparing their case for hearing.

Legal representation

Legal aid in matrimonial proceedings in magistrates' courts became available on 8th May, 1961[1]. This event brought about a significant change in the procedure of magistrates' courts when handling the difficult problem of determining the commission of a matrimonial offence. Nevertheless, a surprisingly large number of complainants and respondents were legally represented in the years immediately before 1961.

Of the orders in the survey sample made before May 1961, relevant information was available for 436. These disclosed that in 144 cases (33%) both parties had the assistance of solicitor or counsel at the hearing of the application; in 149 cases (34%) neither party was legally represented. In 61% of the cases where only one party was represented, it was the wife, in 38% the husband. Overall, wives were represented in 47% of the cases, husbands in 40%.

After May 1961 although the wife-complainant was legally *represented* in (441) 89% of the cases, only 49% of these wives were legally *aided*. The probable explanation of this discrepancy is that some courts failed to record the existence of a legal aid certificate although representation was always noted. Husband-respondents were represented in 52% of cases. In half the cases both parties were represented, and in only 11% of all hearings was neither party represented.

There were insufficient data in the court records to indicate the time taken for the hearing of cases, and it was thus not possible to judge whether legal representation involved more or fewer hours of court time. But the costs awarded against husband-respondents increased considerably after legal aid. Before 1961 only 6% of husband-respondents were ordered to pay costs of £5 or more. Since that date, 34% of husband-respondents were ordered to pay more than £5 costs. If only the latest two years of the survey are taken (1964 and 1965), the figure increases to 41%. This suggests that (*a*) the extra cost of increased representation for wives meant a heavier cost burden to the husbands summoned by legally-represented and, in half of the cases, legally-aided wives; (*b*) proceedings were probably handled less peremptorily, involving fairly lengthy hearings and, perhaps as a consequence, a judicial urge to pass on to the losing party some of the costs of the hearing; and (*c*) an apparent unwillingness on the part of justices to allow the legal aid fund always to shoulder the burden of the costs of the proceedings.

[1] Legal Aid and Advice Act 1949 (Management Order No. 10) Order 1961 (S.I. 1961 No. 554).

Grounds for complaint

Surprisingly, interim orders were made in respect of fewer than 5% of all orders. Table 14 below shows the grounds of complaint in all the Married Women and Married Women and Children orders in the survey for which information was available. The absence of the necessary information in respect of 14% of such orders may be accounted for partly by the long duration of some orders, partly by the transfer of orders from one court to another, and partly by inadequate court records.

TABLE 14   **Grounds for complaint in married women and married women and children orders live on 1st January 1966.**

Complaints	Number of complaints	% of total complaints	% of complainants alleging
Desertion	593	47	70
Wilful neglect to maintain ..	397	31	47
Persistent cruelty	183	14	22
Adultery	94	7	11
Other	4	—	—
Total	1,271	100	

A further breakdown of the data in Table 14 showing multiple complaints (i.e. a summons alleging more than one ground of complaint[1]) suggests that 63% of all complaints alleged only one ground. In these cases, 49% alleged desertion, 21% wilful neglect to maintain, 16% adultery, and 14% persistent cruelty. For all complaints alleging either single or multiple grounds desertion appeared in 70%, wilful neglect in 47%, persistent cruelty in 22%, and adultery in 11%. The data disclose that the majority of cases do not show a finding of wilful neglect on the final order; this is the case with 58% of all orders under which a wife receives a maintenance order for herself.

The separation order

A magistrates' court has power, *inter alia*, to provide that "the complainant be no longer bound to cohabit with the defendant". The non-cohabitation clause in a matrimonial order, alternatively known as a separation order, once the main remedy available to wives ill-used by their husbands, now retains

[1] Many courts make an order only on one ground of complaint, though they may well have been ready to find other grounds proved.

its pre-eminence only in the statutory priority accorded to the orders which the court can make by virtue of section 2 of the Matrimonial Proceedings (Magistrates' Courts) Act 1960[1].

The Committee on Statutory Maintenance Limits in 1968 reflected a widely-held view that "today the main concern of the magistrates' domestic court is to determine issues which will affect the wife's financial position, and only rarely now do justices make an order providing for the non-cohabitation of the spouses"[2]. This is an unexceptionable statement of what the law requires. But the reality of what happens in magistrates' courts hardly bears out such a bald assertion. Separation orders still figure prominently in the exercise of the Justices' matrimonial jurisdiction, to what extent and for what reasons the present study will disclose. The separation order has not yet been consigned to the museum of legal history.

Magistrates are clearly given by the statute a discretion whether or not to include a non-cohabitation clause in any order they might make; and the discretion is absolute. As Sir Jocelyn Simon P. said in *Corton v. Corton*[3] "I do not believe that it would be right to put any such clog on the discretion of the justices". But any discretion must be exercised judicially and therefore in accordance with the principles enunciated by the High Court in decisions over the last sixty years. Until the turn of the century magistrates included, as a matter of course, a non-cohabitation clause in every order for maintenance. Then in 1906, in *Dodd v. Dodd*[4], Sir Gorell Barnes P. condemned the widespread use of separation orders and declared that the intention of the Summary Jurisdiction (Married Woman) Act 1895, consolidating and extending the 1878 and 1886 Acts, was to empower justices to make separation orders only in cases of cruelty and of habitual drunkenness where protection for the spouse could be presumed to be necessary. The *Report* of The Royal Commission on Marriage and Divorce in 1912 explained the automatic insertion by magistrates of non-cohabitation clauses on the basis that "it may be doubted whether the effect of its provisions (section 5(a) of the 1895 Act) were adequately appreciated at the time it was passed"[5]. The Commission went on to condemn the use of separation orders and to endorse the judicial view that they should be made only where necessary for the immediate protection of a wife.

---

[1] Subsection (a) of section 2(1) provides for the granting of a separation order. Subsection (b) deals with maintenance for the wife, and (c) for the husband; subsections (d) to (h) provide for custody and access to, and maintenance for, children.

[2] Cmnd. 3587, para 28, p. 9. A similar view is to be found in the Law Commission's Working Paper No. 9 "Matrimonial and Related Proceedings—Financial Relief" 25th April 1967, p. 10: "But today such clauses (non-cohabitation) clauses are very rare and inserted only when it is clear that they are needed for a spouses' protection."

[3] [1965] P. 1, 3. It had been urged by counsel that a separation order should in general be made in a case of persistent cruelty. The court held that there should be no presumption in favour of separation orders, even in cases of persistent cruelty.

[4] [1906] P. 189, as approved by the Court of Appeal in *Harriman v. Harriman* [1909] P. 123.

[5] Cmd. 6478, 1912, paras 137 and 138 and Cmd. 6479, 1912, *Minutes of Evidence*, Vol I, pp. 348 and 459.

But although separation orders have many disadvantages and lead to irregular connections being formed, and although in many cases their economic consequences are bad both for husband and wife and children, still they are to some extent necessary for the purposes of protection; they are at present the only remedy within the reach of the very poor, and they have been made use of by ill-treated wives for many years. . . . The proper principle to apply to such courts is that their orders should only be granted where they are necessary for the reasonable immediate protection of the wife or husband, or the support of the wife and children with her, and that if it is or becomes necessary for the parties to be permanently separated, application for that purpose should be made to the superior court . . . we are of opinion that no separation order of such courts should be continued for a period of more than two years from the date of the original order. . . .[1]

The one serious consequence of wrongly including a separation order is that it will prevent the period of desertion from running, so as to preclude a deserted spouse from obtaining a divorce on that ground[2]. This consequence will be less serious when the Divorce Reform Act 1969 comes into force, when the irretrievable breakdown of marriage may be presumed from periods of consensual or of non-consensual separation.

The statistical information of the period 1903–1935, after which period the numbers of separation orders were not separately recorded in cases where a maintenance order was also made, tells its own tale. In 1903 the ratio of separation orders to maintenance orders was 93%; this proportion fell from 89% in 1909 to 72% in 1910 and to 65% in 1913. The average for the period 1921–1925 was 53%; but this rose to 62% in 1926–1930 and remained as high as 61% in 1931–1935. These figures suggest a substantial misuse of the power to make a separation order. A constant trickle of cases coming on appeal[3] confirms the suggestion that large numbers of these orders were improperly made. The policy of the appellate court (the Divisional Court of the Probate, Divorce and Admiralty Division, now the Family Division, of the High Court)[4] of restricting separation orders to the rare case where a wife requires the protection of such a legal sanction, reflected in these reported decisions, has never wavered.

---

[1] *Report, op. cit.*, paras 144, 145 and 162.

[2] *Harriman v. Harriman* [1909] P. 123.

[3] *Robinson v. Robinson* [1919] P. 352; *Thomas v. Thomas* (1923) 129 L.T. 575; *Sayers v. Sayers* (1929) 93 J.P. 72; *Smith v. Smith* (1931) 47 T.L.R. 368; *Snow v. Snow* (1932) 96 J.P. 477; *Mackenzie v. Mackenzie* [1940] P. 81; *Cooper v. Cooper* [1940] P. 240; *Perks v. Perks* [1945] P. 1; *Squires v. Squires* (1946) 62 T.L.R. 631; *Cohen v. Cohen* [1947] P. 147; *Bottoms v. Bottoms* [1951] P. 424; *Haynes v. Haynes* [1952] P. 272; *Guinness v. Guinness* [1956] 1 W.L.R. 258; *Corton v. Corton* [1965] P. 1; *Joliffe v. Joliffe* [1965] P. 6; *Vaughan v. Vaughan* [1965] P. 15; *Halden v. Halden* [1966] 1 W.L.R. 1481, 1483; *Wall v. Wall* [1968] 1 W.L.R. 306; this list is not exhaustive of the total number of appeals relating to the inclusion of a non-cohabitation clause.

[4] Section 1, Administration of Justice Act 1970.

In *Corton v. Corton*[1] the President of the Probate, Divorce and Admiralty Division in 1962 compendiously defined the circumstances in which justices could properly insert a non-cohabitation clause:

> The justices should specifically direct their minds to whether a separation order is called for in the circumstances of the particular case. It should be the subject of a separate adjudication on their part. But in coming to their conclusion there are certain questions which I think that they would find it helpful to ask themselves. First, is a separation order really necessary for the protection of the complainant? . . . .
>
> Secondly and closely associated, whether it is a more than ordinarily serious case. . . .
>
> Thirdly, and perhaps most important, the justices should consider whether a reconciliation is reasonably to be looked for.

Faced with such explicit judicial directions, legal commentators have concluded that rarely would it be right for justices to make separation orders, since the need for wives to be physically protected from their husbands hardly arises[2]; and to the extent that a wife may on occasions require protection she can always obtain an injunction from the High Court ordering the husband not to molest his wife, or from the County Court if divorce proceedings are [im]pending.

Since there is no statutory or other power on the justices to enforce a non-cohabitation order, an injunction is the only meaningful legal sanction available to a wife who in reality requires protection. If magistrates are then making separation orders for which there is no legal authority, are the complainants in receipt of these orders in any way jeopardized, or are the orders simply so much legal surplusage?

Section 2(1)(a) of the 1960 Act empowers magistrates to make orders containing a provision "that the complainant be no longer bound to cohabit with the defendant" (which provision while in force shall have effect in all respects as a decree of judicial separation)[3].

---

[1] [1965] P. 1, 3 and 4. A non-cohabitation clause is inappropriate to an order based on the grounds of wilful neglect to maintain in circumstances where the wife did not need protection: *Vaughan v. Vaughan* [1965] P. 15; *Jolliffe v. Jolliffe* [1965] P. 6.

[2] Pugh, *Matrimonial Proceedings before Magistrates* (2nd ed. 1966). p. 36. Bromley, *Family Law* (3rd ed. 1966) p. 236. cautiously states the law without concluding whether the order should rarely be made; and see the Law Commission's view, Working Paper No. 9 "Matrimonial and Related Proceedings—Financial Relief", 25th April 1967, p. 10.

[3] It is perhaps not without significance that the parenthesis in section 2(1)(a) omits words which appeared in the 1895 Act equating the non-cohabitation clause with a decree of judicial separation "on the ground of cruelty". In *Harriman v. Harriman* [1909] P. 123, 132, 135, 141–2 the Court of Appeal did not go quite so far as to say that the provision in the 1895 Act meant that a non-cohabitation clause could be inserted only on an application based upon a case of persistent cruelty. But in that case, where the complaint had been on the ground of desertion, the non-cohabitation clause was held to be valid although, the courts said, only rarely would it be proper to make such an order in the case of desertion, i.e. only when desertion had been accompanied by violence. The dropping of these words in the 1895 Act from the latest provision is unfortunate by indicating that there is no statutory limitation upon the magistrates' discretion.

The court's order itself invariably recites that "the complainant be no longer bound to cohabit with the defendant". It does not order a husband to leave his wife or to remain away from the matrimonial home, but it relieves both spouses from the legal obligation to live together, however unenforceable that obligation may be in practice. It also prevents a husband terminating his matrimonial offence of desertion by offering to cohabit with and maintain his wife. All this is theoretical. What is not theoretical is that the existence of a separation order is a bar to a decree of divorce on the ground of desertion. By obtaining an order of separation, a wife is expressing not only her desire that cohabitation with her husband should not be resumed, but she is also effectually preventing his return to her. The order counteracts the essence of desertion as a ground for divorce because that offence requires one spouse to leave the other without reasonable excuse for a period of three years.

There is little doubt that in many instances the court in making a maintenance order inadvertently omits to strike out from the printed form (which is adaptable to different orders) the non-cohabitation clause. Thus in *Mackenzie v. Mackenzie*[1] a wife who did not want protection and had not asked for it and had never relied on a non-cohabitation clause inserted at the time of her order for maintenance found herself debarred from petitioning for divorce on the ground of desertion. Mackinnon L.J. observed[2] that "on January 12 1934 there were no fewer than nine magistrates sitting at this Petty Sessional Court at Paignton, assisted, no doubt by a Clerk. I do not know whether they have become aware of the fact that owing to their stupid carelessness in putting this formal non-cohabitation clause into an order of the court for maintenance, they have occasioned injustice to this unfortunate petitioner. Unhappily, it is an injustice that we cannot remedy."

So long as the non-cohabitation clause has been inadvertently inserted (or rather unwittingly not struck out of the printed form), either spouse can apply to the magistrates to vary their order by having the non-cohabitation clause struck out[3]. The correct order is the one orally pronounced in court and recorded in the justices' minutes of adjudication, so that if the order when drawn up wrongly includes the non-cohabitation clause, the clause in the order is a nullity and does not preclude a divorce on the grounds of desertion[4], though it might be otherwise if either party had relied on the mistake[5]. The only question then would be whether the three years' desertion would have run again from the date of the amended order or whether the amendment could operate retroactively[6]. Even then the husband might oppose any amendment on the basis that it might effect a change whereby he became

---

[1] [1940] P. 81; see also *Halden v. Halden* [1966] 1 W.L.R. 1481, 1483.
[2] *Mackenzie v. Mackenzie* [1940] P. 81, 87.
[3] *Avon v. Avon* [1939] W. N. 402; *Cooper v. Cooper* [1940] P. 204; *Jolliffe v. Jolliffe* [1965] P. 6, 13.
[4] *Cohen v. Cohen* [1947] P. 147; *Green v. Green* [1946] P. 112, 114; *Jolliffe v. Jolliffe* [1965] P. 6.
[5] *Cohen v. Cohen, supra*, at p. 49.
[6] *Gatward v. Gatward* [1942] P. 97; *Green v. Green* [1946] P. 112.

a deserting spouse liable to divorce on that ground. Suffice it to say, even if the inclusion of a separation order is curable by an amending order, there are complications (not to mention the cost of applying to the magistrates' court to amend the order by deleting the clause) which it would be best to avoid at the outset by not including a non-cohabitation clause.

Curiously, a separation order has one positive virtue for the wife-complainant. Many local authorities are reluctant, if not unwilling to transfer a tenancy from a husband to a separated wife unless she first obtains an order relieving the couple from the obligation to live together. Clearly, to include a non-cohabitation clause in a maintenance order on this ground would be an improper exercise of a magistrates' discretion. But there is some evidence to suggest that legal representatives ask for and obtain a separation order, not for protecting a wife but in order that she may be able to satisfy the local authority that the tenancy of a council house or flat should be transferred into her name[1].

The analysis of those matrimonial orders in the study in which the wife obtained a maintenance order in her own right and did not obtain maintenance solely in right of her child or children shows the present extent of the use of magistrates' power to make a separation order[2]. Of the 549 live orders for which information was available, in 30% a non-cohabitation clause had been inserted in the order of the court. For orders originally made in 1964 and 1965, the two most recent years of the survey, the proportion of non-cohabitation clauses rose to 40% of all orders made. What is perhaps most surprising is that, of all the orders with non-cohabitation clauses, in only 62% of the cases was persistent cruelty either the sole ground or one of two or more grounds for the application by the wife complainant. Tables 15 and 16 show the number of separation orders and the grounds upon which they were made. Those maintenance orders which contained separation orders were then analysed according to the grounds on which they had been made. If cruelty was shown either as the only ground, or as a joint ground, that order was recorded as cruelty. The same analysis was then applied to the other grounds and the results are shown in Table 16.

This information suggests that in the two years 1964 and 1965 non-cohabitation clauses were inserted in matrimonial orders in 5,000 cases each year of which some 1,100 were made on a ground of application other than

---

[1] In *Montgomery v. Montgomery* [1965] P. 46 the High Court held that the court could grant an injunction only to support a legal right, and since the wife had no proprietary right in the matrimonial home the court had no jurisdiction to make a mandatory order excluding the husband from the premises. The court, of course, had jurisdiction to prevent the husband from molesting his wife who had earlier obtained a decree of judicial separation. In the course of the case it was revealed that the Wandsworth Borough Council had written to the wife to say that the tenancy of the flat would be transferred to her provided that the court would grant her an injunction to compel the husband to leave the flat.

[2] It would be rare (although not inconceivable) that a wife who for one reason or another—for example, if she had private means or was in gainful employment and her husband had committed adultery—was disqualified from maintenance for herself would obtain a separation order.

TABLE 15   **Number and proportion of maintenance orders with separation orders live on 1st January 1966.**

Date order made	Number and proportion of maintenance orders with separation orders		All maintenance orders made	
	No.	%	No.	%
Pre-1961	74	24	307	100
1961–63	39	36	109	100
1964–65	53	40	133	100
Total	166	30	549	100

persistent cruelty[1]. Further analysis by area showed that some courts were more inclined to insert non-cohabitation clauses than others. Two of the larger courts in the North of England were examined. In Court A 37% of orders contained a non-cohabitation clause; in Court B the figure was 33%. Only 55% of the separation orders made by Court A showed persistent cruelty as the ground of application as compared with 86% in Court B. For the three London courts in the survey only 14% of the maintenance orders contained a non-cohabitation clause. Persistent cruelty was the ground of application in 73% of these cases. One large court in South-west England had only one instance of a separation order out of fifty-five maintenance orders.

What are the reasons for so great a disparity between legal rules and the law in action? One explanation, suggested by the cases which have appeared in the law reports, is that the non-cohabitation clause is inadvertently not struck out from the printed form. If this were the explanation for most cases, one would expect to find a higher proportion of applications on the grounds of adultery, desertion and wilful neglect to maintain containing non-cohabitation

TABLE 16   **Grounds on which maintenance orders with separation orders live on 1st January 1966, had been made.**

Grounds for separation order	Date order made			Total	
	Pre-1961	1961–63	1964–65	No.	%
Persistent cruelty	41	23	33	97	62
Adultery	18	7	10	35	22
Desertion*	6	5	6	17	11
Wilful neglect to maintain ..	8	—	—	8	5
Total	73	35	49	157	100
Grounds not known	1	4	4	9	

*It is possible that these cases were constructive desertion, involving a finding of cruelty against the husband so as to make him the deserting spouse although the wife in fact left him.

[1] For the two years 1964 and 1965, 32,206 maintenance orders were made. 77·6% of such orders (24,992) provided for the direct benefit of the wife. 39·8% of all such orders contained a non-cohabitation order, i.e. 9,947, of which 22·7% were not made on the ground of cruelty, i.e. 2,258 or 1,129 for each year.

clauses. It might be that inadvertence explains the inclusion of a separation order at least in the non-cruelty cases, and that where a maintenance order is made on the ground of persistent cruelty magistrates' courts, either defiant or oblivious of the rulings of the High Court, automatically include the non-cohabitation clause. Observation of the courts at work suggests that it is the Justices' Clerks rather than the justices who are responsible. Justices may be blindly making separation orders, if only in cases of persistent cruelty. In this respect they are failing in their duty to deal with a separation order as "a separate adjudication" from the decision to award maintenance. If that is so, it is probably because the Justices' Clerks who guide the Bench are themselves failing in their duty to ensure a deliberate consideration by justices of their power to make a separation order.

CHAPTER 5

The social and demographic characteristics of complainants and defendants

The materials for sketching a social profile of the people who resort to magistrates' courts when their marriages run on to the rocks, can be drawn only from information in court records. This information was recorded for legal and not for social purposes. The records contain some details of the economic and demographic characteristics of spouses who pass through the courts, though, from a statistical point of view, they are inadequate, incomplete and imprecise. Despite the imperfections of court records for the purposes of social analysis, they tell enough to establish in rough outline the main characteristics of the couples whose failures are recorded and regulated by the summary matrimonial jurisdiction. Wherever possible in the analysis which follows, these husbands and wives are compared with those in the general or in the divorcing population in order to discover how far they are similar to and how far they differ from the generality of married people.

The occupations and incomes of defendants

Court records contain some information about the occupations and incomes of defendant husbands and thus provide a rough guide to their social class. Since the Census of 1911, it has been customary for the Registrar General and for social commentators to use a fivefold classification of occupations and to relate the categories to social classes in the following scheme:

Social Class	Occupation
I	Professional
II	Intermediate
III	Skilled
IV	Partly skilled
V	Unskilled

The records contained occupational data for about 68% of defendants in the

TABLE 17 Social class distribution of husbands by type of order.

| Type of order | Social class of husband | | | | | | |
	I	II	III	IV	V	VI	Total
Guardianship of infants or children only ..		9	71	39	35	14	168
% of total		6	42	23	21	8	100
Married women and children	1	19	238	88	74	41	461
% of total	—	4	52	19	16	9	100
Married women only ..	4	13	113	39	33	10	212
% of total	2	6	53	18	16	5	100
Total	5	41	422	166	142	65	841
% of total	1	5	50	20	17	7	100

sample; the information is tabulated in Table 17 in accordance with this crude classification, to which we have added a sixth category to cover those instances where husbands have retired or were unemployed or in prison.

The information about the occupational distribution of defendants presented in Table 17 must be treated with caution because the inadequate descriptions of occupations in court records tend to result in an upgrading of all occupations which fall above social class category V[1]. Even if this distortion is ignored, comparison with the occupational distribution of the whole male population as shown by the census of 1961 in Table 18 emphasizes the extent to which the Registrar General's social classes I and II are under-represented among the population of husbands appearing as defendants in matrimonial complaints in magistrates' courts. Only $5\frac{1}{2}\%$ of the defendant husbands fell into social class I and II (and this percentage is certainly an overestimate) whereas 21% of all married men in the country were so classified by the 1961 census.

In order to test whether the social class distribution of husbands varied in

TABLE 18 Social class distribution of married males in England and Wales at the census of 1961[2].

Social class	Percentage
I	4
II	17
III	51
IV	20
V	8

[1] Court records usually state occupations in such stark terms as "miner" or "engineer" with no indication of whether the work requires considerable and specific skill or no skill. The difficulties of interpretation led to a tendency to code ambiguous occupational descriptions as higher rather than lower social class categories. This conclusion is supported by detailed examination of a number of cases where additional information was available, for example, as the result of a challenge to a defendant's statement of his means.

[2] *Census of England and Wales* 1961, Occupation Tables, Table 20.

TABLE 19[1] **Social class distribution of husbands by area.**

Area	I	II	Social class of husband III	IV	V	VI	Total
A	3	20	204	72	83	23	405
%	1	5	50	18	20	6	100
B	2	20	205	91	58	39	415
%	—	5	50	22	14	9	100

different parts of the country, the data were tabulated according to the geographical distribution of the courts which made the orders. Area A comprises all courts within the Registrar General's Standard Regions 1 to 5 and 10, the North, the North-west, the Midlands and Wales. Area B covers the remainder of the country in regions 6 to 9, the East, the South and the South-West.[2] There are no significant differences between the two areas although the south shows a higher proportion of husbands in social class IV and the north a higher proportion in social class V.

These occupational data suggest that the upper social classes make little use of the matrimonial jurisdiction of the magistrates' courts. The conclusion is strongly reinforced by what is known about the incomes of defendants. Again, this information is thinly spread in court records. Surprisingly, the courts are under no obligation to obtain details of a defendant's financial resources, and their only specific power in this respect is to call for a probation officer's report.[3] Moreover, the court learns only what complainants know or defendants volunteer about their earnings and must make its own judgment of the truth of what it is told. The high proportion of court records which contained no information about defendants' incomes ranged from one-third in the case of Married Women and Children orders to 45% of Married Women Only orders. Table 20 shows the weekly income of the 60% of defendants for whom the information was available, but there are no grounds for believing that these are not representative of all defendants.

TABLE 20 **Defendant's income at date of order for orders live on 1st January 1966.**

Weekly income at time of making the order	Matrimonial and guardianship orders Number	Percentage
Under £10	317	43
£10 but under £16	330	44
£16 but under £20	67	9
£20 and over	29	4
Total	743	100

[1] The factors of occupation and area were available for only 820 cases, some two-thirds of the total.   [2] See Appendix B, Part 3, for the full classification.
[3] Section 60, Magistrates' Courts Act, 1952.

TABLE 21 **Defendant's income by duration of all types of order for orders live on 1st January 1966.**

| Weekly income | Period when order was made | | | | | | | | Total | Cumulative total % |
	1965 No.	%	1964–1961 No.	%	1960–1954 No.	%	1953 or before No.	%		
Under £10	11	11	49	19	114	50	143	91	317	43
£10 but under £16 ..	58	59	162	63	97	43	13	8	330	87
£16 but under £20 ..	22	22	30	11	13	6	2	1	67	96
£20 and over	8	8	18	7	3	1			29	100
Total	99	100	259	100	227	100	158	100	743	
Average income ..	£14 8s.		£13 6s.		£10 9s.		£7 13s.		£11 7s.	

87% of defendants under an obligation to pay maintenance under magistrates' order at the beginning of 1966 had incomes of less than £16 a week when the order against them was made. Table 21 breaks down the data in Table 20 by the duration of the orders and, in particular, shows the distribution of incomes among the most recent group of defendants. Even allowing for the strong incentive of defendants to understate their earnings and the inadequate means of checking in many courts, we can record that 70% of the defendants against whom orders were made in 1965 had incomes of less than £16 a week. This may be compared with the average earnings of men in manufacturing industry of £18 a week in 1965.

The available information permitted the incomes of rather more than half the defendants in the sample to be tabulated by their social class. The result is shown in Table 22.

The conviction that the rough and ready description of defendants' occupations in court records has resulted in an upgrading of those falling into the categories above social class V, is strengthened by the relationship between income and social class demonstrated by Table 22. 60% of the small number of defendants in social classes I and II and 84% of the defendants in social class III had incomes of less than £16 a week. Further, one-third of the defendants in social class III are shown to have incomes of less than £10 a week.

These data relating to the occupations and incomes of defendants are crude but they demonstrate clearly that the matrimonial jurisdiction of magistrates is used almost entirely by the working class and very largely by the lowest paid among them.

Duration of the marriage at the time of complaint to the magistrates' court

Information was available about the status of one-third of the complainants and defendants immediately before their marriages. This is shown in Table 23,

TABLE 22 Defendant's income and social class when the order was made; all orders live on 1st January 1966.

Income	Social class											Sub Total IV, V, VI		Total	
	I	II	%	III	%	IV	%	V	%	VI*	%	IV, V, VI	%	Total	%
Under £10		5	16	117	33	68	46	73	58	25	78	166	54	288	42
£10 but under £16		14	44	176	50	74	50	44	35	5	16	123	40	313	46
£16 but under £20	1	7	22	42	12	4	3	3	2	1	3	8	3	58	8
£20 but under £25	1	4	12	13	4	2	1	2	2	1	3	5	2	23	3
£25 and over		2	6	3	1			2	2			2	1	7	1
Total	2	32	100	351	100	148	100	124	100	32	100	304	100	689	100
%	—	5		51		21		18		5				100	

* Unemployed, armed forces, and others (e.g. prisoners) not codeable into social classes I–V.

TABLE 23   Status of parties at marriage.

Women		Single	Men Divorced	Widower	Total	%	All marriages England and Wales 1966[1] %
Single	..	419	7	1	427	94	89
Divorced	..	12	8	2	22	5	7
Widow	..	3		3	6	1	4
Total		434	15	6	455		
%		95	3	1		100	
All marriages[1] %		88	7	5			100

Percentage totals may not add up to 100 due to rounding.

which also compares them with the rest of the married population in England and Wales in 1966.

The duration of the marriage at the time the order was made was known for two-thirds of the orders[2]. Table 24 sets out the distribution of orders made by type of order and duration of marriage.

TABLE 24   Distribution of orders made by type of order and duration of marriage.

Type of order	Duration of marriage						
	Under 3 yrs.	Under 5 yrs.	Under 9 yrs.	Under 12 yrs.	Under 15 yrs.	Under 20 yrs.	Over 20 years
	Cumulative percentages						
Married women only ..	14	25	35	41	50	67	100
Married women and Children	15	27	52	67	80	92	100
Guardianship of Infants and children only ..	20	35	62	80	86	93	100
All orders	16	28	50	63	73	86	100

The marriages of the shortest duration were those of wives who obtained Guardianship of Infants orders. In this group, 35% of the marriages broke down within five years. Among the wives with Married Women and Children orders, 27% of the marriages lasted for less than five years; and in the Married Women Only Group the proportion was 25%. The longest surviving marriages were those of wives who obtained Married Women Only orders: 59% of these had lasted for more than twelve years and 33% for more than twenty years before they came to court. Among the Married Women and Children

[1] *Registrar General's Statistical Review . . . for* 1966, Part II, Table G.
[2] For all orders, the proportion was 68%. For Guardianship of Infants and Children orders, it was 70%; for Married Women Only orders, it was 65%; and for Married Women and Children orders, it was 69%.

orders, one-third of the marriages had lasted for more than twelve years and 8% for more than twenty. One-fifth of the wives with Guardianship of Infants orders had been married for more than twelve years and 7% for more than twenty years before seeking the help of the court.

Table 24 provides no support for the view that wives rush quickly and heedlessly to magistrates' courts at the first sign of matrimonial rift. The average length of marriage for Guardianship of Infants and Children orders was eight years; for Married Women and Children orders it was ten years; and for Married Women only orders it was fourteen years. Orders of all types were obtained after less than one year of marriage in only 3% of the instances and in less than three years in 16%. At the other extreme, 14% of the marriages had survived for more than twenty years before the wife went to court.

Table 25 compares the duration of marriages before the making of a matrimonial order by magistrates with the duration of marriages before divorce. When allowance is made for the number of magistrates' court orders obtained in respect of marriages which collapsed within their first three years, the durations of the marriages of complainants before magistrates and of petitioners to the High Court are remarkably similar.

TABLE 25 Duration of marriages (i) at date of making a magistrates' matrimonial order, all orders live on 1st January 1966, and (ii) before decree absolute in 1966.

Duration of marriage				Orders made by magistrates' courts %		Decrees absolute[1] %	
Under 3 months	..	..	..	0·1			
3 months but under 6 months	..	..	..	0·3			
6 months but under 1 year	..	..	..	2·6	16		1
1 year but under 2 years	..	..	..	7			
2 years but under 3 years	..	..	..	6			
3 years but under 5 years	..	..	..	12		12	
5 years but under 7 years	..	..	..	12	34	14	38
7 years but under 9 years	..	..	..	10		12	
9 years but under 12 years	..	..	..	13		15	
12 years but under 15 years	..	..	..	10	36	11	41
15 years but under 20 years	..	..	..	13		15	
Over 20 years	..	..	..	14		20	

Age of survey wives and husbands at the time of their marriage

Table 26 compares the age of marriage of the survey husbands and wives and the age at marriage of all couples marrying in 1956[2].

[1] *Registrar General's Statistical Review . . . for* 1966, Part II, Table P. 4.
[2] 1956 was selected because analysis of the data showed that half the marriages of the sample couples occurred before 1956.

TABLE 26 **Age at marriage of survey husbands and wives compared with all husbands and wives marrying in 1956.**

Survey Wives	All wives marrying in 1956[1]	Age at marriage	All husbands marrying in 1956[1]	Survey husbands
percentages			percentages	
31	23	Under 20	4	14
43	53	20–24	50	48
13	14	25–29	29	19
7	5	30–34	9	9
6	5	Over 35	8	10

Table 26 shows that 31% of the wives in the magistrates' courts sample married before they were twenty compared with the 23% of all brides in 1956. The corresponding figure for husbands in the survey was 14%; among all bridegrooms in 1956, it was only 4%. There was thus a significantly higher proportion of teenage brides and grooms in the sample than among those who married in 1956. Accordingly the data in Table 26 may be interpreted in the light of the strongly marked social class differential of age at marriage displayed in Table 27.

TABLE 27 **1961 census of England and Wales, women married once only and enumerated with their husbands[2].**

Husband's occupational group	Age at marriage	Percentages of women marrying in		
		1947/51	1955/56	1960/61
Unskilled manual	Under 20	20	29	41
	20–24	45	46	42
	25–29	19	13	9
	30–34	8	6	4
	up to 45	8	6	4
Skilled manual	Under 20	19	26	32
	20–24	55	55	53
	25–29	18	12	10
	30–34	5	4	3
	up to 45	3	3	2
Self-employed professional ..	Under 20	4	2	4
	20–24	45	48	49
	25–29	36	35	31
	30–34	8	8	12
	up to 45	7	7	4

Table 27 shows that, in the period during which most of the survey marriages took place, the proportion of women marrying in their teens rose from 20% between 1947 and 1951 to 41% in 1960/1961 for the brides of unskilled manual workers; from 19% to 32% for the brides of skilled manual workers,

[1] *Registrar General's Statistical Review ... for* 1964, Part III, Table C9.
[2] *Registrar General's Statistical Review ... for* 1965, Part III, Table C17.

and remained unchanged at 4% for the brides of self-employed professional workers. 31% of the survey wives married in their teens compared with 29% of the brides of unskilled manual workers in the population at large in 1956. The strikingly low age at marriage of the survey brides and grooms reinforces the conclusion derived from the occupational and financial data that the population bringing its matrimonial troubles to magistrates' courts is drawn mainly from the lowest stratum of the working class.

The young age at marriage of the survey wives helps to explain why nearly three-quarters of all the orders shown in Table 28 were made before the wife had reached the age of forty.

TABLE 28   Age of wife at time the order was made.

Type of order	Below 40	40 and above	Total number
	Age of wife		
	percentages		
Guardianship of infants orders and matrimonial orders with provision only for children ..	91	9	43
Matrimonial orders with provision for wife and children	46	54	68
Matrimonial orders with provision only for wife	83	17	124
Total	74	26	235 (100%)

Duration of the order

Table 29 shows for how long all orders live on 1st January 1966 had lasted.

On 1st January 1966, one-eighth of all orders had existed for under one year, nearly one-half had lasted for less than five years, and only 18% had been made before 1951.

TABLE 29   Duration of all orders live on 1st January 1966.

Duration of order	Guardianship and children only No.	%	Married women only No.	%	Married women and children No.	%	All orders No.	%
Under 1 year	39	16	39	11	76	12	156	12
1 year but under 3 years	62	25	41	11	129	21	232	19
3 years but under 5 years ..	42	17	45	12	88	14	175	14
5 years but under 9 years ..	53	21	57	16	121	19	231	19
9 years but under 15 years ..	44	18	63	18	113	18	220	18
15 years and over	7	3	115	32	100	16	222	18
Total	247	100	360	100	629	100	1,236	100
%	20		29		51		100	

Family size of survey couples at the time the order was made

The average number of dependant children in each family at the time of making the order was 1·35. Applying this to our calculation that the total number of live orders amounted to some 165,000[1], we estimate that women with matrimonial orders from magistrates' courts were responsible on 1st January 1966 for some 223,000 children under sixteen. The number of children by family size and type of order is shown in Table 30.

TABLE 30   **Number of children under sixteen by family size and type of order at the time the order was made.**

Type of order	Number of children					
	1	2	3	4	5 or more	Total
Guardianship of infants and children only..	127	69	33	13	6	248
Married women and children[2]	314	210	80	30	21	657
Total number of orders	442	280	113	43	27	905
%	49	31	12	5	3	100
Total number of children	442	560	339	172	149	1,662

Nearly three-quarters of the wives who obtained orders had children under the age of sixteen. Nearly half of these mothers had one child, nearly one-third had two children, and one-fifth had three or more. The average size of family among survey couples at the time their marriage collapsed was 1·8 dependant children. This figure may be compared with an average family size of 1·9 for wives whose husbands were unskilled manual workers at the time of the 1961 Census of England and Wales.[3]

Table 31 shows the size of family of survey couples by duration of marriage for the 68% of orders for which the information was available. The table shows that childless wives resort to the court significantly earlier than those wives with children. For marriages which lasted less than three years, the childless wife is twice as likely as any other to seek an order. This finding indicates that childlessness is as much a factor in the breakdown of marriages which come to the magistrates' court as it is in those which result in divorce. 18% of all wives in the survey were childless. The same percentage of childlessness was found at the 1961 Census of England and Wales[4] among

[1] See Appendix B, Part 2.
[2] This category includes thirty orders originally and mistakenly classified as Married Women Only orders although they contained children.
[3] Fertility Table 14. The average duration of survey marriages before their border was made and cohabitation ceased was ten years. Accordingly, when comparing their fertility experience with that of the wives of unskilled manual workers in the general population, only marriages that had existed for less than ten years were included.
[4] *Ibid* 14.

TABLE 31[1] **Number of children of marriage by duration of marriage, for all orders.**

Number of childless marriages	C.T. %	Duration of marriage	1	2	3	4	5 or more	Total	C.T. %
						Number of chlidren			
32	26	Under 3 years	73	25	3			101	14
24	45	3 years but under 5 years ..	37	37	7			81	25
12	54	5 years but under 7 years ..	41	26	16	5		88	38
16	67	7 years but under 12 years	51	84	25	11	10	181	63
41	100	12 years and over	77	73	50	37	28	265	100
125		Total	279	245	101	53	38	716	
		C.T. %	39	73	87	95	100		

C.T.: cumulative total

all the wives of unskilled manual workers. This suggests that women resorting to the magistrates' courts with matrimonial complaints and the wives of unskilled workers are the same population.

[1] The discrepancy between the 905 orders with children, shown in Table 14 and the 716 orders with children in this table results from the fact that 189 orders did not show the date of marriage.

CHAPTER 6

Amounts of maintenance and regularity of payment

This chapter presents the statistical results of the survey which show the amounts of maintenance awarded by the courts, the frequency with which orders are varied, the extent to which payments fall into arrears and the amount of arrears formally remitted. The Home Office undertook an investigation on behalf of the Committee on Statutory Maintenance Limits[1] (the Graham Hall Committee) and the survey findings are compared wherever possible with the Home Office findings. The Committee made considerable use of the survey results in its *Report*. Inescapably, the content of this chapter is severely statistical.

Table 32 shows the amounts of maintenance awarded to wives. As the Bedford College sample contains orders made over a long period of time[2] and the Home Office sample consists of all orders made in England and Wales in September and October 1966, it is to be expected that average amounts payable under orders in the Bedford College survey will be lower than those in the Home Office survey. The difference of twenty shillings

TABLE 32   Average amounts payable to wives under matrimonial orders. Bedford College sample of orders live on 1st January 1966, compared with the Home Office sample of orders made during September and October 1966. Original orders only.

	Number of children on order					
Sample	0	1	2	3	4 or more	Total
Bedford College						
Number of orders ..	519	174	120	40	23	876
Average amount payable to wife	£1 18s.	£2 1s.	£1 19s.	£1 18s.	£1 8s.	£1 18s.
Home Office						
Number of orders ..	635	755	649	328	256	2,623
Average amount payable to wife	£2 19s.	£3 2s.	£2 19s.	£2 14s.	£2 7s.	£2 18s.

Amounts rounded to nearest shilling.

[1] Cmnd. 3587, 1968. The Home Office survey is described in Chapter 3, p. 49–50.
[2] There were ninety orders in the sample older than twenty years. The earliest order was made in 1920.

TABLE 33 Amounts payable to wives under matrimonial orders. Bedford College sample of orders live on 1st January 1966, compared with Home Office sample of orders made during September and October 1966. Original orders only.

Sample	*Amount payable to wife	Number of children on order											
		No children		One child		Two children		Three children		Four or more children		Total orders	
		No.	%	No.	%	No.	%	No.	%	No.	%	No.	%
Bedford College	Under £1 15s.	274	53	83	48	61	51	18	45	14	61	450	52
	£1 15s. but under £3 5s. ..	173	33	61	35	42	35	17	43	9	39	302	35
	£3 5s. but under £5 10s. ..	70	13	24	14	13	11	5	12			112	12
	£5 10s. and over	2	1	6	3	4	3					12	1
	Total	519	100	174	100	120	100	40	100	23	100	876	100
	%		59		20		14		4		3		100
Home Office	Up to £1 15s.	139	22	164	21	129	20	90	27	73	29	595	22
	More than £1 15s. up to £3 5s.	228	36	283	37	299	46	139	42	130	51	1,079	41
	More than £3 5s. up to £5 10s.	212	33	261	36	184	28	76	23	49	19	782	30
	Over £5 10s.	56	9	47	6	37	6	23	7	4	1	167	6
	Total	635	100	755	100	649	100	328	100	256	100	2,623	100
	%		24		29		24		13		10		100

* It should be noted that the amounts payable to wives in the two samples are not strictly comparable because the intervals are different.

between the two samples is reduced to two shillings when the amounts awarded on the orders made in 1964 and 1965 in the Bedford College sample are compared with the average of those in the Home Office sample of 1966.

More detailed information about the amounts payable to wives is given in Table 33.

The significance of the statutory maximum of £7 10s. for wives[1] may be judged by the 2% of wives in the Home Office sample and the 0·4% in the Bedford College sample with orders for £6 10s. or over. Indeed, in the Home Office sample only 1·9% of the wives were awarded the maximum and, in the Bedford College sample, none had achieved £7 10s.

The amounts payable for children under guardianship orders and orders with provision only for children are shown in Table 34.

TABLE 34   Average amounts payable for children under guardianship orders and matrimonial orders with provision only for children. Bedford College sample of orders live on 1st January 1966, compared with Home Office sample of orders made during September and October 1966. Original orders only.

| | Number of children on order | | | | |
Sample	1	2	3	4 or more	Total
Bedford College					
Number of orders	166	79	29	15	289
Average amount payable	£1 10s.	£2 13s.	£3 12s.	£4 8s.	£2 3s.
Average amount payable for each child	£1 10s.	£1 6s.	£1 4s.	£1 0s.	£1 6s.
Home Office					
Number of orders	417	275	114	53	859
Average amount payable	£2 0s.	£3 17s.	£4 18s.	£5 7s.	£3 0s.
Average amount payable for each child	£2 0s.	£1 18s.	£1 12s.	£1 7s.	£1 14s.

Amounts rounded to nearest shilling.

Again, the average amounts awarded in the Home Office sample of 1966 orders are higher than those in the Bedford College sample. Both samples show a steady decline in the amount awarded per child as family size increases and both demonstrate that average amounts for children fell far short of the then statutory maximum of £2 10s. More detailed information about the amounts payable to children is shown in Table 35.

The maximum amount was more frequently ordered for children than for wives. Nevertheless, it did not apply to more than one-fifth of the children in the Home Office sample. Even among the single child orders which bear the highest amounts of maintenance, only 45% of the Home Office sample exceeded £2 a week and only 36% of those in the Bedford College sample exceeded £1 15s.

The Home Office survey also covered all High Court Orders for maintenance made in September and October 1966. Here too, the large majority

[1] The limits were abolished in 1968.

TABLE 35 Amounts payable under guardianship orders and matrimonial orders with provision only for children. Bedford College samples of orders live on 1st January 1966, compared with Home Office sample of orders made during September and October 1966. Original orders only.

Sample / Amount	Number of children on order								Total	%
	1		2		3		4 or more			
	No.	%	No.	%	No.	%	No.	%		
Bedford College										
Under 15s.	10	6	2	3	2	7	1	7	15	5
15s. but under £1 15s.	97	58	19	24	3	10	2	13	121	43
£1 15s. but under £2 15s.	59	36	22	28	4	14	2	13	87	30
£2 15s. but under £4 10s.	—	—	28	35	11	38	5	34	44	15
£4 10s. but under £6 10s.	—	—	8	10	7	24	3	20	18	6
£6 10s. and over	—	—	—	—	2	7	2	13	4	1
Total	166	100	79	100	29	100	15	100	289	100
Percentage of orders	58		27		10		5		100	
Home Office										
Up to £1	41	10	5	2	4	3	4	8	50	6
More than £1 up to £2	190	45	25	9	2	2	5	9	221	26
More than £2 up to £3	186	45	64	23	11	10	19	36	266	31
More than £3 up to £5	—	—	181	66	45	39	18	34	245	28
More than £5 up to £7	—	—	—	—	35	31	18	34	53	6
Over £7	—	—	—	—	17	15	7	13	25	3
Total	417	100	275	100	114	100	53	100	860	100
Percentage of orders	49		32		13		6		100	

of orders fell well within the then statutory limits applying to magistrates' courts. 87% of High Court orders for wives were for less than £7 10s. a week, and 87% of High Court orders for children were for less than £2 10s.

Originally, the power to vary the amounts of maintenance awarded depended on the submission of "fresh evidence", but this requirement was repealed by the Money Payments (Justices' Procedure) Act 1935. Thus, magistrates' courts have been able for more than a generation to allow for changes in the value of money as well as for alterations in the circumstances of the parties. Accordingly, the rapid inflation of the last quarter of a century might have been expected to produce a high rate of complaint for variation orders.

Table 36 shows the period of time between the making of a matrimonial order and the first variation. A comparison of the variation orders with the complete Bedford College sample of 1,212 original orders for which the necessary information was available shows that 6% of orders were varied within one year of being made, 20% within three years, 32% within five years and 39% within nine years.

In a quarter of all complaints for variation the amount is increased, and in about three-quarters it is reduced. 70% of all increases were heard within five years of the original order, and 71% of all reductions were heard in the same period.

The chances that a complaint for variation will result in an increase do not alter significantly over different periods of time. 26% of variation orders made within two years of the original order were increased, 24% made within three and five years were increased, and 28% of those varied after nine years or more were increased.

Table 37 shows amounts by which matrimonial orders were varied in relation to the amounts of the original orders. As the average amount originally awarded in the 1,212 orders for which the relevant information is available was £3 4s. 8d., the data have been tabulated to show increases and decreases in amounts ranging below and above the average. In 46% of all orders there has been at least one variation order. When allowance is made for the automatic termination (technically not a variation because it requires no complaint) of payments for children who reach the age of sixteen, this percentage falls to 37.

The size of the original order has little effect upon the likelihood of its being varied. 47% of orders for more than £5 10s. were varied, and 43% of orders for less than £2 5s. were varied. 11% of all orders were increased and 33% reduced at their first variation hearing, whilst 1% remained the same (Table 37).

The discrepancy between the 550 variation orders shown on Table 36 and the 556 on Table 37 is explained by lack of information in six instances about the period between the making of the order and the first variation.

An analysis of variation orders in the Home Office sample showed the same experience both in terms of the incidence of variation by duration of the

TABLE 36 Variation proceedings for all types of matrimonial order live on 1st January 1966, including orders in respect of dependant children. Length of time between making of order and first variation.

Variation in amount	Length of time up to first variation (in years)										
	Under 1	1 but under 3	3 but under 5	Under 5 No.	%	5 but under 9	9 but under 15	15 and over	5 and over No.	%	Total No.	%
(1) *Amount remains same*	2	3	1	6	2	4	6	1	11	6	17	3
(2) *Decrease*												
Under 15s	22	42	18	82		22	20	3	45		127	
15s but under 25s	27	38	21	86		18	10	5	33		119	
25s but under 35s	17	14	9	40		13	9	—	22		62	
35s but under 40s	11	9	2	22		4	1	—	5		27	
45s and over	18	22	14	54		8	1	—	9		63	
Sub-total	95	125	64	284	74	65	41	8	114	69	398	72
(3) *Increase*												
Under 15s	24	17	14	55		10	7	1	18		73	
15s but under 25s	9	10	5	24		5	5	2	12		36	
25s but under 35s	1	3	—	4		2	2	2	6		10	
35s but under 45s	6	—	1	7		2	1	1	4		11	
45s and over	2	1	1	4		—	—	1	1		5	
Sub-total	42	31	21	94	24	19	15	7	41	25	135	25
(4)=(1)+(2)+(3) Total	139	159	86	384	100	88	62	16	166	100	550	100

TABLE 37 Variation proceedings for all matrimonial orders live on 1st January 1966, including orders in respect of dependant children. Variation of amount by amount originally ordered.

Variation in amount (per week)	Under £1 5s	£1 5s but under £2 5s	£2 5s but under £3 5s	Under £3 5s No.	Under £3 5s %	£3 5s but under £5 10s	£5 10s and over	£3 5s and over No.	£3 5s and over %	Total No.	Total %
(1) *Amount remains same*	2	5	4	11	1	4	2	6	1	17	1
(2) *Decrease*											
Under 15s	14	63	30	107		18	5	23		30	
15s but under 25s	7	18	44	69		34	18	52		121	
25s but under 35s	—	11	15	26		23	9	32		58	
35s but under 45s	—	2	6	8		14	10	24		32	
45s and over	—	2	7	9		23	31	54		63	
Sub-total	21	96	102	219	29	112	73	185	40	404	33
(3) *Increase*											
Under 15s	24	32	7	63		6	4	10		73	
15s but under 25s	9	13	8	30		4	2	6		36	
25s but under 35s	3	3	2	8		2	—	2		10	
35s but under 45s	3	2	2	7		4	1	5		12	
45s and over	2	2	—	4		—	—	—		4	
Sub-total	41	52	19	112	15	16	7	23	5	135	11
(4)=(1)+(2)+(3) Variations' total	64	153	125	342	45	132	82	214	47*	556	46*
No variation	109	182	122	413	55	152	91	243	53	656	54
Total (4)+(5)	173	335	247	755	100	284	173	457	100	1,212	100

Total amount originally ordered (per week)

* Percentages may not add up to the shown figure due to rounding. Information was not available in 24 cases.

TABLE 38 Outstanding arrears of over £20 on 1st January 1966, on all live matrimonial orders including orders in respect of dependant children.

Amount of order per week	Amount of arrears												Arrears		
	£20 £40	£40 £60	£60 £80	£80 £100	£100 £120	£120 but under £150	£150 £200	£200 £300	£300 £500	£500 £700	£700 £1000	Over £1000	£20 and over	Nil or under £20	All orders: Total
Under 5s.	—	—	—	—	—	—	—	—	—	—	—	—	—	13	13
5s. but under 15s. ..	3	1	2	1	1	1	1	—	—	1	—	—	11	29	40
15s. " £1 5s. ..	13	2	2	1	1	1	3	3	—	—	—	—	26	92	118
£1 5s. " £1 15s. ..	12	8	6	3	—	2	3	5	4	3	—	—	46	122	168
£1 15s. " £2 5s. ..	20	7	9	6	5	6	3	5	6	1	—	1	69	97	166
£2 5s. " £2 15s. ..	7	4	4	2	4	2	5	5	1	2	—	—	36	82	118
£2 15s. " £3 5s. ..	9	7	6	2	6	3	6	6	1	1	3	1	51	76	127
£3 5s. " £4 10s. ..	13	8	5	3	2	9	7	12	8	5	1	1	74	82	156
£4 10s. " £5 10s. ..	10	5	3	3	6	3	12	7	7	3	2	1	62	64	126
£5 10s. " £6 10s. ..	9	7	6	2	2	—	4	6	7	1	—	—	44	41	85
£6 10s. and over ..	6	5	3	3	3	4	4	9	5	6	—	2	50	37	87
Total	102	54	46	26	30	31	48	58	39	23	6	6	469	735	1,204

Note: The necessary information about arrears was not available in respect of twenty-six orders in the sample.

original order and of the majority of all variations resulting in a decrease in the amount of the order[1].

Tables 36 and 37 underestimate the number of complaints for variation because court records do not reliably show complaints dismissed. Further, it it sometimes difficult to distinguish arrears from variation hearings. Nevertheless, the investigators' impression is that the amount of such underestimation is small and would not significantly change the picture of an astonishingly little used variation procedure.

In order to check the findings of Tables 36 and 37 a detailed hand analysis was made of all orders showing variation proceedings or changes of amount in 1965. None showed more than one variation within the year. In 2% the amount remained the same, in 26% it was increased and in 72% it was reduced. These proportions for orders varied in 1965 are remarkably similar to those for the whole sample.

The information available in court records does not permit the "changing circumstances" given as the reason for 59% of all variation orders to be broken down satisfactorily. 8% of variations result either from a wife's adultery or from her subsequent marriage. Between a fifth and a quarter of all changes in the amount of orders result from children reaching their sixteenth birthdays and orders for children are extended beyond that time for fewer than 3%.

Table 38 shows that 39% of all orders live on 1st January 1966 were in arrears for amounts of more than £20. Slightly more than one-fifth of all original orders for amounts under £1 5s. fell into arrears of more than £20 and half the original orders for amounts of £3 5s. or over were similarly in arrears.

Table 39 shows the proportion of orders for different amounts in arrears. Tables 38 and 39 suggest strongly that the factor most likely to shape the arrears history of an order is not its duration but the amount for which it was first made.

TABLE 39 **Proportion of orders, for different amounts in arrears, of over £20 on 1st January 1966, on all live matrimonial orders including orders in respect of dependant children.**

Amount of order	% in arrears
£6 10s. and over	57
£5 10s. but under £6 10s.	52
£4 10s. but under £5 10s.	49
£3 5s. but under £4 10s.	47
£2 15s. but under £3 5s.	40
£2 5s. but under £2 15s.	31
£1 15s. but under £2 5s.	42
£1 5s. but under £1 15s.	27
15s. but under £1 5s.	22
5s. but under 15s.	28

[1] Cmnd. 3587, paras 143–145.

TABLE 40 Outstanding arrears of over £20 on 1st January 1966, on all live orders made before 1956.

Amount per week	Arrears on 1st January 1966												Arrears total	No arrears	Total
	£20 £40	£40 £60	£60 £80	£80 £100	£100 £120	£120 but under £150	£150 £200	£200 £300	£300 £500	£500 £700	£700 £1,000	£1000 and over			
Under 5s.	—	—	—	—	—	—	—	—	—	—	—	—	—	4	4
5s. but under 15s. ..	3	—	—	1	—	1	—	—	—	1	—	—	6	20	26
15s. " £1 5s. ..	4	1	2	1	—	—	1	2	—	—	—	—	11	52	63
£1 5s. " £1 15s. ..	6	3	5	1	—	—	2	2	2	2	—	—	23	73	96
£1 15s. " £2 5s. ..	8	2	6	1	2	1	1	3	5	—	—	—	29	43	72
£2 5s. " £2 15s. ..	1	1	—	—	1	1	2	3	—	1	—	—	10	39	49
£2 15s. " £3 5s. ..	4	—	5	—	2	1	3	2	—	—	—	—	17	29	46
£3 5s. " £4 10s. ..	1	—	—	1	—	1	1	1	1	—	1	1	7	13	20
£4 10s. " £5 10s. ..	1	—	—	—	—	—	—	1	—	—	1	1	4	9	13
£5 10s. " £6 10s. ..	—	—	—	1	—	—	1	—	—	1	—	—	2	4	6
£6 10s. and over ..	—	—	—	—	—	—	—	—	—	—	—	—	—	2	2
Total ..	28	7	18	6	5	5	11	14	8	4	1	2	109	288	397
* % of all orders ..	7	2	5	2	1	1	3	4	2	1	1 }		27	73	100
% of arrears orders ..	26	6	17	6	5	5	10	13	7	4	3 }		100	—	

* Percentages shown to nearest whole number.

TABLE 41 Outstanding arrears of over £20 on 1st January 1966, on all live orders made in the period 1956–1962.

Amount per week	Arrears on 1st January 1966												Arrears total	No arrears	Total
	£20 £40	£40 £60	£60 £80	£80 £100	£100 £120	£120 but under £150	£150 £200	£200 £300	£300 £500	£500 £700	£700 £1,000	£1,000 and over			
Under 5s.	—	—	—	—	—	—	—	—	—	—	—	—	—	1	1
5s. but under 15s. ..	1	1	2	—	1	—	1	—	—	—	—	—	5	5	10
15s. „ £1 5s. ..	4	1	—	—	—	1	2	1	—	—	—	—	9	20	29
£1 5s. „ £1 15s. ..	4	2	—	2	—	1	—	3	2	1	—	—	15	33	48
£1 15s. „ £2 5s. ..	7	2	—	3	2	3	1	2	1	1	—	1	23	30	53
£2 5s. „ £2 15s. ..	2	1	3	1	2	1	2	1	1	1	—	—	15	24	39
£2 15s. „ £3 5s. ..	3	2	—	2	4	1	3	3	1	1	3	1	24	24	48
£3 5s. „ £4 10s. ..	7	1	2	—	2	3	4	10	5	5	1	—	40	45	85
£4 10s. „ £5 10s. ..	3	2	—	1	1	3	3	4	5	2	1	—	24	28	52
£5 10s. „ £6 10s. ..	2	2	4	1	1	—	—	6	4	1	—	—	21	17	38
£6 10s. and over	1	1	2	1	2	—	—	4	1	4	—	2	18	10	28
Total	33	15	13	10	15	13	16	34	20	16	5	4	194	237	431
* % of all orders ..	8	3	3	2	3	3	4	8	5	4	1	1	45	55	100
% of arrears orders ..	17	8	7	5	8	7	8	18	10	8	3	2	100	—	—

* Percentages shown to nearest whole number.

TABLE 42 Outstanding arrears of over £20 on 1st January 1966, on all live orders made in the years 1963 and 1964.

Amount per week	Arrears on 1st January 1966										Arrears total	No arrears	Total
	£20 £40	£40 £60	£60 £80	£80 £100	£100 but under £120	£120 £150	£150 £200	£200 £300	£300 £500	£500 £700			
Under 5s.	—	—	—	—	—	—	—	—	—	—	—	3	3
5s. but under 15s.	—	—	—	—	—	—	—	—	—	—	—	2	2
15s. " £1 5s.	5	—	—	—	1	—	—	—	—	—	6	8	14
£1 5s. " £1 15s.	1	3	1	—	1	1	1	—	—	—	7	10	17
£1 15s. " £2 5s.	5	2	2	1	1	2	1	—	—	—	14	12	26
£2 5s. " £2 15s.	2	1	1	1	—	—	1	1	—	—	7	12	19
£2 15s. " £3 5s.	1	3	—	—	—	—	—	1	—	—	5	14	19
£3 5s. " £4 10s.	8	6	—	2	—	1	2	—	2	—	16	15	31
£4 10s. " £5 10s.	1	2	3	2	2	—	6	2	2	1	21	11	32
£5 10s. " £6 10s.	6	4	1	—	—	—	3	—	3	—	17	11	28
£6 10s. and over	3	—	1	2	1	2	2	4	4	2	21	14	35
Total	27	21	9	8	5	6	16	8	11	3	114	112	226
* % of all orders	12	9	4	4	2	3	7	4	5	1	50	50	100
% of arrears orders	24	18	8	7	4	5	14	7	10	3	100	—	—

* Percentages shown to nearest whole number.

TABLE 43 Outstanding arrears of over £20 on all live orders made during 1965.

Amount per week	Arrears at 1st January 1966										
	£20 £40	£40 £60	£60 £80	£80 but under £100	£100 £120	£120 £150	£150 £200	£200 £300	Arrears total	No arrears	Total
Under 5s.	—	—	—	—	—	—	—	—	—	5	5
5s. but under 15s.	—	—	1	—	—	—	—	—	1	2	3
15s. „ £1 5s.	—	—	—	—	—	—	—	—	—	12	12
£1 5s. „ £1 15s.	1	—	—	—	—	—	—	—	1	6	7
£1 15s. „ £2 5s.	—	1	1	1	—	—	—	—	3	12	15
£2 5s. „ £2 15s.	2	1	—	—	1	—	—	—	4	7	11
£2 15s. „ £3 5s.	1	2	1	—	—	1	—	—	5	9	14
£3 5s. „ £4 10s.	2	1	3	—	—	4	—	1	11	9	20
£4 10s. „ £5 10s.	5	1	—	1	3	—	3	—	13	16	29
£5 10s. „ £6 10s.	1	1	1	—	1	—	—	—	4	9	13
£6 10s. and over	2	4	—	—	—	2	2	1	11	11	22
Total	14	11	7	2	5	7	5	2	53	98	151
* % of all orders	9	7	5	1	3	5	3	1	35	65	100
% of arrears orders	26	20	13	4	9	13	9	4	100	—	—

* Percentages shown to nearest whole number.

TABLE 44 Amounts by which outstanding arrears of more than £20 on 1st January 1965 had changed by 1st January 1966, for all orders in arrears on 1st January 1965.

Change during 1965 in amounts of arrears on 1st January 1965	Outstanding arrears on 1st January 1965									
	£20 £60	£60 £100	£100 but under £150	£150 £200	£200 £300	£300 £500	£500 and over	Total	C.T. %	%
Decrease										
Under £40	27	6	3	—	—	—	—	36	40	
£40 but under £100	5	11	4	3	1	—	—	24	67	
£100 but under £200	—	—	2	4	5	3	—	14	82	
£200 and over	—	—	—	—	1	5	10	16	100	
Sub-total	32	17	9	7	7	8	10	90		25
C.T. %	36	54	64	72	80	89	100			
Increase										
Under £40	17	10	6	—	—	—	—	33	24	
£40 but under £100	18	15	7	8	—	—	—	48	60	
£100 but under £200	8	4	5	—	5	—	2	24	77	
£200 and over	7	2	2	2	—	13	5	31	100	
Sub-total	50	31	20	10	5	13	7	136		37
C.T. %	37	60	74	82	85	95	100			
Arrears remain the same	39	18	7	15	25	19	16	139		38
C.T. %	28	41	46	57	75	88	100			
Total	121	66	36	32	37	40	33	365		100
C.T. %	33	51	61	70	80	91	100			

C.T.: Cumulative total.

The data presented in Table 38 have been broken down in Tables 40, 41, 42 and 43 to show the arrears history of orders made in different periods; before 1956, between 1956 and 1962, in 1963 and 1964, and in 1965.

The proportion of orders for amounts of £3 5s. 0d. or more has risen from 10% for orders made before 1956, to 47% for orders made between 1956 and 1962 and to 56% for orders made after 1962.

These tables show a steady increase in the proportion of orders in arrears among the more recently made orders. The percentages are:

Orders	%
Made before 1956	27
between 1956 and 1962	45
in 1963 and 1964	50

Of the orders made in 1965 a very high proportion had fallen into arrears by the beginning of 1966. Table 44 has therefore been constructed to provide a detailed analysis of the history during 1965 of all orders in arrears for more than £20 on 1st January 1965. It shows that by 1st January 1966 a quarter of all arrears had been reduced, 37% had increased and 38% remained the same during 1965.

Table 45 tabulates the data in terms of the number of weekly payments in arrears. By this measure, 38% of all orders live on 1st January 1966 had been in arrears for more than six weeks and one-quarter for more than six months.

Information was available about remittance of arrears for more than 90% of orders in the survey. Some part of the arrears have been remitted for one-fifth of the orders live on 1st January 1966[1].

TABLE 45   Number of weekly payments in arrears on 1st January 1966 by duration of order.

Number of weekly payments in arrears	Year order was made				All orders
	Before 1956	1956–62	1963–64	1965	
More than 104	26	38	3	—	68
70 to 104	8	22	10	—	40
52 to 70	16	28	13	—	57
36 to 52	14	26	12	6	57
28 to 36	14	19	21	8	62
20 to 28	15	15	10	9	49
12 to 20	10	23	27	13	73
6 to 12	6	20	9	14	49
Sub-total	109	191	105	50	455
None or less than 6	288	237	112	98	750
Total	397	428	217	148	1,205

The necessary information about arrears was not available in respect of 25 orders in the sample.

[1] The remittal of arrears is discussed in more detail in Chapter 7.

CHAPTER 7

Enforcement of maintenance

The *Report* of the Graham Hall Committee observed that "a notable feature of the magistrates' machinery is the status of the clerk. His role as collecting officer is central to the efficiency of the procedure. It involves two functions: enforcement and bookkeeping"[1]. It is almost universal practice throughout the country for all payments to be made through the clerk who, at the complainant's request, will take enforcement proceedings in his own name[2]. Enforcement proceedings are initiated by a summons requiring the defendant to appear before the court. If he fails to appear, the court may either proceed in his absence or issue a warrant for his arrest. There are then four courses open to the court. It may remit all or part of the arrears; it may issue a distress warrant; it may make an attachment of earnings order; or it may commit the defendant to prison. Enforcement by attachment of earnings order and by committal are considered at length in the main sections of this chapter. The two other procedures may be examined more briefly.

The court may remit arrears of maintenance on its own initiative. Information was available about the remittance history of more than 90% of the orders in the survey. Arrears were remitted in respect of one-fifth of the orders which were live on 1st January 1966, the amounts are shown in Table 46.

Table 47 divides the amounts remitted into three bands.

The practice of courts in dealing with arrears varies widely throughout the country. Some follow the High Court practice recommended by Lord Merriman in 1956[3] of enforcing one year's arrears and remitting the remainder. Others allow them to accumulate. In some courts, justices' clerks deal informally with arrears by a stroke of the pen, and there would seem to be great advantage in giving them the formal power to regulate the accumulation of arrears in accordance with their knowledge of defendants' circumstances and ability to pay.

---

[1] Cmnd. 3587, para 57.

[2] If payments fall into arrear by an amount equal to four weekly payments, the clerk must notify the beneficiary (Rule 33, Magistrates' Courts' Rules 1952). If the beneficiary asks the clerk in writing and there is no reasonable ground for refusing, he must take proceedings for enforcement in his own name. Magistrates' Court Act 1952, s. 52(3).

[3] *Pilcher v. Pilcher (No. 2)* [1956] 1 All E.R. 463.

TABLE 46   Amount remitted by year remitted, on orders live on 1st January 1966.

Amount remitted	Year remitted								
	Pre-1960	1960	1961	1962	1963	1964	1965	Total	Cumulative total
£20 but under £40 ..	16	1	5	3	4	10	7	46	46
£40 but under £60 ..	7	2	—	4	4	4	4	25	71
£60 but under £80 ..	5	2	2	2	2	1	6	20	91
£80 but under £100..	1	—	—	3	2	1	3	10	101
£100 but under £120	3	—	2	2	2	2	4	15	116
£120 but under £150	3	1	3	1	—	2	1	11	127
£150 but under £200	3	1	1	—	—	2	4	11	138
£200 but under £300	4	1	2	1	1	7	3	19	157
£300 but under £500	1	2	1	2	2	4	3	15	172
£500 but under £700	2	—	—	1	—	2	2	7	179
£700 but under £1000	1	—	—	—	1	1	3	6	185
Over £1000	—	—	—	—	—	1	1	2	187
Total	46	10	16	19	18	37	41	187	

TABLE 47   Amounts remitted below £100, between £100 and £200, and above £200, by year remitted.

Amount remitted	Pre-1960 %	1960/61 %	1962/63 %	1964/65 %	Total %
Below £100	63	46	65	46	54
£100–£200	20	31	13	19	20
Above £200	17	23	22	35	26

If the court issues a distress warrant, it must be executed by or under the direction of the police[1]. Execution consists of taking the defaulter's money or of selling his goods. This method of enforcement is now very rarely used.[2] The police disliked it, and it rarely satisfied the beneficiary's claim because the goods seized were hardly ever saleable.

Attachment of earnings

HISTORY

The Common Law Procedure Act 1854 for the first time enabled a creditor to attach monies due to his debtor but in the hands of a third party. This so called "garnishee procedure" was restricted by the early development of a rule that future earnings could not be seized[3] and by statutory exclusions of

[1] L. M. Pugh, *Matrimonial Proceedings Before Magistrates* (2nd ed. 1966) p. 332.
[2] *Report of the Committee on the Enforcement of Judgment Debts*, Cmnd. 3909 (1969) paras 182 and 183.
[3] J. C. Wood, "Attachment of Wages", *Modern Law Review*, Vol. 26, 1963, p. 52.

certain wages, pensions and bank deposits[1]. Further restrictions were imposed by the long-standing working class hatred of truck (the reward of labour in the form of goods, or of vouchers encashable only at shops owned or controlled by the employer) and by the series of Truck Acts designed to protect workers from abuses inherent in the system. At one level, experience of truck helped to establish consumers' co-operation as a means of providing working class housewives with honest measures and unadulterated goods. At another level, the trade union attack on truck resulted in the Wages Attachment (Abolition) Act 1870 which protected "servants, labourers, or workmen" and provided that "no order for the attachment of wages of any servant, labourer or workman shall be made by the judge of any court of record or inferior court"[2]. From 1870 until the late 1950s, the maintenance of the integrity of the wage packet was a constant object of trade union policy; and national insurance and P.A.Y.E. payments were the only permitted deductions from wages.

The first statutory provision for attachment of earnings was made by the Select Vestry Act of 1819 which enacted some of the recommendations of the Select Committee set up under Sturges Bourne in 1817 to inquire into the Poor Law[3]. The Act empowered justices who were satisfied that an applicant for poor relief

> might but for his extravagance, neglect, or wilful misconduct, have been able to maintain himself or support his family (as the case may be) . . . to advance money, weekly or otherwise as may be requisite, to the person so applying, by way of loan only, and to take his receipt for, and engagement to repay the same[4].

Failure to repay could result in an instalment order or finally in imprisonment. The power to grant relief by way of a loan was also extended to pensioners in the army and navy who were enabled to assign their pensions to the overseers of the poor in repayment. Similarly, the Act made the wages of merchant seamen liable for attachment in respect of poor relief afforded to their families in their absence. These provisions were not widely used because, as Sir George Nicholls observed, "facility of borrowing, whether it be of the pawnbroker or of the parish officer, is not calculated to give rise to or encourage provident habits in the working classes, on the existence of which their comfort and general well-being so much depend"[5].

[1] *Ibid.*, p. 54. The most important were the pay of the armed forces and the wages of merchant seamen. The pensions of the forces and of the police were also protected as were deposits in the Post Office Savings Bank which Gladstone set up in 1861 in order to provide thrifty working men with a safe deposit.

[2] Section 1.

[3] An account of the Committee is contained in Sidney and Beatrice Webb, *English Poor Law History: Part II: The Last Hundred Years*, (1929) Vol. 1, pp. 40–3.

[4] Section 29.

[5] George Nicholls, *A History of the English Poor Law, in Connexion with the Legislation and Other Circumstances Affecting the Condition of the People* (1854), Vol. 2, p. 199.

The first extension of this principle beyond the poor law came eighty-nine years later. The Children Act 1908 provided, with regard to the enforcement of contribution orders on parents to support their children in Industrial or Reformatory Schools, that

> any court making an order . . . for contribution by a parent or other such person may, in case where there is any pension or income payable to such parent or other person and capable of being attached, after giving the person by whom the pension or income is payable an opportunity of being heard, further order that such part as the court may see fit of the pension or income be attached and be paid to the person named by the court. Such further order shall be an authority to the person by whom such pension or other income is payable to make the payment so ordered, and the receipt of the person to whom the payment is ordered to be paid shall be a good discharge to such first-named person.[1]

The following year a Select Committee[2] reported on the law relating to the making and enforcement of Bastardy Orders and urged attachment as a method of enforcement. Its proposal became section 2 of the Affiliation Orders Act 1914 under which any pension or income "capable of being attached" could be attached for the benefit of the person to whom the affiliation payments were due. This facility remained until 1958; but it was a dead letter from the beginning because the power of attachment was limited to pensions or incomes "capable of being attached". This phrase was carried over from the Children Act 1908. It operated to put the whole range of pensions, excluded from attachment by statute as well as the wages of the mass of the population covered by the Wages Attachment (Abolition) Act of 1870, beyond the reach of the sanction.

The first weighty suggestion for the use of attachment to enforce the maintenance of wives came in the *Report* of the Gorrell Commission in 1912.

> We think that power should be given to the court, in its discretion, to make an order, but that the order should merely authorise the employer to pay the amount ordered to be paid out of the husband's wages, and that the employer should be at liberty to assent or decline to act on the order . . .[3]

The proposal for a permissive power of attachment reflected the hostility of the majority of employers consulted by the Commission[4]. But opinion in favour of attachment for the benefit of wives strengthened during the next twenty years. The subject was examined again in 1934 in the lucid *Report*

---

[1] Section 75(11).   [2] 1909 (236) vi. 717.
[3] [Cd. 6478] (1912), para 174.
[4] Appendices to the Minutes of evidence [Cd. 6482] (1912). The employers' replies are printed as Appendix XXIV.

of the Departmental Committee on Imprisonment by Courts of Summary Jurisdiction in Default of Payment of Fines and Other Sums of Money (the Fischer Williams Committee). The *Report* summarized the conflict of opinion.

"The main objections which have been raised to the proposal are the following:

(i) It is contended that an employer would dispense with a man's services rather than be put to the trouble of making the necessary deductions and paying the amount deducted to the Collecting Officer of the Court or that the employer would object on principle to continuing to employ a man against whom such an order had been made.

(ii) The same objection is sometimes put in the more general form—that any system of attachment of wages would tend to upset generally the relations between employers and employees.

(iii) It is said that as any system of attachment could be applied to the regular wage-earner only, it would constitute an unfair discrimination against him as compared with the casual labourer or the man working on his own account.

(iv) It is also pointed out that the attachment of wages will not be of any assistance in cases where the man is out of work, and it is precisely the fact that he is out of work which is the usual cause of failure to pay.

(v) Lastly, the proposal has to meet a general predisposition to regard with suspicion and even hostility anything that seems to savour of an attack upon the income of the wage-earner.

On the other hand, in favour of the proposal it is argued that as a matter of principle there can be no valid reason against a measure which does nothing more than ensure that a man discharge out of his earnings a liability which ranks very high in the scale of his social obligations and which will have been fixed, if the law has been observed, with special reference to those earnings. If any valid objections exist, they are objections of detail and of practical arrangement which it is not impossible to overcome."[1]

The Committee recommended legislation to provide that

when payments under a maintenance or affiliation order are in arrears for four weeks or longer and the Court after hearing the defendant are satisfied that his default is due to wilful refusal or culpable neglect to pay the amount due, the Court may, if it thinks fit, make an order requiring any person, firm or company (including the Post Office or any Government Department) by whom the defendant is employed, to pay to the Collecting Officer, by way of deduction from wages or salary, such sum weekly or otherwise as the Court shall specify in discharge or part discharge of the liability under the order[2].

[1] Cmd. 4649 (1934), paras 185 and 186.   [2] *Ibid.*, para 194.

Only one member, Miss Annie Loughlin, a trade unionist, dissented on the ground that attachment would be "a dangerous innovation" which "might be taken as a precedent, and . . . be extended in future to debts in general"[1]. However, it was the minority view which prevailed, and it became a commonplace that attachment would imperil good industrial relations. Thus, the *Final Report* of the Committee on Supreme Court Practice and Procedure (the Evershed Committee) in 1953 had

> no doubt that any general adoption of the attachment of wages as an ordinary form of execution would be strongly opposed both by employers and employees as an undue interference in industrial relations and as being in opposition to the known antagonism of employees' organisations to any deduction from wages[2].

The Royal Commission on Marriage and Divorce (the Morton Commission) went over the same ground and concluded in 1956 that "there has been little, if any, change in the views expressed to the Fischer Williams Committee by representatives of the employers and of the wage earners . . . "[3] But the same evidence led this Commission to the opposite conclusion to that of the Fischer Williams Committee; and it recommended against attachment[4].

The following year a *Report* of the Advisory Council on the Treatment of Offenders under the title, *Alternatives to Short Terms of Imprisonment*, expressed the hope of easing the difficulties of deserted wives and of economizing on scarce prison accommodation by recommending attachment of wages as a substitute for the imprisonment of maintenance defaulters[5]. In the early post-war period two private members' Bills sought to introduce attachment of earnings: the first was promoted by Dr. Edith (now Lady) Summerskill and Mr. J. E. S. (now Sir Jocelyn) Simon; the second, The Maintenance Orders (Attachment of Income) Bill, introduced by Miss (now Dame) Joan Vickers, was given a second reading by the House of Commons but foundered in Committee. During the next session the Government introduced similar legislation which the Home Secretary, Mr. R. A. Butler, commended because

> the hardship to the women, the burden thrown upon the taxpayer in supporting those who are compelled to apply for National Assistance

---

[1] *Ibid.*, p. 92.   [2] Cmd. 8878 (1953) para 429.

[3] Cmd. 9678 (1956) para 1105. In an *Appendix to Minutes of Evidence*, the Commission printed the views of the British Employers' Federation and of the T.U.C. The Employers thought that attachment would "be inimical to the interests both of employers and their workpeople". Further, that "it might well be applied at a later date to the recovery of fines and other debts" (p. 31). The T.U.C. thought that it would be "wrong to impose upon an employer an obligation to make a deduction from the wages of any of his employees in respect of a matter which does not arise from and has no obvious relationship to the man's employment" (p. 32).

[4] The Chairman, Lord Morton of Henryton, later changed his mind and thought that the advantages of attachment would outweigh the disadvantages, see Hansard, House of Commons, 12th December 1957, col. 1555.   [5] *Op. cit.*, pp. 13–16.

and the futility of putting men in prison, constitutes a unique combination of circumstances which justifies, in our view, a resort to attachment for the enforcement of maintenance obligations[1].

The debate demonstrated the beginning of a shift in the attitude of some trade unionists. Mr. Charles Pannell declared that

this Bill will deal with the non-unionists in our society—the defaulters, the escapists and . . . the people whom we call the knobsticks, the black legs, the rats and the scabs . . . Those members of the trade union movement who can claim the greatest degree of knowledge of the problem are on the side of the Bill.[2]

The Bill was widely approved inside and outside Parliament; it passed into law, and the Act came into operation in 1958. It provided that the employer of a defendant who is subject to a maintenance or an affiliation order and who is four weeks in arrears with weekly payments (or in any other case in arrear with two payments), can be ordered by the court to pay part of the earnings directly to the court. The court may make an attachment of earnings order only if the defendant's failure to pay was due to his wilful refusal or culpable neglect. When making the order, the court must specify two rates: first, "the normal deduction rate" which is the amount thought reasonable to satisfy the affiliation or maintenance order and to reduce the arrears; second, "the protected earnings rate" which is the amount thought adequate to remain in the hands of the defendant for his needs and inescapable responsibilities.

An employer against whom an attachment of earnings order is directed must normally pay to the court the normal deduction rate; but if his employee's weekly wage is less than the normal deduction rate, what is attached is the difference between the protected earnings rate and the employee's net earnings. Each attachment order must be directed against a particular employer and, if the employee changes his employer, the current order lapses and the court must make a new order.

The fear and disapproval of attachment of earnings as a method of enforcing payments have largely evaporated. The Maintenance Orders Act 1958 was followed by the Criminal Justice Act 1967 which authorized the use of attachment against defaulters on fines, and the Administration of Justice Act 1970 extends attachment to the whole area of civil debt, as recommended by the Committee on the Enforcement of Judgment Debts (the Payne Committee) in 1969. The Truck Acts have even proved an embarrassment; because strong trade unions and full employment have, for some workers at least, converted the harshness of truck payments into the indulgence of fringe benefits. As the

---

[1] Hansard, House of Commons, 12th December 1957, col. 1547.
[2] *Ibid.*, col. 1585.

British Employers' Confederation explained to the Committee on the Truck Acts (the Karmel Committee) in 1961, "in modern conditions . . . there are many instances in which the Truck Acts have prevented employers from providing amenities which would be of value to their employees"[1]. It is against this background that section 2 of this chapter reports the findings of the survey of attachment of earnings orders for maintenance and affiliation payments under the 1958 Act which was undertaken for the Payne Committee as part of the present research project[2].

THE SURVEY OF ATTACHMENT OF EARNINGS ORDERS

Statistically, an examination of 600-odd attachment orders would have yielded reliable conclusions, but it was decided to reduce the sampling error by increasing the number of orders in the sample to between 900 and 1,000. The types of attachment of earnings orders and the categories of courts in which they were held are shown in Table 9 in Chapter 3. The duration before the maintenance orders were enforced after 1959 by attachment of earnings orders in the sample is shown by Table 48.

TABLE 48   **Duration, before attachment, of the maintenance orders enforced by the attachment orders in the sample.**

Duration of maintenance order before attachment	Period when maintenance order was made					
	Before 1959	%	1959 and after	%	Total	%
Less than 1 year	18	6	305	50	323	35
1 year but less than 3	51	16	221	36	272	29
3 years but less than 7	119	37	83	14	202	22
7 years but less than 10	69	21	—	—	69	7
Over 10 years	63	20	—	—	63	7
Not known	—	—	—	—	22	—
Total	320	100	609	100	951	100

The above durations are not shown by type of order because the differences are insignificant. The table demonstrates how quickly the new procedure was adopted. Half the attachment orders made after 1959 applied to maintenance orders which had lasted no longer than their first year. Almost two-thirds of the attachment orders in the sample were enforcing maintenance orders which were less than three years old.

The discharge and duration of attachment of earnings orders

A very high proportion of the 951 orders in the sample are discharged.

[1] p. 8.   [2] See Chapter 3, p. 47.

TABLE 49 Proportion of orders discharged.

Orders	Number	%
Discharged	677	71
In force	245	26
Not known	29	3
Total	951	100

Of the 677 discharged orders, 300 had been "remade". Their distribution by reference to the number of times the order was "remade" was as follows:

TABLE 50 Number of times discharged orders have been "remade".

Number of further Attachment Orders made	Number of instances	%
1	175	58
2	78	26
3	27	9
4	7	
5	6	
6	5	7
7	2	
Total	300	100

As a number of the orders in the sample would have been discharged too near in date to 1st January 1966 to allow sufficient time for them to have been "remade", it seems reasonable to assume that around 50% of discharged orders will be "remade".

Most discharged orders have lasted for very short periods Nearly three-quarters of the orders made were discharged and, of these, more than one-third lasted less than four months, half lasted less than six months, and three-quarters were discharged within a year of being made. Only 11% of discharged attachment orders have survived for more than two years before discharge.

The distribution by duration of the orders that were live on 1st January 1966 may be compared with the similar distribution of the discharged orders shown in Table 51.

Of the orders in force on 1st January 1966 slightly fewer than half have been in operation for more than two years. Table 52 shows that live orders with a survival period of more than two years constituted 45% of the total of live orders. This compares with the 11% of discharged orders with the same survival rate shown in Table 51.

TABLE 51 Duration of attachment orders before discharge.*

Duration of Orders	Affiliation	Married women	Guardianship	National Assistance	Children and Young Persons	Total	Cumulative total	Cumulative %
Never enforced	1	9	—	—	—	10	10	2
Less than 2 months	13	74	16	—	6	109	119	18
2 months but less than 4 months	17	66	25	1	11	120	239	35
4 months but less than 6 months	14	63	22	—	10	109	348	51
Between 6 months and 1 year ..	22	100	22	2	11	157	505	75
Between 1 year and 2	13	55	19	—	9	96	601	89
Between 2 years and 3	6	20	6	—	8	40	641	95
Between 3 years and 5	2	15	3	—	4	24	665	98
Between 5 years and 7	1	5	4	—	2	12	677	100
Total	89	407	117	3	61	677		

* Table 49 shows the derivation of such orders.

TABLE 52   Duration of attachment orders in force on 1st January 1966.

Duration of orders	Affiliation	Married women	Guardianship	National Assistance	Children and Young Persons	Total	Cumulative total	Cumulative %
Less than 2 months ..	4	7	1	1	1	14	14	6
2 months but less than 4 ..	3	16	2	—	2	23	37	15
4 months but less than 6 ..	4	12	1	—	—	17	54	22
Between 6 months and 1 year	6	25	5	—	4	40	94	38
Between 1 year and 2 ..	6	30	3	—	1	40	134	55
Between 2 years and 3 ..	4	10	4	—	1	19	153	67
Between 3 years and 5 ..	6	30	11	—	5	52	205	84
Between 5 years and 7 ..	4	31	3	1	1	40	245	100
Total	37	161	30	2	15	245		

Reasons for the discharge of attachment orders

Overwhelmingly, the reason for the discharge of orders was that men whose earnings had been attached changed their employers.

TABLE 53   Reasons for the discharge of attachment orders.

Reason	Number of instances
Respondent left work and employer obtained discharge of the order	507
Maintenance order revoked or discharged	44
Respondent dismissed and employer obtained discharge of the order	33
Maintenance order varied	10
Order discharged on respondent's application after arrears had been cleared	6
Reason not known	77
Total	677

In the 600 cases in which the reason for the discharge of the order was known, 85% of the respondents (507) had changed their jobs. With a further 6% (33) the employer took the initiative by dismissing the respondent and then having the order discharged, but in only 1% (6) of the cases was the order revoked on the respondent's application because the arrears of maintenance had been cleared.

Social characteristics of men whose earnings have been attached and of employers against whom orders were directed.

It was hoped to provide an occupational classification of men whose earnings had been attached and to determine the size of the labour force of employers against whom orders had been directed. Regrettably, the relevant data in court records proved ambiguous or uncertain and did not permit well grounded conclusions. It is clear, though, that attachment of earnings is a method of enforcement which applies almost exclusively to the working class.

Court records yielded no useful information about employers save that only eleven instances were found in which an employer had complained to court officials about his obligations when an attachment of earnings order had been directed against him.

Arrears of maintenance

The data permit a detailed analysis of arrears of maintenance and of the contribution which attachment orders made to their reduction.

First, the amount of arrears of maintenance when the attachment order was made can be shown.

TABLE 54 **Amount of arrears of maintenance when the attachment of earnings order was made.**

Amount of arrears			Total number of orders	Cumulative %
Less than £40	..	..	120	13
£40 but less than £60		..	365	53
£60 but less than £100		..	169	71
£100 but less than £200		..	149	87
£200 but less than £500		..	106	99
£500 and over		..	13	100
Total			922	
Not known			29	

Table 54 shows that half the attachments were made upon arrears of under £60 and two-thirds upon arrears of less than £100. The range of arrears within which an attachment order was most likely to be made was between £40 and £60.

When, as in Table 55, the data are broken down to show the detail of arrears among different types of order, they suggest that courts might be more willing to tolerate higher arrears in wife-maintenance than in other forms of maintenance.

Table 56 shows the proportion of orders in which arrears had been cleared.

These data can be broken down to show:

(*a*) the proportion of discharged orders in which arrears had been cleared by type of order;

TABLE 55[1] **Seeming propensity of magistrates to tolerate larger arrears of maintenance before making attachment orders for wife maintenance than for other types of order.**

Amount of arrears at time of attachment order						Married women orders %	Other orders %
Less than £100	..	..	..	..	..	67	83
Between £100 and £200	..	..	..	..		17	14
Over £200	..	..	..	..	..	16	3

TABLE 56 **Proportion of orders in which arrears have been cleared.**

Orders					Arrears cleared %	Arrears standing %
In force on 1st January 1966	..	..	..	..	41	59
Discharged ..	..	..	..	..	10	90

[1] Total in sample 922.

TABLE 57 **Discharged orders: Arrears by type of order at time of discharge.**

Type of order	Arrears standing %	Arrears cleared %
Affiliation	87	13
Married Women and Guardianship	92	8
National Assistance and Children and Young Persons ..	76	24
Total	90	10

TABLE 58 **All orders: proportion in which arrears were cleared.**

Type of order	Arrears standing %	Arrears cleared %
Affiliation	77	23
Married Woman and Guardianship	84	16
National Assistance and Children and Young Persons ..	73	27
Total	82	18

(*b*) the experience of discharged orders can be combined with that of orders remaining in force to provide a picture of the arrears situation of all orders.

The data provide information about the remission of arrears when attachment orders were made. 13% of the courts in the sample remitted part of the arrears of maintenance when making the attachment order. In half the instances, the amount remitted was less than £70, in a quarter the amount was between £70 and £120, and in 14% more than £200.

It seems a reasonable test of the success or failure of an attachment order to consider whether it secured either (*a*) a reduction of outstanding arrears or (*b*) at least the regular payment of the weekly amount fixed by the maintenance order. A laborious analysis was undertaken in order to apply these tests to all orders made in 1960. The procedure was to compare the arrears on 1st January 1962 with those accumulated at the time the attachment order was made. First, the orders were analysed to show how many had been discharged by 1st January 1962.

In line with the experience demonstrated in Table 51, more than two-thirds of the orders made in 1960 had been discharged by the beginning of 1962.

Second, the attachment orders discharged by 1st January 1962 were examined in order to discover if the arrears accumulated at the time the order was made had been reduced or cleared when it was discharged.

In only one instance had arrears been cleared when the order was discharged. Third, the orders still in force on 1st January 1962 were examined in order to determine the number in which arrears had been cleared by that date.

TABLE 59 Number[1] of attachment orders made during 1960 in force on, or discharged by, 1st January 1962.

Type of order (made during 1960)	In force on 1st January 1962	Discharged by 1st January 1962	Total
Affiliation	1	13	14
Married women and guardianship	29	62	91
National assistance and children and young persons	5	7	12
Total	35	82	117

Tables 60 and 61 show a total of eight orders in which arrears had been cleared. Thus, of the 117 orders made in 1960, and for which the necessary information was available, one had been discharged without arrears, 81 had been discharged with arrears and, of the remaining 35 in force on 1st January 1962, only seven had cleared their arrears. Thus, the final step in the analysis is to examine the experience of the 28 orders made in 1960 and still in force with arrears at the beginning of 1962.

TABLE 60 Arrears cleared before discharge of orders made in 1960 and discharged before 1st January 1962.

Type of order	Number of orders in which arrears had been cleared before discharge	Number of orders discharged with standing arrears	Total
Affiliation	—	13	13
Married women and guardianship of infants ..	1	61	62
National assistance and children and young persons	—	7	7
Total	1	81	82

Of the 28 1960 orders with arrears still in force at the beginning of 1962, 8 had larger arrears than when the attachment order was made, in 4 the arrears were unchanged, and in 16 they had been reduced. So in only 28 cases (8 in which arrears were cleared altogether and 20 in which they remained the same or were reduced) could attachment orders have resulted in greater regularity of payment, and only in these 28 cases could the attachment orders be regarded as achieving their object. Thus, fewer than one-quarter of the attachment orders made in 1960 did all that could be hoped of them.

[1] The number was 130; but the necessary information was not recorded, or was unsatisfactorily recorded, in thirteen cases.

TABLE 61   Arrears cleared by orders in force on 1st January 1962.

Type of order	Number of orders with arrears cleared	Number of orders with arrears standing	Total
Affiliation	—	1	1
Married women and guardianship of infants ..	5	24	29
National assistance and 'children and young persons	2	3	5
Total	7	28	35

TABLE 62   Reduction or increase of arrears among orders made in 1960 and still in force on 1st January 1962.

Arrears	Affiliation	Married women and guardianship of infants	National assistance and children and young persons	Total
Increases in outstanding arrears ..	—	8	—	8
Arrears unchanged	—	4	—	4
Arrears reduced by more than £40	—	4	1	5
Arrears reduced by less than £40	1	8	2	11
Total	1	24	3	28

TABLE 63   Arrears at time of attachment order.

Duration of maintenance order at time of attachment	Arrears £					
	up to 59	60 to 99	100 to 199	200 to 499	500 and over	Total
Less than 6 months	22	2	—	—	—	24
6 months but less than 1 year ..	18	2	2	1	—	23
1 year but less than 5	17	6	10	12	—	45
5 years but less than 10	14	5	7	—	1	27
10 years or over	4	2	2	3	—	11
Total	75	17	21	16	1	130

Duration of maintenance order at time of attachment	Arrears				
	Under £100	%	£100 and over	%	Total
Less than 5 years	67	73	25	66	92
More than 5 years..	25	27	13	34	38
Total	92	100	38	100	130

All orders made in 1960 were analysed to find out if the amount of arrears outstanding on maintenance orders at the time of attachment could be related to the duration of the orders.

Orders with less than £100 arrears constituted 73% of the orders that had existed for less than five years, and 66% of those lasting more than five years before attachment. These proportions suggest that the duration of an order is not a significant factor in determining the amount of arrears.

Respondents' incomes at the time of making the attachment of earnings order

The data permit a comparison of respondents' incomes with the protected earnings rates specified by courts under section 6 of the Maintenance Orders Act 1958. The financial data shown in Table 64 relate to all the orders made in 1960.

TABLE 64 **Respondents whose incomes were attached in 1960, classified by the different ranges of protected earnings specified by the courts.**

| | Income per week | | | |
Protected earnings rate	Less than £10	£10 but less than £14	More than £14	Total
Under £4 10s.	7	5	1	13
£4 10s. but less than £7 10s. ..	31	46	9	86
£7 10s. „ „ „ £10 10s. ..	5	17	8	30
More than £10 10s.	—	—	1	1
Total	43	68	19	130

This table reinforces the view that attachment of earnings as used in magistrates' courts applies exclusively to the working class. In 85% of the cases the respondents' earnings were less than £14 a week in a year in which the average weekly earnings of male manual workers were £14 1s. Indeed, it is clear that most of the men whose earnings had been attached must have worked in partly skilled or unskilled occupations. The low rate of protected earnings—some two-thirds of the men had only £7 a week and a substantial proportion less—must be seen in the context of what is known about the other commitments of men whose earnings have been attached. This is shown in Table 65.

For nearly a third of the whole sample the court had no record of additional commitments but almost a third were supporting paramours, relatives or new wives. It is striking that one-fifth of the men with attached earnings were supporting paramours and their offspring. As this proportion includes only those men about whom courts had knowledge, the true proportion is likely to be considerably larger.

TABLE 65   **Additional financial commitments of men whose earnings have been attached.**

Commitment	Affiliation	Type of order	
		Married women and guardianship	National assistance and local authority
None	31	228	22
Supporting paramour and her children	46	144	12
Marriage after divorce from complainant	—	51	—
Supporting relatives	8	22	15
Mortgage repayments	5	13	—
Debt repayments	8	62	10
Other—unclassified	15	42	12

THE EXTENSION OF THE USE AND THE LIMITATIONS OF ATTACHMENT

The Criminal Justice Act 1967 provided that attachment of earnings orders could be made against defaulters on fines. The Home Office has as yet published no statistics to show the extent to which the courts have used the new facility, although it is likely that very few attachment orders have been made for this purpose. The explanation may be that scepticism about the usefulness of attachment is widespread among Justices and their clerks. This scepticism is demonstrated by Table 66 which shows the number of attachment orders in existence on 1st January 1966 in the London Stipendiary courts.

Chapter 6 showed[1] that 38% of all orders live on 1st January 1966 had been in arrears for more than six weeks and 25% for more than six months. If a similar proportion had been in arrears in London as in the rest of the country and if attachment orders had been made only in respect of arrears of more than six months, there would have been more than 3,500 attachment orders in the London courts. Clearly, attachment is not the enforcement method of choice in London.

The Criminal Justice Act has done nothing to cure the defects of the system created by the Maintenance Orders Act 1958, which are presented in quantitative detail in our survey originally undertaken for the Committee on the Enforcement of Judgment Debts (the Payne Committee). Its *Report* concludec that "two main features of the present system tend to inhibit its successful operation.

   (*a*) There is no provision whereby an attachment of earnings order can be made by consent, either immediately on a maintenance order being made or at any other stage. The defendant therefore, rather

[1] Table 45.

TABLE 66 Number of live matrimonial orders and attachment of earnings orders in London Stipendiary courts on 1st January 1966[1].

	Number of live matrimonial orders on 1st January 1966	Number of attachment orders on 1st January 1966
North London	2,250	100
Lambeth	1,800	10
Marylebone	1,700	12
West London	1,450	45
South Western	1,420	50
Greenwich	1,200	12
Old Street	1,000	6
Clerkenwell	875	25
Thames	800	10
Tower Bridge	635	3
Woolwich	590	10
Balham	575	0
Bow Street	180	2
Marlborough Street	130	12
Wells Street	6	2
Total	14,611	299

than being encouraged to see it as a convenient method of payment, is brought to regard attachment of earnings as a penalty imposed when he is in default.

(b) The other is that the procedure is virtually powerless against the defendant who is determined to avoid payment, in that he can thwart the order for the time being by terminating his employment, whether he subsequently remains unemployed or takes on new employment. If he changes his employment, the order lapses and any variation in earnings requires a recalculation of the normal deduction rate and the protected earnings rate. The whole order, therefore, has to be considered anew by the court and the relevant court procedures have to be followed all over again."[2]

The Administration of Justice Act 1970 accepts some of the recommendations of the Payne Committee, including the abolition of imprisonment for civil debt[3] and the extension of attachment of earnings to secure the payment of civil debts. The Act seeks to correct the chief disadvantages of the 1958 procedure by substituting a composite code which includes provisions for

(a) a debtor to apply on his own behalf in respect of payments under a maintenance order;[4]

[1] Attachment orders include only those made by the court named. Orders transferred from other courts (20 in all) are excluded.
[2] Cmnd. 3909, para 601.
[3] Imprisonment for default on certain debts to the Crown and on maintenance obligations remains.   [4] Section 14(1)(d)(i).

(b) an order to remain in force even though it has lapsed as a result of the debtor's change of employer[1];

(c) a debtor to notify the court on every occasion of change of employment and to include in the notification particulars of his actual and anticipated earnings[2]; and

(d) any person who becomes a debtor's employer and has knowledge of the existence of an attachment of earnings order to notify the court that he is the debtor's employer[3].

It would be idle to speculate whether the altered procedure will significantly improve the success-rate of attachment of earnings as a method of enforcing maintenance. Half the debts sued for in the county courts are for amounts of £20 or less. The debtor may regard attachment as a convenient method of settling such once-and-for-all commitments. On the other hand, the unending obligation of maintenance raises entirely different problems of collection. The fundamental difficulty is that English[4] notions of liberty are happily not compatible with the degree of control over the citizen by the police which is customary in some countries where attachment works satisfactorily.

Imprisonment of maintenance defaulters

Magistrates can commit a defaulter for a period not exceeding six weeks, but they must be certain as a result of inquiries made in his presence that the default resulted from his wilful refusal or culpable neglect to pay. They may suspend the committal order for so long as the defendant continues to pay a stated amount which will include the current maintenance and a reduction of the arrears. The number of maintenance defaulters sent to prison in the last few years is shown in Table 67.

There can be no doubt that the reduction to half in prison committals of maintenance defaulters in 1959 resulted from the immediate use of attachment orders by the courts. Nevertheless, there has been a reversal of the earlier downward trend in the number of committals since 1959. The size of the group of maintenance defaulters among civil prisoners has changed over the period chiefly because the number of debtors committed by county courts increased six-fold between 1955 and 1963.

THE EFFECT OF ATTACHMENT OF EARNINGS UPON THE
NUMBER OF MAINTENANCE DEFAULTERS IMPRISONED

The extent to which the courts used committal against defaulters in the sample is shown by Table 68

---

[1] Section 18(4).   [2] Section 21 (a) (b).   [3] Section 21 (c).

[4] We discuss briefly the efficacy of assessment as a diligence for enforcing payment of ailment in Scotland in Chapter 12, pp. 204–205.

TABLE 67[1]   Receptions in prison of maintenance defaulters committed by magistrates' courts, 1955–1967.

Year	Number	Maintenance defaulters as percentage of civil process prisoners
1955	4,333	72
1956	4,314	68
1957	4,597	62
1958	4,910	52
1959	2,358	29
1960	2,379	28
1961	2,867	30
1962	3,194	27
1963	3,013	26
1964	3,304	34
1965	3,465	43
1966	3,664	47
1967[2]	3,511	45

Twelve per cent of the men (113) whose earnings had been attached had been sent to prison before for default on maintenance payments. Of these, some two-thirds had been committed once and one-third twice or more. A further 11% of the men (107) had had suspended committal orders made against them. It should be noted that the committal orders shown in Table 68 include those made in respect of defaults on maintenance orders before 1959. (It was shown in Table 1 that one-third of the sample related to maintenance orders made before the Maintenance Orders Act 1958, came into force.)

However, further analysis of the data shows that, of the 200 committals classified in Table 68, rather more than half had been ordered before the Maintenance Orders Act 1958 came into force but before the attachment order was made. Thus, in that half of the total number of suspended and prison committals made after the Act, the magistrates seem to have reversed the intention of the Act and to have used attachment orders after committal

TABLE 68   Attachment orders with a record of committal proceedings before attachment.

Type of order	Committal		Total orders
	Suspended	Prison	
Affiliation	17	12	131
Married women and guardianship	86	93	737
National assistance and young persons	4	8	83
Total	107	113	951

[1] *Report on the Work of the Prison Department*, Statistical Tables, Cmnd. 3788, 1968, Table C.9. (The number of receptions in 1964 is not strictly comparable with the figures for other years.)
[2] In this year, the total includes four women.

had failed to produce payment of maintenance. Attachment orders made in these circumstances constituted 13% of the sample for which the relevant information is available.

This analysis of the data relating to committal produces few conclusions because the records of many courts in the sample were inadequate or unusable.

THE FINDINGS OF THE MAIN SURVEY

The quality of court records varies considerably in different parts of the country and among the categories of information recorded. Data relating to imprisonment were thin and unreliable in many of the survey courts, especially in respect of such decisions as the making of suspended committal orders about which complete and accurate records might have been expected. In some courts, the decision of the bench to make a suspended committal order is not recorded in the case file and can be discovered only from the transcript of the hearing.

Table 69 shows the number of committals by type of order in the survey.

TABLE 69   **Prison committals by type of order.**

| Type of order | Number of committals | | | | | | Total committals | Total orders | Committals as a percentage of orders |
	1	2	3	4	5	6			
Married women and children	29	6	2	3	2		42	627	7
Married women only ..	12					1	13	355	4
Children only	5	2					7	248	3
Total	46	8	2	3	2	1	62	1,230	5

This table shows that 5% of the matrimonial orders in the survey had led to the imprisonment of the defaulting husband[1]. A detailed examination of the orders made in 1965 disclosed only nine with a record of committal to prison. In accordance with our estimate[2] of 165,000 live orders on the 1st January 1966, this would give a national total of some 1,250 imprisonments in 1965, only half the actual number of 2,664 for that year. It is therefore clear that court records underestimate the number of committals to a significant extent. Nevertheless, there is no reason to suppose that Table 68 does not reflect accurately the distribution of committals among the different types of

[1] The difference of 7% between the main survey imprisonment rate of 5% and the 12% shown in the attachment survey in Table 68 is explained by the differing populations of these two surveys. The prison committal rate of 12% results from a survey, carried out for the Committee on the Enforcement of Judgment Debts (The Payne Committee), that concentrated exclusively on respondents who had had attachment of earnings orders made against them. As these respondents were all maintenance defaulters it could be expected that a higher rate of committal would be found amongst them than in the main survey population in which only 13% of all respondents had had attachment of earnings orders made against them.

[2] Appendix B, Part 2.

order. The low proportion of imprisonments in cases of children only orders might measure the likelihood that men will try harder to keep up maintenance payments on behalf of their children. But, if this were the case, the proportion of imprisonments might be expected to be highest for married women only orders where the reluctance to pay might be keenest. However, the proportion is in fact highest with the married women and children orders. There are two possible explanations. In the first place, these orders are generally for larger amounts of money, so that the financial hardship for the husband and the chances of his falling into arrears are greater. Second, magistrates may react more punitively if wives and children are jointly suffering from the default.

We had hoped to obtain detailed information about the use of suspended committal orders as a method of enforcement. Regrettably, we have concluded that our data are too unreliable to permit conclusions. They show that 11% of orders made since 1959 have been enforced at least once by suspended committals. The probability is that this figure seriously underestimates the reliance which magistrates place upon this sanction.

These data do not permit firmly based conclusions about the efficacy or deterrent effect of imprisoning maintenance defaulters. Those who wish to retain imprisonment often argue that more husbands than at present would neglect their obligations towards their families if they were not restrained by the ultimate sanction of imprisonment. This view can only have the status of an unprovable assertion, because we know very little about general deterrence. Moreover, factual information, however extensive and elaborate, can no more help one to decide the question of abolishing or retaining imprisonment for maintenance defaulters than to settle the conflict between the opponents and proponents of capital punishment. Moral questions do not admit of quantitative answers. We hold that the imprisonment of maintenance defaulters is both immoral and an obstacle to the desirable development of family law; but we think it more appropriate to argue our views in the final chapter of this book where they can be judged on their practical and ethical merits[1].

[1] The Committee on the Enforcement of Judgment Debts divided on this issue, and most of the arguments on both sides are set out in its *Report* (Cmnd. 3909, 1969, paras 952–1108). As the Committee, in making its case for recommending the abolition of imprisonment for civil debt, unanimously rejected the argument from general deterrence none of the members who urged the retention of imprisonment for maintenance defaulters was able to use this argument. We examine the views of the Committee in Chapter 12, pp. 200–207. One of the authors of this book was a member of the Committee and signed the recommendation that the imprisonment of maintenance defaulters should be abolished forthwith.

Imprisonment of fine-defaulters, which involves the same practical and ethical considerations, is discussed in the report of the Advisory Council on the Penal System on Non-Custodial and Semi-Custodial Penalties (1970). A minority recommended abolition, with the replacement of a specific criminal offence of wilful default.

CHAPTER 8

How wives and husbands perceive the courts

The hearing by magistrates of matrimonial complaints are "domestic proceedings" governed by the special provisions of the Magistrates' Courts Act 1952 and the Administration of Justice Act 1964. These require that a domestic court with lay justices shall include, so far as practicable, a man and a woman. The general public is excluded; but the press may attend, although reports of the proceedings must be restricted in much the same way as those of divorce cases. In practice, the press hardly ever attend domestic proceedings. The Magistrates' Court Act 1952 provides that

> the business of magistrates' courts shall, so far as is consistent with the due dispatch of business, be arranged in such manner as may be requisite for separating the hearing and determination of domestic proceedings from other business[1].

This requirement is not always met. In 1952, the National Association of Probation Officers collected information from 256 courts and found

> 74 in which matrimonial cases are dealt with by special courts or on special days; 177 in which these cases are dealt with by the ordinary courts.
>
> In the latter cases there is evidence of very serious delay in the hearing of cases and in 94 of them matrimonial cases are always taken at the *end* of the day's list.
>
> In only 6 cases are the people concerned asked to come at a later hour than that at which the court commences its business, and so there are many cases in which the parties wait from 10 or 10.30 a.m. to 3, 4 or 5 p.m. before their cases are heard[2].

On the basis of this and similar evidence, the Morton Commission commented in its *Report* that

[1] Section 57(1).
[2] *Minutes of Evidence* taken before the Royal Commission on Marriage and Divorce, Day 11, p. 334.

taking the country as a whole, the present arrangements for hearing matrimonial cases are not satisfactory. In our view it is essential that there should be a complete separation of matrimonial business from the other business of the courts. We do not think that the solution lies along the lines of trying to fix times for the hearings of matrimonial cases . . . We . . . recommend that steps should be taken to ensure that in all courts the work of hearing domestic proceedings is handled by itself and apart from the other work of the courts. This can be done by hearing such cases on a day or a half-day when no other business is taken. Alternatively, where this is feasible, they can be heard in a separate court room or in a different building.[1]

When the Graham Hall Committee reported twelve years afterwards, the position had not improved.

Many courts arrange for domestic proceedings to be held in a building separate from the ordinary criminal court and for the collecting office to be located in the same place. In many others, however, arrangements of this kind will not become practicable until out-of-date premises can be replaced. The fault is not always attributable solely to the inadequate accommodation available. We understand that some magistrates are reluctant to organise their sittings in such a way as to enable domestic proceedings to be heard on a separate day. This may on occasion be because they are reluctant to sit in the afternoon as well as the morning, or because they are unwilling or unable to sit on more than one day a week. The evidence we received made it clear how unwilling women often are for their matrimonial breakdowns or the determination of the paternity of their children to be a subject of judicial proceedings at all, and how this unwillingness is increased when courts have a criminal atmosphere. One large court with an inadequate and out-of-date court building was vividly described to us in which the parties to both criminal and domestic proceedings had to assemble in a large, crowded and cheerless waiting room which was the only place available for them to arrange last minute consultations with their legal advisers. We were told that similar conditions prevail in other courts. There is little doubt of the adverse effect conditions like these have on parties to domestic proceedings in many parts of the country.[2]

The fifty two courts which constituted the survey sample of courts were all visited by research staff, and court officials were interviewed wherever possible. Notes of all interviews were taken and details relating to court premises, use of staff, type and quality of records, the methods of collection

[1] Cmnd. 9678, 1956, para 1079.
[2] Cmnd. 3587, 1968, para 112.

and payment of money were recorded. Unhappily, we failed to ensure that all relevant information was collected and the only comment that we can make upon the Graham Hall Committee's findings is that only fourteen of the courts set aside a special time for hearing domestic cases, and such special provision was more likely to be made by the smaller courts.

The courts in our survey ranged in size from Leeds with 3,000 live orders to Longtown with eight live orders. The type of record used in the courts and the amount of information recorded in court files varied as widely. We have already noted in different chapters that the records of some courts contain serious gaps. For example, we found that there was no record of defendant's incomes in around 40% of all orders and that the court files were decidedly defective in recording court decisions about committal. Evidence from the survey was submitted to the Graham Hall, the Adams and the Payne Committees and their *Reports* have all emphasised that the administration of justice as well as the improvement of official statistics alike require good records.

We made no attempt to collect information about court staff. The larger courts have a structured staff under the authority of the chief clerk and the deputy chief clerk. The smaller courts may have only one or two officials working under a part-time clerk who also practises as a solicitor. Only a minority of courts in the survey had a member of the staff who gave all his time to the matrimonial work, though a further five courts carried staff which spent most of their time in this way. Many courts complained of shortage of staff.

Only a minority of the fifty-two courts had a separate office for the collection and payment of maintenance. For the rest, maintenance payments are dealt with as part of the general work of a collecting office which handled all court fines and payments. Even where new courts had been built, only one possessed a separate office. Two courts had plans to provide a separate office For the rest, husbands and wives waited in the queue with those paying fines for criminal offences, and the like. Collecting offices are generally housed within the court building, but in a number of cases the offices are separate from the court, sometimes adjoining the office of a local solicitor if he is part-time clerk of the court. They are usually centrally situated in the town and reasonably accessible to the public.

Most court collecting offices are open daily during normal office hours 9.0 or 9.30 to 5.0 or 5.30 for paying in by defendants. Only three of the fifty-two courts visited stay open late enough on one night of the week to enable men to pay in after work. Seven of the fifty-two courts open their collecting offices for one or two hours on Saturday mornings. Some collecting offices open for paying in for shorter periods. The hours during which a wife may collect her maintenance are generally shorter than those for husbands paying in. Of the fifty-two court collecting offices, sixteen open daily; the rest range from four days a week to eleven which open for seven hours or less a week. These last include one court with 820 live orders, open on Monday, Wednesday and Friday afternoons, and another with 365 live orders, open from

2.0 p.m. until 4.0 p.m. on Tuesdays and Fridays. Only three of the fifty-two court offices stay open on one evening a week for collection. Twelve courts, mainly in rural areas, send most of their payments to the wives by post, but some, including four very large courts, do not allow a woman to receive her money by post unless she lives outside the city.[1] The majority of courts allow telephone enquiries to find out if money has arrived, but seven, including two large courts, refuse to accept or strongly discourage, telephone calls.

It is certain that the convenience and feelings of litigants have hardly ever been considered in the administration of this branch of summary justice. Such details as the opening hours of collecting offices or the willingness of court staff to save a woman the loss of half a day's earnings by giving her information over the telephone seem too trivial to be considered in legal dis-cussion of the jurisdiction. But these are the sort of trivia that mean for the mostly very poor and unhappy citizens who meet family law in the magistrates' courts, the difference between dignity and humiliation, between decency and squalor. This survey has drawn the bulk of its information from court records which throw no light on the feelings and attitudes of the wives and husbands who have failed to make a go of their marriages. A full-scale study of this population designed to establish with rigorous statistical reliability how com-plainants and defendants viewed their experience of marriage breakdown and their treatment by the courts could not have been undertaken within the resources available for this research. Nevertheless, we regarded their reactions as too important an element in the social results of the exercise of matrimonial jurisdiction by magistrates' courts to be wholly neglected. We decided by means of newspaper publicity to attempt to obtain a sample of those who had been through the courts, and to administer a postal questionnaire to them. We therefore sought the help of Mr. Graham Stanford, at that time a colum-nist writing for the *News of the World*. On 21st May 1967, he generously gave his weekly article the title *Wanted: victims of broken homes*; it opened with the following paragraphs.

> Are you a broken marriage casualty? A deserted mother who can't possibly manage on her maintenance allowance? Or a husband ready but unable to meet the court order made against him?
>
> If so the Legal Research Unit of the Department of Sociology of Bedford College, London, would like to know.
>
> Backed by the Nuffield Foundation they are completing an analysis of a nationwide investigation into the circumstances of husbands, wives and children when their home is broken by separation.
>
> But before doing so they're anxious to receive first-hand accounts from wives and husbands. They've asked me to help by putting them in touch with you.

[1] *Fair Shares for the Fair Sex* (Conservative Political Centre, 1969) recommends that all payments under maintenance orders should be sent by post if so requested by recipients as a "civilised alternative to methods generally in use . . ."

An official of the unit told me they wanted to know whether wives or husbands felt they had been given a fair court hearing. Or whether they were unhappy about any aspect of the procedure.

Investigators have scoured records at magistrates' courts all over the country and thousands of questionnaires have been completed. But before closing their files the unit would like to hear from more of you.

If you have anything to say PLEASE DON'T WRITE TO ME. Address your letters to the Dept. of Sociology, Legal Research Unit, Bedford College, Regent's Park, London, N.W.1.

Keep them short, factual and don't make them mere hymns of hate against your one-time partner.

As a result, we received some 1,300 letters within a fortnight. Surprisingly, very few were written by cranks or by people pathologically obsessed by their difficulties. Most were clear but lengthy accounts of marriage breakdown and its aftermath. After eliminating the letters of those who had been through the divorce court or who had had no experience of the magistrates' court, we were left with 1,007 correspondents of whom 523 were husbands and 484 were wives. To these, we sent out questionnaires[1], one devised for the men and another for the women. Nearly 700 questionnaires were returned: the husband's response rate was 60% and the wives' was 71%. Nearly all the questionnaires were completed competently. We also received a very large number of requests for help and advice. Of the 700 completed questionnaires, 544 related to court hearings at which orders had been made. In order to compare this material with the findings of the main survey, we restricted the analysis to these 544 questionnaires of which 263 were sent in by husbands and 281 by wives.

A letter was sent with each questionnaire asking if the respondent would agree to be interviewed. Almost all were willing. Our only available interviewers were seventeen first year sociology undergraduates (nine women and eight men) who volunteered to work for a short period at the end of the summer term and the beginning of the long vacation. Thus it was feasible to interview only the hundred odd respondents living within an area of London reasonably accessible for the student interviewers, who finally managed to complete eighty-seven interviews. They were always welcomed; but all were inexperienced, and most were overwhelmed by the flood of talk from respondents anxious to make full use of a sympathetic listener. For this reason, many of the interviews took several hours to complete. Seventy-two of the completed interview questionnaires[2] were analysed.

The data thus obtained from a self-selected sample cannot provide a statistically representative picture of the population which takes its matrimonial

---

[1] The husband and wife postal questionnaires are printed as Appendix E.

[2] The husband and wife interview schedules are printed as Appendix F; 35 were with wives and 37 with husbands. One consequence of using undergraduate interviewers available only for a limited period was the impossibility of testing and revising the schedules.

disputes to the magistrates' courts. On the other hand, the comparison of the characteristics of the *News of the World* and of the main survey sample set out in Appendix F suggest that the findings drawn from the readers of the newspaper may be used with some confidence as a guide to the attitudes generally of complainants and defendants to the courts and their procedures. In any case, whatever its limitations, the account that follows at least represents the views of 544 husbands and wives who have experienced the system.

Table 70 sets out the statements made in the postal questionnaires as to which spouse took the initiative in leaving home.

TABLE 70   **Which spouse first left home.**

Answers of		Husband left	Wife left	Mutual	Total
Men		100	142	9	251
	%	40	57	3	100
Women		213	60	1	274
	%	78	22		100
	Total	313	202	10	525[1]
	%	60	38	2	100

40% of the husbands but only 22% of the wives admitted that they had been the first to leave home. It may be that the combined total of 39% of the marriages collapsing because the wife left gives a truer guide.

Table 71 shows the number of husbands and wives who sought advice when their spouses left them. Only three husbands and two wives failed to answer the question. Almost all the wives sought advice but over one quarter of the husbands did not.

TABLE 71   **Proportion of husbands and wives seeking advice on the breakdown of their marriages.**

	Husbands		Wives		Total
	No.	%	No.	%	
Sought no advice ..	72	28	11	4	83
Sought advice ..	188	72	268	96	456
Total	260	100	279	100	539

Table 72 shows the extent and sources of advice used by the 188 husbands and the 267 wives shown in Table 71.

Solicitors were quantitatively the most important source of advice for husbands and wives, accounting for roughly one-quarter of all the consultations and seeing nearly half the spouses. They were closely followed by probation officers who provided nearly one-fifth of the consultations and

[1] In the tables which follow, the total refers to the respondents who answered the relevant question(s).

TABLE 72 Sources of advice used by husbands and wives after the collapse of their marriages.

Source of advice	Husbands			Wives			Total		
	All con-sultations No.	%	% who consulted	All con-sultations No.	%	% who consulted	All con-sultations No.	%	% who consulted
Solicitor	90	24	48	130	27	49	220	25	48
Probation Officer ..	68	18	36	88	18	33	156	18	34
Doctor	49	13	26	66	14	25	115	13	25
Relative/friend ..	35	9	18	45	9	17	80	9	18
Citizens' Advice Bureaux.. ..	40	10	21	34	7	13	74	9	16
Clergyman ..	38	10	20	34	7	13	72	8	16
Marriage Guidance agency ..	22	6	11	28	6	10	50	6	11
Social work agency	16	4	9	29	6	11	45	5	10
Magistrates' court official	8	2	4	25	5	9	33	4	7
Other	17	4	9	8	2	3	25	3	5
Total	383	100		487	100		870	100	

advised more than one-third of husbands and wives. One-quarter of the spouses consulted their doctors, and some 16% saw a clergyman. Marriage guidance and social work agencies played only a small part among advice-giving services, being responsible for some 10% of the consultations, although some part of the work of probation officers would have to be included under this heading. There were no significant differences between the sources of advice utilized by husbands and by wives.

Three-quarters of the wives reported that a summons had been issued immediately upon their application to the court[1]; of the remainder, only some 9% felt that they had been delayed unreasonably as a result of undue slowness or inefficiency on the part of court staff. Those couples involved in complaints heard since 1961 were asked if they had obtained legal aid. The result is shown in Table 73. Those who did not have legal aid were asked if they knew about the scheme. The answers are shown in Table 74.

TABLE 73 Husbands and wives with legal aid.

	Husbands		Wives		Total	
	No.	%	No.	%	No.	%
Had legal aid	53	31	163	81	216	58
Did not have legal aid	119	69	38	19	157	42
Total	172	100	201	100	373	100

[1] 9% of these wives had made private agreements about maintenance with their husbands; they applied to the court because the agreement was persistently dishonoured.

TABLE 74 Husbands and wives with and without knowledge of the legal aid scheme.

				Husbands		Wives		Total	
				No.	%	No.	%	No.	%
With knowledge	..	..	..	50	44	21	57	71	47
Without knowledge	..	..	..	63	56	16	43	79	53
		Total		113	100	37	100	150	100

Rather more than half the wives and husbands who did not have legal aid said that they were ignorant of the possible availability. In terms of all couples in the sample who were involved in court proceedings after 1961, only 8% of the wives but 36% of the husbands said that they did not know of the scheme. This striking inequality in respect of the penetration of knowledge about legal aid to men and women underlines the emphasis which the recent *Report* of the Advisory Committee on the better provision of Legal Advice and Assistance placed upon "the need for advertising the available facilities"[1]. In particular, it is important that information should be available at places of employment.

The seventy-two husbands and wives whose interviews produced service-able questionnaires were questioned in detail about what happened to them at the court. Table 75 shows how long they had to wait before their hearing. Nearly half the couples had to spend two hours or more in the court waiting-room. More than one-third of those who had to wait sat in a crowded waiting-room containing more than twenty people. All the couples com-mented on the discomfort and lack of seats.

TABLE 75 Length of waiting time before hearing.

Length of time waiting at court before the hearing	Wives' answers	Husbands' answers	Total	%
Under 15 minutes	3	3	6	11
15 but under 30 minutes	2	2	4	7
30 minutes but under 1 hour	4	8	12	22
1 hour but under 2 hours	1	7	8	15
2 hours but under 3 hours	12	6	18	32
3 hours but under 5 hours	—	6	6	11
5 hours and over	—	1	1	2
Total	22	33	55[2]	100

Table 76 shows how long the hearings lasted.

Only one-third of the hearings lasted for more than one hour. It is difficult to calculate the minimum length of hearing compatible with the proper administration of justice. Even if all the complainants' allegations were

[1] Cmnd. 4249, 1970.
[2] 17 had no recollection. In all tables relating to the interview sample, the total relates to the number of spouses who answered the relevant question.

TABLE 76 Length of hearing.

Length of hearing				Wives' answers	Husbands' answers	Total	%
Under 15 minutes	..	..	..	4	6	10	16
15 but under 30 minutes	..	..	..	5	11	16	26
30 minutes but under 1 hour		..	..	7	10	17	27
1 hour but under 2 hours	..	..	..	6	3	9	15
2 hours but under 3 hours	..	..	..	3	—	3	5
3 hours but under 5 hours	..	..	..	3	3	6	10
5 hours and over	..	..	..	—	1	1	1
		Total		28	34	62	100

admitted and the amount of maintenance agreed beforehand, the matrimonial offence must still be proved and both parties' means inquired into. Thus, it is very surprising that 16% of the hearings were completed in less than a quarter, and 26% in less than half an hour.

The sample was asked if they had known before their hearing what the court and its procedure would be like. Table 77 shows the answers. Three-quarters of these spouses went to court with no understanding of the procedure.

TABLE 77 Husbands and wives with prior information about court procedure.

Spouses				Wives' answers	Husbands' answers	Total	%
Well informed	..	..	..	8	3	11	16
Partly informed	..	..	..	2	6	8	12
Uninformed ..	..	..	..	23	27	50	72
		Total		33	36	69	100

Husbands and wives who completed the postal questionnaire were asked if they felt that the atmosphere of the court assisted towards securing a fair hearing. Table 78 sets out their answers.

TABLE 78 Views of husbands and wives about the atmosphere of the court.

Court atmosphere			Husbands' answers		Wives' answers		Total	
			No.	%	No.	%	No.	%
Conducive to a fair hearing	..	..	35	15	104	42	139	28
Adverse to a fair hearing ..	..	..	206	85	143	58	349	72
	Total		241	100	247	100	488	100

It is only to be expected that a higher proportion of wives than of husbands should have felt that the atmosphere of the court conduced to a fair hearing because the former were the successful parties; it is unexpected that more than half the wives thought that the atmosphere of the court was adverse to a fair hearing. They were then asked to assess the fairness or unfairness of the hearing itself, and their replies are shown in Table 79.

TABLE 79   **Views of husbands and wives about the fairness or unfairness of the court hearing.**

Assessment of hearing	Husbands No.	%	Wives No.	%	Total No.	%
Fair	22	10	102	38	124	24
Not Fair	233	90	166	62	399	76
Total	255	100	268	100	523	100

Again, it may not be surprising that a high proportion of the men against whom maintenance orders were made thought the hearing unfair, although 90% is a very high proportion. But almost two-thirds of the wives felt similarly about the hearing. Table 80 sets out the main reasons given by both parties for their dissatisfaction with the hearing.

TABLE 80   **Reasons given by husbands and wives for thinking that their court hearing was unfair.**

Reason	Husbands No.	%	Wives No.	%	Total No.	%
Court failed to examine the other party fully	126	48	92	47	218	48
Court accepted untruthful evidence from the other party	47	18	59	30	106	23
No legal representation and other party represented	31	12	4	2	35	8
Did not understand court procedure ..	12	5	9	5	21	5
Short time spent on the hearing	12	5	9	5	21	5
Lack of time to prepare case	9	3	2	1	11	2
Other	23	9	19	10	42	9
Total reasons	260	100	194	100	454	100
Number giving reasons	216		166		382	

The main ground of complaint advanced by almost half the husbands and wives was that the court had failed to examine the other party fully. Of course, it is impossible with such an assertion to distinguish factual from emotional claims but this widespread feeling among husbands and wives is itself significant. The distribution of reasons for thinking the hearing unfair between spouses is remarkably similar save in the already noted instance of access to legal aid.

An obvious explanation of the complaint by half the spouses that the court had not properly examined the other party would be that the husbands were aggrieved because they had been required to pay too much to wives who, in their turn, felt they were getting too little. Table 81 clarifies this point.

TABLE 81 **Proportion of husbands and wives who regarded the amount of the maintenance order as fair or unfair.**

Assessment of amount	Husbands No.	%	Wives No.	%	Total No.	%
Fair	49	19	71	26	120	22
Unfair	211	81	203	74	414	78
Total	260	100	274	100	534	100

Although a very large number of spouses, four-fifths of the husbands and three-quarters of the wives, regarded the amount of maintenance awarded as unfair, 19% of the husbands thought it fair. It is significant that this is more than double the proportion of husbands who thought that the court hearing was fair.

Table 82 sets out the reasons given by husbands for holding that the maintenance they were required to pay by the court order was too much. 59% of the defendants said that they could not afford to pay the amount asked of them. In 1967, at the time of the survey, 42% said that they had incomes of less than £12 a week, 64% had incomes of less than £15 a week, and 86% of less than £20 a week. At this time, the average weekly earnings of manual workers in manufacturing industry were £20 12s. These figures of defendants' incomes are entirely in line with those of the main survey discussed in Chapter 5.

TABLE 82 **Reasons advanced by defendants for holding that the amount they were required to pay on the maintenance order against them was too high.**

	No.	% giving reason	% reasons
Amount of order unrealistic in terms of defendant's income	118	44	59
Wife receiving sufficient income from her own earnings, from another man or from her own family	67	24	33
Amount unjustly large because wife was responsible for the breakdown of the marriage ..	34	13	17
Defendant has to support other dependants ..	14	5	7
Defendant has been unemployed or sick ..	12	4	6
In-laws were responsible for the breakdown of the marriage	7	3	3
Other	17	7	8
Total reasons	269	100	
Number giving reasons			201 (100%)

Of the 201 defendants shown in Table 82, ninety-five had at least one dependant other than their first wives. These are shown in Table 83.

TABLE 83   Defendants with dependants other than their first wives.

	Defendants with dependants	
	Nos.	%
Paramour	41	43
Child or children of paramour or second wife ..	40	42
Second wife	16	17
Relatives	15	16
Other children	13	14
Housekeeper	13	14
Child or children of first marriage	9	9
Other	3	3
Total dependants	150	
Total defendants	95 (100%)	

Thus, 17% of the defendants had subsequently become divorced and had married another person, 43% were living with a paramour, and 40% of them had produced children in their new unions. Given the incomes of the men concerned, there was no possibility that they could discharge both their legal obligations towards the families from whom they had parted and at the same time maintain those with whom they were actually living.

The seventy-two husbands and wives who were interviewed were asked if they had established a liaison since the collapse of their marriage. Table 84 presents their replies. 65% of the husbands but only 17% of the wives established an illicit relationship. Only two of the husbands said that the other woman was the reason for their leaving home in the first place. Nearly half of the husbands who had acquired paramours had fathered children upon them.

TABLE 84   Number of separated husbands and wives who established liaisons after the collapse of their marriages.

	Husbands		Wives		Total	
	No.	%	No.	%	No.	%
Liaison	24	65	6	17	30	42
No liaison	13	35	29	83	42	58
Total	37	100	35	100	72	100

All the husbands who answered the postal questionnaire were asked if they had been employed or sick since their wife's maintenance order had been made. Of the 260 who replied, 197 (76%) said that they had been off work for these reasons at some time. They were then asked what action they took over their payments under the order. Their replies are set out in Table 85.

Just over one-third of the men whose earnings were interrupted by sickness or

TABLE 85 **Action taken over payments under maintenance orders by sick or unemployed defendants.**

	No. of defendants	%
Continued paying	54	28
Did not pay, but took no action to have maintenance order reduced	64	33
Asked court to reduce payment and reduction made	30	16
Asked court to reduce payment and reduction refused. ..	32	16
Asked court to reduce payment, and proceedings pending ..	10	5
Court cancelled arrears	2	1
Paid maintenance for child but not for wife.	2	1
Total	194	100

unemployment asked the court to reduce the size of the order. Another third simply stopped paying and did nothing about it, while one-quarter tried to keep up their payments. Of those who applied to the court and knew the result of the hearing, a slightly higher number had the application refused than had it accepted.

This confirms the conclusion of Chapter VI that the variation procedure works very badly. That one-third of the present sample took no action when they found themselves unable to continue their payments suggests extensive ignorance[1].

The sample of wives were asked what they did if their husbands failed to pay. Their actions are set out in Table 86.

TABLE 86 **Action taken by wives when husbands fail to meet payments under maintenance orders.**

	No. of wives	%
Contacted court for advice	10	5
Asked court for hearing	93	46
Asked advice of any other person or body	2	1
Went to Supplementary Benefits Commission for financial help	42	21
Went to other welfare agency for financial help	1	—
Borrowed from relatives or friends	5	3
Contacted husband directly	2	1
Tried to manage on money she had, and took no other action ..	44	23
Total	199	100

Almost three-quarters of the wives went either directly to the court or to agencies which would direct them to the court. Nevertheless, it is striking that nearly a quarter tried to manage without maintenance and took no further action.

The sample of wives who completed the postal questionnaire were asked how they had fared financially after the separation from their husbands. Table 87 sets out the results.

[1] This might be interpreted as showing a preference for taking the law into their own hands.

TABLE 87   **Financial position of wives separated from their husbands.**

	Wives No.	%
Improved	1	—
Little change	12	4
Occasional periods of great difficulty	11	4
Constantly short of money but can afford necessities	216	78
Constantly a struggle even for necessities	23	8
Financial difficulties so acute that health has deteriorated ..	16	6
Total	279	100

Almost all the wives had suffered financial hardship as a result of the collapse of their marriages, and Table 88 shows that more than two-thirds were working.

More than one-third of the separated women were working full-time. In the population as a whole in 1965, nearly half the married women were working, and a little over one-fifth were working full-time[1]. There was clearly a stronger pressure upon separated than upon still-married women to go out to work. Inevitably, a high proportion of wives in our sample found it necessary to apply to the Supplementary Benefits Commission after their husbands had left them. Indeed, only 13% of the 273 wives for whom we have information did not become applicants as a result of the breakdown of their marriage.

TABLE 88   **Proportion of separated wives at work.**

	No.	%
Not working	48	17
Wishes but unable to work	37	14
Working part-time	83	30
Working full-time	105	39
Total	273	100

The seventy-two husbands and wives who were interviewed spoke unanimously of harsh penury as the chief consequence of their separation. For the women, loneliness was the other chief anxiety; for the men, it was the absence of children. Half the fathers ceased altogether to see their children, and only 15% of them made regular weekly visits. Of the sample who answered the postal questionnaire, 230 (88%) of the men and 262 (93%) of the women had at least one child under sixteen. In all these cases wives had been given custody of the children, and we asked husbands if they were able to see their children as often as they wished. Only 30% said that they experienced no difficulty. The remainder complained of such obstacles as distance or the

[1] Audrey Hunt, *A Survey of Women's Employment* (1965), Vol. I, p. 9.

TABLE 89 Attitudes of husbands and wives to the breakdown of their marriages.

		Husbands		Wives		Total	
		No.	%	No.	%	No.	%
Had regretted breakdown	..	18	50	16	46	34	48
Had not regretted breakdown	..	18	50	19	54	37	52
Total		36	100	35	100	71	100

unwillingness of the children to see their fathers; but the overwhelming consideration was that wives disliked the visits.

The interview sample was questioned about attitudes to reconciliation. Half the spouses had no regrets. They were then asked if they would have welcomed facilities for reconciliation before the court hearing and if they would welcome such facilities at the present time.

TABLE 90 Attitudes of husbands and wives to reconciliation.

Attitudes to reconciliation			Husbands		Wives		Total	
			No.	%	No.	%	No.	%
Before the court hearing								
Welcome	..	..	..	19	54	21	64	40	59
Not welcome	..	..	..	16	46	12	36	28	41
Total			35	100	33	100	68	100
At present time								
Welcome	..	..	..	10	28	7	21	17	25
Not welcome	..	..	..	26	72	26	79	52	75
Total			36	100	33	100	69	100

Finally, the whole sample were asked for their views about the court and its personnel. Table 91 presents the answers to questions about the helpfulness of court officials. The wives were asked if the court officials were generally helpful in letting them know of the payment or non-payment of maintenance orders, and the husbands were asked if the officials were generally helpful in giving advice about the order.

TABLE 91 Views of husbands and wives about the helpfulness of court officials.

				Husbands		Wives		Total	
				No.	%	No.	%	No.	%
Helpful	..	..	..	..	64	27	86	42	150	34
Not helpful	..	..	..	127	55	110	55	237	55
No contact	..	..	..	43	18	7	3	50	11
Total			234	100	204	100	437	100

Slightly more than half the husbands and wives whose marriage breakdowns fell to be regulated by magistrates' courts found court officials unhelpful.

Table 92 shows what the sample of husbands and wives most disliked about their experience of the matrimonial jurisdiction of the magistrates' court.

TABLE 92   **What husbands and wives most disliked about the magistrates' court.**

	Husbands			Wives			Total		
Dislikes	No.	% (R)	% (S)	No.	% (R)	% (S)	No.	% (R)	% (S)
Attitude of magistrates	110	34	50	71	23	32	181	29	41
Attitude of court officials	36	11	16	15	5	7	51	8	11
Attitude of own solicitor/counsel	31	10	14	10	3	5	41	7	9
Lack of care by court	40	13	18	41	14	18	81	13	18
Lack of privacy in court	20	6	9	22	7	10	42	7	9
Made to feel a criminal by court	66	21	30	49	16	22	115	18	26
Procedure for collecting/paying money	4	1	2	37	12	17	41	7	9
Slowness taking action when money not paid	—	—	—	47	16	21	47	8	10
Other	13	4	6	11	3	5	24	4	5
Total dislikes	320	100		303	99		623	101	
Total sample	220		100	224		100	444		100

R = %age of responses   S = %age of sample

Percentages may not total 100 due to rounding

Table 92 suggests that magistrates' courts do not obtain the confidence of those using them to sort out their matrimonial difficulties. The outstanding dislike of litigants is for the attitude of the bench; this was the view of half the husbands and one-third of the wives. The second major dislike is that nearly a third of the husbands and more than one-fifth of the wives felt that they were being treated like criminals.

CHAPTER 9

The number of complainants for maintenance who became petitioners for divorce

The *Introduction* to the Civil Judicial Statistics for 1968 observed that "it is not possible to draw reliable conclusions from the statistics about the rate at which marriages are breaking down. In the first place, it is not known what proportion of *de facto* broken marriages leave a record in court proceedings. Secondly, there is no knowledge of the relationship between the jurisdictions of the High Court and of Magistrates' Courts. For some complainants, a Magistrates' Court is a staging post on the way to the High Court; for other complainants, it is a terminus at which marital journeys will end."[1] Since the early years of this century, divorce petitions have increased sixtyfold; in the same period, applications to magistrates' courts for matrimonial orders have trebled.[2] The proportion of spouses resorting to the divorce court rather than to the magistrates' courts has risen significantly in the last generation. In 1935, for every 100 petitions for divorce by husbands and wives there were 259 applications for maintenance to magistrates; by 1966, for every 100 petitions there were only fifty-nine applications. As applications are almost always made by wives, it is more relevant to compare wife-petitioners with applicants for maintenance. On this basis, there were 480 applications for maintenance for every 100 wife-petitions in 1935; thirty years later, the ratio was ninety-seven applications to every 100 petitions.

This striking change can be explained in part by the achievement in recent years of greater equality before the law. Writing in 1955, Barbara Wootton found that nothing precise could be said about the distribution of divorces among different social classes although she thought it "not unreasonable to suppose that there has been a change in . . . the penetration of divorce proceedings to the lower social classes"[3]. In 1958, Mr. Carrier and Miss Rowntree published their study of *The Resort to Divorce in England and Wales*, which was based on statistics extracted from all petitions filed in 1871 and a sample of those in 1951. This provided the first information available

---

[1] Cmnd. 4112, para 45.
[2] See Chapter 2, Figure 1, p. 32.
[3] "Holiness or Happiness", *The Twentieth Century*, November 1955, p. 414.

since 1921 about the occupational structure of the divorcing population. It is set out in Table 93.[1]

TABLE 93   Occupational structure of the divorcing and the continuing married populations in England and Wales in 1951.

	Husband's present occupation			
Couples	Professional and managerial %	Farmers and shopkeepers %	Black-coated workers %	Manual workers %
Divorcing	13·5	8·0	9·0	69·5
Continuing married[2] ..	13·9	8·4	8·1	69·6

This table showed a remarkable similarity in the occupational structure of the divorcing and the still-married populations, and permitted "the inference that a manual worker (or his wife) may soon be as likely to seek a remedy for his matrimonial difficulties by divorce as his employer (or his wife)"[3]. The authors urged that their findings should be treated with caution because the number of manual workers' petitions must have been inflated by the backlog of cases brought to court in the first full year after the Legal Aid and Advice Act came into force in the autumn of 1950. Poverty had been the main factor barring most working class people from access to the divorce court, but it hindered wives more than husbands. Thus, it was only to be expected that working class wives previously too poor to contemplate a petition would be the immediate and most numerous beneficiaries of the legal aid scheme. Though the number of divorce petitions filed between 1949 and 1951 increased by 9%, those presented by wives rose by 21%. In 1951, 65% of petitioners were legally aided and, of these, 71% were wives and 56% were husbands. Between 1950 and 1968, the proportion of divorce petitions filed by husbands declined from 46% to 37%.

During the 1950s the number of divorce petitions fell. The proportion of legally aided petitioners fell from 65% of the total in 1951 to only 38% in 1959. This decline cannot be interpreted as evidence of greater unwillingness among spouses to resort to divorce, rather it was one of the consequences of inflation. As financial assistance under the Legal Aid Act was related to an applicant's nominal disposable income, inflation reduced the value of legal aid for any given level of real income. The benefits of legal aid were thus steadily eroded throughout the 1950s. This process was reversed when the Legal Aid Act 1960 raised the limits of disposable income and capital for assisted persons and therefore brought a larger section of the population

[1] *Population Studies*, Vol. 11, No. 3, 1958, p. 223.
[2] *Census 1951*, Occupation Tables, Table 18, p. 149.
[3] O. R. McGregor and Griselda Rowntree, "The Family" in A. T. Welford *et al.* (eds.), *Society* (1962), p. 406.

within the scheme. Moreover, applicants were helped by a change in 1959 in the procedure for assessing means which reduced the amount of contribution which a legally aided litigant could be called upon to make. There is sound evidence for the view of the Law Commission "that these fluctuations in the number of divorces were caused mainly by the availability of legal aid and that there would not have been a continued fall in numbers prior to 1960 but for the fact that fewer couples could afford a divorce if they wanted it"[1]. This greater generosity in the provision of legal aid was immediately reflected in the divorce statistics. In 1958, husband-petitioners constituted only 18% of all legally aided petitioners; in 1961, they accounted for almost half. Between 1959 and 1968 the number of divorce petitions more than doubled, rising from some 26,000 to 55,000. Rather more than one-third of all petitioners were legally aided in 1959 but nearly two-thirds of them were legally aided in 1968[2].

Since 1950, the legal aid scheme has enabled many working class spouses to move out of the class described by Lady Wootton as "homeless spirits, neither married nor unmarried, but suspended between the chance of heaven in a happy marriage with a new partner and the certainty of hell in life with the old one"[3] by obtaining a licence to marry again from the divorce court in place of a magistrates' order. But the flight of couples from the disadvantages of the indeterminate status conferred by the summary jurisdiction has also been hastened by the wider acceptance of divorce as a socially respectable method of mending broken marital earthenware. The only systematic study so far attempted of the change in public opinion from absolute disapproval to the point where divorce has ceased to be an obstacle even to a politician's chances of becoming prime minister is that contained in the article of Mr. Carrier and Miss Rowntree. They conclude that "many would now subscribe to the view, boldly advanced by a metropolitan magistrate in his evidence to the (Gorell) Commission that 'marriage cannot hope to be a working success unless divorce is in the background as a reserve. With divorce as a protection against unforeseen calamities . . . marriage becomes a wise investment . . . Without divorce I look on marriage as a dangerous, mad gamble'."[4] There is no doubt that this attitude represents the view of most middle class people. But we are still ignorant of the extent to which knowledge or acceptance of divorce as a means of ending broken marriages has spread among the working class. Table 94 suggests that the occupational structure of the divorcing and still married populations shows as comparable a similarity in 1961 as in 1951.

Tables 93 and 94 suggest that, since the introduction of the legal aid scheme in 1950, petitioners for divorce have become a cross-section of the whole population and now reflect accurately its occupational and social composition.

---

[1] Cmnd. 3123 (1966), *Reform of the Grounds of Divorce: The Field of Choice*, p. 8.
[2] Cmnd. 4112, *Civil Judicial Statistics for* 1968, Table J, p. 16.
[3] *Op. cit.*, p. 415.   [4] *Op. cit.*, p. 199.

TABLE 94[1] Occupational structure by social class of the divorcing and continuing married populations in England and Wales in 1961.

Couples	Husband's social class by present occupation[2]				
	Professional Intermediate %	Skilled %	Partly skilled %	Unskilled %	Total number
Divorcing ..	17	56	16	11	599 (100%)
Continuing married[3]	21	51	20	8	11,471,000 (100%)

Many well-informed observers agree with the explanation of the sustained vitality of the matrimonial jurisdiction of magistrates' courts which Mr. G. S. Green, Clerk to the County of Manchester Justices, put forward in a letter to *The Times*. "What enables a divorce to be granted speedily is that in most cases a previous hearing in a magistrates' court has already taken place—a hearing which in these days is all too often a prelude to divorce."[4] On this view, the magistrates' court is a staging post at which wives quickly obtain maintenance orders at the beginning of their journeys to the High Court. The purpose of this chapter is to present the results of an analysis of the relationship between the two jurisdictions, and to quantify the extent to which they overlap.

The direct method of obtaining the relevant data for this purpose would have been to determine the proportion of orders in our survey which subsequently resulted in petitions to the High Court. This proved impossible because investigation showed that, in a significant number of instances, the magistrates' court records contained no indication of the fact that the marriage had been subsequently dissolved although it was known from other sources that a divorce decree had been made absolute. Accordingly, we were driven to rely exclusively upon the very full information in divorce petitions. The rules relating to petitions prescribe that any previous court proceedings between the parties in respect of their matrimonial affairs shall be disclosed. Hence the petitions filed in the Divorce Registries contain full details of any prior maintenance proceedings. We selected for study petitions which were filed in 1955 and 1961; and we know of no reason for thinking that, if any other two years in the recent past had been chosen, the findings would have been significantly different. By 1955, the increase in the number of petitions which followed the introduction of legal aid had subsided. Although 1961

[1] This table has been extracted from the findings of a study of divorce petitions in 1961. These will be published separately.

[2] Social class based upon occupations of husband recorded on the petition, and subsequently coded by the Registrar General's Classification of Occupations manual.

[3] *Census 1961*, Occupation Tables, Table 20, p. 125.

[4] 10th December 1965.

saw the further increase in petitioning which followed the more generous legal aid provisions of 1960, that year gave the overwhelming advantage of comparison with new census data. A one in twenty sample of all divorce petitions filed at Somerset House and in the ninety-five District Registries throughout the country was taken[1]. This sampling fraction was adequate to provide valid statistical conclusions for the two years under review.

Table 95 shows the proportion of successful divorce petitions having a previous history of proceedings before magistrates. The two years show a strikingly similar pattern. In nearly 28% and 29% respectively of the petitions filed in the two years, the wife had earlier obtained a maintenance order for herself together with her dependant children, or for her children alone.

TABLE 95   Percentage distribution of divorce petitions heard in London and the provinces in which there were prior proceedings before magistrates' courts, 1955 and 1961.

Location of court	Divorce petitions showing									
	*Prior hearing before magistrates but no order		Maintenance Order made by magistrates		No prior hearing before magistrates		Total			
	1955 %	1961 %	1955 %	1961 %	1955 %	1961 %	1955 No.	%	1961 No.	%
Provinces ..	8	6	32	34	60	60	862	100	1,015	100
London ..	5	5	22	20	73	75	516	100	563	100
Total	7	6	28	29	65	65	1,378	100	1,578	100

*Includes complaints dismissed and withdrawn before hearing, and applications for interim orders of maintenance, and for custody orders.

Regrettably, it is impossible to work back from the national figure of 35% of divorce petitions shown by Table 95 to have a history of prior complaints before magistrates to calculate the proportion of magistrates' court orders which end up as petitions in the High Court. For example, the 5% sample of divorce petitions for 1955 contained 482 petitions with an earlier history of complaint before magistrates. On a national basis (allowing for the destruction by fire of 401 petitions in the Portsmouth Registry) this represents 9,780 petitions which can be compared with the 22,727 applications to magistrates' courts for maintenance orders in 1955. Similarly, for 1961, 10,900 petitions can be compared with 25,471 maintenance applications. The proportion of petitions to applications on this basis is 43% for both years, 1955 and 1961. On the other hand, if the petitions are compared with maintenance[2] orders, the proportion increases to 47% for 1955 and to 48% for 1961. This sort of juggling is unsatisfactory for many reasons, not least because the figures for

[1] Our own research staff extracted the data from the petitions filed at Somerset House. The County Courts Branch of the Lord Chancellor's Department very kindly arranged for officials in the District Registries to extract data on our behalf.
[2] Married Women and Guardianship of Infants orders combined for each year, (a 15% reduction for the latter allowing for wives with joint orders).

applications for magistrates' orders are unreliable for the reason stated in Chapter 2.

The best estimate which we can make suggests that about one half of all wives in receipt of magistrates' maintenance orders find themselves in the divorce court subsequently, either as petitioners or respondents. To the extent that the wives with maintenance orders are divorce petitioners, there is an irresistible inference that the magistrates' court is a first step towards divorce, even though this statement must be qualified if the grounds for divorce were different from the grounds for a maintenance order. If wives with maintenance orders are respondents to their husband's petitions, with or without cross-petitioning, the conclusion that the magistrates' court is a prelude to divorce cannot be so readily drawn. We proceed, therefore, to examine the intentions of the one-third of divorce petitioners who had previously appeared before the justices. Were they then contemplating divorce?

Table 95 indicates a higher proportion of divorce petitioners appearing before magistrates' courts in the provinces than in London. Table 96 provides a further breakdown of these figures according to geographical distribution.

TABLE 96   **Geographical distribution of divorce petitions with previous history of complaint before magistrates' courts, 1955 and 1961.**

Area in which petition was filed	Percentage of petitions with previous magistrates' hearing		
	1955	1961	1955 + 1961
Northern and Midland Counties and Wales (1–5; 10)*	46	45	45
Eastern and Southern Counties (6–9)*	23	28	26
London	27	25	26
All England and Wales	35	35	35

* By the Registrar-General's Standard Regions (1–10).

A significantly higher proportion of divorce petitions filed in registries in the Midlands, the North, and Wales were preceded by hearings before magistrates' courts than was the case with those filed in either London or in the Eastern and Southern counties of England. The marked regional differences clearly reflect the familiar higher socio-economic level of the population in London and the South-east, and are in line with the conclusions of Chapter 5.

Table 97 compares the grounds of divorce used by petitioners with the grounds on which maintenance orders had been granted. Section 3(2) of the Matrimonial Causes Act 1965 provides that, on a petition for divorce, the court may treat the magistrates' order as sufficient proof of the adultery, cruelty, desertion or other ground on which the order was granted. A finding by a magistrates' court constitutes *prima facie* evidence or corroboration of the commission of a matrimonial offence but it does not absolve the divorce court from examining all the evidence at the divorce hearing. It might seem reasonable to assume, therefore, that petitioning wives would have proceeded on the ground or grounds for divorce which they used as a basis for obtaining their maintenance orders. But the results of our research provide no evidence for such an assumption. We analysed 658 petitions (constituting 78% of all decrees in the sample) in which wives had successfully petitioned for divorce. Information showing the ground on which both the maintenance order and the divorce petitions were based was available in all but twenty-nine cases. This information is set out in Table 97 which must be read with the knowledge that 629 wives had obtained magistrates' courts' orders on a total of 648 grounds because nineteen of them had orders on multiple grounds. Sixty-seven of the 629 decrees nisi also showed multiple grounds.

TABLE 97 **Grounds for divorce by wife compared with grounds for maintenance order.**

Grounds for order	Maintenance order			Divorce		
				Percentage distribution of grounds for decree nisi		
	Number	Percentage		Adultery	Cruelty	Desertion
Adultery	51	8		7	1	1
Cruelty	129	21		3	17	2
Desertion ..	296	47		15	7	29
*Wilful neglect to maintain ..	89	14		4	2	9
†Guardianship of infants	77	12		6	4	4
Other	6	1				
Total	648	103		(222) 35	(193) 31	(281) 45

* as a ground on its own.   Sample size: 629 (100%).
† alone.

Table 97 shows the breakdown of maintenance orders according to the ground upon which the complainant proceeded. Each of these orders is followed through to see which ground was advanced by the complainant when she became petitioner in her divorce proceedings. If more than one ground was used by the complainant or the petitioner respectively each ground was counted separately, except that wilful neglect to maintain as a ground for a maintenance order was not counted if it was used in conjunction with either adultery, desertion or cruelty.

Desertion headed the list of grounds for maintenance in the magistrates' courts in 47% of the instances, cruelty in 21% and adultery in 8%. Desertion was the most common ground for petitions for divorce, appearing in 45% of petitions; adultery came next in 35% and cruelty in 31%. In 11% of the cases there was a combination of two or three grounds (no grounds other than desertion, adultery and cruelty figured in the decrees of divorce).

A quarter of the petitioning wives had obtained maintenance orders, /

either for themselves or for their children, on a ground that provided no basis for a divorce—wilful neglect to maintain or an application under the Guardianship of Infants Act. Sixty-two per cent of those with orders obtained on the ground of wilful neglect to maintain petitioned the divorce court on the ground of desertion; but only 32% of those with guardianship of infants orders petitioned for divorce on the ground of desertion. Adultery was the most common ground for this group of wives, appearing in 48% of the instances. Whatever the ground for divorce, if these wives had intended to employ the jurisdiction of the magistrates' court as a first step on the road to the divorce court, they would have established an appropriate matrimonial offence at their first appearance in court. Twenty-one per cent of the wives with maintenance orders based on adultery, cruelty or desertion alone or in combination did not proceed to the divorce court on that basis.

Altogether, of the wives successfully petitioning for divorce, 47% of our sample did not use as their ground the matrimonial offence upon which they had obtained their maintenance order. In addition, 186 husbands whose wives had obtained maintenance orders, obtained divorce. Thus, in 57% of all divorce petitions which disclosed that there had been prior proceedings before the magistrates' courts, a ground for divorce was used which was other than the ground advanced in the maintenance proceedings.

The next stage in the analysis is to compare the occasions upon which a wife petitioning the divorce court on the ground of adultery, cruelty or desertion used the same ground in the divorce proceedings as that upon which she had obtained her maintenance order.

Table 98 shows that in 83% of the maintenance orders obtained upon the ground either of adultery or of cruelty, the same ground was the basis of the subsequent divorce petition. This figure dropped to 66% in the case of desertion. The difference between the percentages for adultery and cruelty on the one hand and for desertion on the other is explicable on the ground that desertion in the magistrates' court is not dependent upon a time element. That desertion must run for three years before a petition for divorce can be presented necessarily requires some wives to proceed on a different ground

TABLE 98   **A comparison of the grounds upon the wife's successful petition with those of the original maintenance order.**

Successful ground in magistrates' court			Each ground as % of total	% of wives using the same ground as appeared on the magistrates' order
Adultery	..	..	..	10	83
Cruelty	..	..	..	28	83
Sub total	..	..	..	38	83
Desertion	..	..	..	62	66
	Total		100	72
	Number		406	292

when petitioning for divorce. The comparable percentage in adultery and cruelty cases strongly suggests that the ground upon which the maintenance order is made will largely predetermine the ground for divorce.

Table 99 shows the period of delay between obtaining the maintenance order and petitioning for divorce. If an order were obtained by a wife in the magistrates' court, partly at least with one eye cocked on the divorce court, it could be expected that the divorce proceedings would follow hard on the heels of the maintenance order. Any lengthy delay would tend to suggest that the separated wife when applying to the magistrates' court did not at that time contemplate divorce proceedings.

TABLE 99 **Delay between the maintenance order and the divorce petition by ground of maintenance order.**

Successful ground in magistrates' court	Percentage distribution of orders by a period of time from making of maintenance order to filing of petition			Total number	*Average period of time	
	Under 3 years %	3 years but under 9 years %	9 years and over %		Years	Months
Adultery	62	21	17	29	4	
Cruelty	59	31	10	59	4	
Sub total	60	27	13	88	4	
Desertion ..	31	53	16	134	5	8
Total	95	95	32	222†	5	
% Distribution	43	43	14	100		

* Averages are derived from a more detailed 12-point breakdown.
† The total is less than 406 because the necessary information was not available in 184 cases.

It is reasonable to suppose that when a wife obtains a maintenance order as a preliminary step to divorce, she will petition within three years. In fact our sample shows that 60% of the adultery and cruelty cases proceeded to divorce within three years, and 74% within five years. In the case of desertion, the proportion of wives proceeding to divorce within three years was only 31%. There was a slight difference in the period of delay between the 1955 and 1961 samples; the latter showed a marginally shorter delay.

Any study of the relationship between the two jurisdictions must include the comparative periods of time that elapse before the spouses resort to the magistrates' courts and/or to the divorce court. Table 100 records the number of years from marriage until a maintenance order is obtained for those wives resorting solely to the magistrates' court and for those cases where there is a divorce after a prior hearing before the magistrates.

Table 100 shows that where the parties ultimately went on to the divorce court, their marriages endured for a shorter period before maintenance was obtained than in those cases where there were no divorce proceedings after the maintenance order. Just over a quarter of the non-divorcing population obtained a maintenance order within five years of the marriage, whereas

TABLE 100   Duration of marriage up to the obtaining of a maintenance order for divorcing and non-divorcing wives.

Duration of marriage	(A) Maintenance order only		(B) Divorce after maintenance		(C) Percentage differences (B-A)	
	%	C.P.D.*	%	C.P.D.*	%	C.P.D.*
Under 3 years	16	16	29	29	+13	13
Over 3 years and under 5 years ..	12	28	15	44	+ 3	16
Over 5 years and under 9 years ..	22	50	23	67	+ 1	17
Over 9 years and under 15 years ..	23	73	20	87	— 3	14
Over 15 years and under 20 years	13	86	9	96	— 4	10
20 years and over	14	100	4	100	—10	0
Size of sample (100%)	834		281			

* *Cumulative percentage distribution.*

44% of those spouses who went on to the divorce court obtained their maintenance order within five years of marriage. If a maintenance order was obtained within five years of the marriage, dissolution of the marriage was more likely to occur than when the maintenance order was made more than five years after the marriage.

The average duration of undissolved marriages until the maintenance order was 10·6 years. In the case of those who petitioned for divorce, the duration of marriage until the maintenance order averaged 7·6 years. This significant difference might be accounted for by the type of maintenance order sought. The possibility that maintenance orders might have been more or less often granted in respect of dependant children only, is examined in Table 101.

TABLE 101   Length of marriage to magistrates' court hearing by type of order.

Duration of marriage	Type of maintenance order made					
	(1) for wife		(2) for children only		Total	
	Group * A	B	A	B	A	B
	%	%	%	%	%	%
Under 5 years	26	43	35	45	28	44
5 years but under 15 years ..	44	43	51	47	45	43
15 years and over	30	14	14	8	27	13
Size of sample (100%)	659	206	175	75	834	281

* Group as Table 100.
A. Maintenance order only.
B. maintenance order proceeding to divorce court.

Marriages were of shorter duration for both groups of wives who did not establish a matrimonial offence against their husband. but obtained maintenance for their dependant children. Where the maintenance order was for the wife, the average duration of the marriage in the cases with no subsequent divorce proceeding was 11·1 years compared with 7·8 years in the cases where divorce followed. Where the maintenance order was for the child only, the difference in the duration of marriages which did or did not go on to the divorce court was much less marked—8·3 years compared with 7·0 years.

The totality of this evidence suggests that, of the divorcing population, those marriages which had passed through the magistrates' court were of shorter duration than those which went straight to the divorce court. This might indicate that an application to the magistrates' court, with its first taste of matrimonial court proceedings for the wife, hastened the spouses on their way to divorce. But it would be incautious to draw such an inference, since only one half of wives with maintenance orders petition the divorce court and these constitute only one third of all annual divorce petitions. Of those petitions disclosing previous proceedings in the magistrates' courts, a high percentage (92%) relate to working class people. Only 1% of our sample population was classified under social class I, while the majority (57%) came under social class III. We proceed to examine the duration of marriages by social class where there was a divorce following proceedings in the magistrates' court. The data are set out in Table 102.

TABLE 102 **Duration of marriage by social class for petitions showing previous proceedings in magistrates' courts, and continuing married population in England and Wales in 1961.**

Duration of marriage to divorce	Social class				
	Professional Intermediate I and II	Skilled III	Partly skilled IV	Unskilled V	Total
	cumulative		percentage		distribution
Under 5 years	13	15	21	25	17
5 years but under 9 years ..	36	45	40	58	45
9 years but under 15 years ..	66	69	69	77	70
15 years but under 20 years ..	89	80	87	86	83
20 years and over	100	100	100	100	100
Total numbers	30	221	77	57	385
Percentage distribution ..	8	57	20	15	100
Continuing married* percentage distribution	21	51	20	8	11,471,000 (100%)

* *Census 1961*, Occupation Tables, Table 20, p. 215.

This table demonstrates that there is a strongly marked social class differential in marriage breakdown. Nearly twice as many divorcing couples in social class V ended their marriages within five years as did those in social classes I and II. In social class III and IV 8% more marriages existed for fifteen years or more than among those in social class V. Of marriages lasting for nine or more years, 57% were from social classes III and IV but only 42% from social class V. As the duration of marriage shortened, the proportion of lower social class husbands increased. This was more marked among the 1961 population than among the 1955 population where there was greater similarity between the three working class groups.

Table 102 provides a further comparison of the distribution by social class between the divorcing and non-divorcing population. The 1961 census shows that just over half the marriage population fell into social class III, the professional and intermediate social classes accounted for 21%, and the semi-skilled and unskilled social classes made up the residue of 28%.

The distribution of successful grounds for divorce is examined in Table 103 in order to disclose any significant factors.

TABLE 103　Distribution of successful grounds for decree nisi shown by petitioner, as a percentage, by years 1955 and 1961.

| | | | | Petitioner | | | | | |
| | | | | Wife | | Husband | | Total | |
Ground of petition				1955 %	1961 %	1955 %	1961 %	1955 %	1961 %
Adultery ..	..	..	..	27	37	60	59	36	42
Desertion	..	..	..	47	34	36	36	44	35
Cruelty ..	..	..	..	26	28	4	5	20	23
Sample size (100%)	..			266	328	86	97	352	425

The most popular ground for divorce in 1961 for those petitioners who had previously gone through the magistrates' courts was adultery. Of all such petitions 42% were for adultery, 35% for desertion and 23% for cruelty. In 1955, desertion was the most popular ground with 44%, adultery followed with 36% and cruelty with 20%. These differences are wholly accountable for by changes in the grounds used by wife-petitioners. Between 1955 and 1961 there was a marked shift from desertion to adultery. The explanation may be the growing awareness that there is no time bar to a divorce on the grounds of adultery as there is with desertion[1]. Table 104 shows these petitions by the husbands' social class.

The table discloses the same shift from the use of desertion to that of adultery

TABLE 104　Petitioners' grounds for social classes III, IV and V, as percentages of all petitions.

Year	A 1955		B 1961		Percentage difference	A–B
Social class	III and IV %	V %	III and IV %	V %	III and IV %	V %
Grounds of petition						
Adultery	31	4	38	4	+ 7	0
Desertion	33	7	23	5	—10	— 2
Cruelty	12	7	17	6	+ 5	— 1
Total	76	18	77	14	+ 2	— 3
All petitions	288 (100%)		358 (100%)			

(The sum of the individual percentages may not equal "total" or "difference" due to rounding.)

[1] It is unlikely that there could have been a marked increase in the readiness to commit adultery between 1955 and 1961.

as a ground for divorce, but the shift is more pronounced among social classes III and IV. Adultery was the least popular ground among social class V petitioners, though it was the most widely used by social classes III and IV. Desertion grew less popular with the three classes from 1955 to 1961. As husband-petitioners had not changed their grounds for divorce over the two years, the transfer from desertion to adultery has occurred among working class wife-petitioners. With this exception, there was little change between 1955 and 1961 in the pattern of petitioning for divorce by working class couples. What change there was occurred mainly among social classes III and IV and emerged as an increase of 8% in adultery petitions and of 6% in cruelty petitions but a decrease of 13% in petitions on the ground of desertion.

In 1961, 23,369 decrees absolute were made. Adultery was the ground in half of them, desertion the ground in one-third and cruelty in 15%. A similar proportion of petitioners in social classes III and IV in our sample, as in the whole divorcing population, used adultery as their ground. On the other hand, the unskilled working class in our sample used adultery in only one-quarter of their petitions. But even here there is a trend towards greater use of adultery and less reliance upon desertion. This may reasonably be interpreted as a slow adoption of middle class habits by working class petitioners.

The findings set out in this chapter suggest one hypothesis which should be tested by further research. We now know that there was remarkable similarity in the social composition of the divorcing and still married populations of 1951 and 1961. There is no evidence to suggest that poverty itself still bars access to the High Court[1]. We know, too, that extensive use is still made of the matrimonial jurisdiction of magistrates' courts by the poorest section of the working class. We have estimated that somewhere in the region of half the marriages which leave a record of their collapse in the files of the magistrates' courts remain broken but never end in divorce. These facts suggest that the likelihood that the incidence of marriage breakdowns which leave a legal record is highest among the lowest social class[2].

[1] This does not imply that such correlates of poverty as poor education and fear of courts and lawyers do not serve as bars.

[2] Such a conclusion would be in line with American studies of the incidence of divorce among differential occupational groups. See William J. Goode, "Marital Satisfaction and Instability: A Cross-Cultural Analysis of Divorce", *International Social Science Journal*, Vol. XIV, No. 3, 1962. In theory, the incidence of recorded breakdown in England might be the same throughout all social strata. It could be held that the breakdowns in the lowest social class are very likely to come to magistrates' courts because (*a*) the couples are most unlikely to make private financial agreements and (*b*) the wives are likely to seek financial help from the Supplementary Benefits Commission and thus to be required by the Commission to seek a court order. On the other hand, the higher social classes are in a better position to avoid the courts and to make their own private agreements with or without the help of solicitors. So the situation might be that the disproportionate rate of applications to courts by the lower social classes will be balanced by the rate of recourse to private agreements or to solicitors by the higher social classes. This is a possible explanation but informed opinion rejects it on the ground that separation agreements are increasingly rare and are nowadays made chiefly in relation to divorce. Regrettably, there is little knowledge of the arrangements made by the parties to broken marriages which are not brought before the courts.

CHAPTER 10

Maintenance and social security

The liability to maintain one's family under poor law and social security legislation

The Ministry of Social Security Act 1966 gives the Supplementary Benefits Commission power to recover the amount of benefit which it may pay from any person liable to maintain the beneficiary. This provision had its origins in the poor law.

The Elizabethan poor law was one element in a national policy designed to protect the weaker members of the community from the insecurities flowing from economic change. With the poor law went measures to prevent evictions, to control food supplies and prices, and to provide employment. The Act of 1601 consolidated the steps which had been taken after the suppression of the monasteries into a national code which laid down legal sanctions for the observance of what were then accepted as the ordinary duties of kinship. Section 6 required that

> the father and grandfather, and the mother and grandmother, and the children of every poor, old, blind, lame and impotent person, . . . being of sufficient ability, shall at their own charges relieve and maintain every such poor person, in that manner and according to that rate, as by the justices of the peace of that county, where such sufficient persons dwell, or the greater number of them, at their general quarter sessions shall be assessed; upon pain that every one of them shall forfeit twenty shillings for every month which they shall fail therein.[1]

This provision made no mention of husbands and only imposed the obligation to maintain their kinfolk on those of sufficient ability. At that time, if one member of a family was destitute, the likelihood would have been that all the liable relatives were in the same position with no chance of enforcing

[1] Quoted in the very helpful article of L. Neville Brown, "National Assistance and the Liability to Maintain One's Family", *Modern Law Review*, Vol. 18, p. 113. We have drawn heavily in this section on Professor Brown's discussion. We also found the analysis of "California's Dual System of Family Law: its Origin, Development and Present Status", by Jacobus Ten Broek, *Stanford Law Review*, Vols. 16 and 17, 1963–1965, illuminating and relevant.

an order against any of them. For this reason, deserted wives gained no benefit from the Poor Relief (Destitute Wives and Children) Act 1718, which allowed the property of absconding husbands to be seized as a source of maintenance for any family chargeable to the parish. Civil procedure against defaulters was extended by the Poor Law (Naval and Merchant Seamen) Act 1819 which, in the aftermath of the Napoleonic Wars, introduced attachment of naval and military pensions and of merchant seamen's wages as a procedure for use against husbands who left their families chargeable to the parish[1]. The Vagrancy Act 1824 extended the criminal sanctions provided in the legislation which stemmed from the *Report* of a Committee of the House of Commons set up in 1735 to consider the laws relating to the maintenance and settlement of the poor. An Act[2] of 1739 made "a distinction between idle and disorderly persons, rogues and vagabonds, and incorrigible rogues. In the first category (it placed) all persons who threaten to run away and leave their wives and children to the parish . . ."[3] The 1824 Act created for such persons what Professor Neville Brown has described as a "tryptych of villainy"[4]. A deserting husband would become, on his first conviction, a "rogue and vagabond"; his second conviction would turn him into an "idle and disorderly person"; and, on his third conviction, he would be designated an "incorrigible rogue" and go to gaol for three months.

Neither the *Report* of the Royal Commission of 1834 nor the major reform which followed it made any reference to the situation of unsupported wives or their children. Sidney and Beatrice Webb observe that

> the wife is treated throughout exactly as is the child; and it is assumed that she follows her husband, both with regard to the continuance of outdoor relief to the aged, the impotent and the sick; and with regard to its abolition in the case of the able-bodied . . . With regard to the really baffling problems presented by the widow, the deserted wife, the wife of the absentee soldier or sailor, the wife of a husband resident in another parish or another country—in each case whether with or without dependant children—the Report is silent.[5]

The Poor Law Amendment Act 1834 assumed that husband and wife constituted one legal personality and provided[6] that outdoor relief given to a wife or to children under sixteen was to be "considered as being given to the husband of such wife or the father of such child or children, as the case may be", and so allowed the Guardians to recover the amount which they had expended from the husband. The system varied widely in its operation

[1] For further discussion of this legislation, see Chapter 7, p. 97.
[2] 13. Geo. II., c. 24.
[3] C. J. Ribton-Turner, *A History of Vagrants and Vagrancy* (1887), p. 199.
[4] *Op*. cit., p. 114, fn. 14.
[5] *English Poor Law Policy* (1910), p. 6.
[6] Section 56.

throughout the country. In 1909, the Minority *Report* of the Poor Law Commission stated "that it depends on the mood of the Guardians, or even on which Guardians happen to be present, whether, in any particular case, much or little or nothing at all is demanded from relations known to be legally liable"[1]. But if the Guardians had required a contribution and it had not been paid, they could proceed against the defaulting relative in the magistrates' court. Strict proof of marriage was not necessary in such proceedings, and cohabitation was sufficient *prima facie* evidence to justify an order. If a court order was ignored, the husband could be committed for contempt of court. The annual *Judicial Statistics* show the extent of proceedings under this poor law offence of "deserting or neglecting to support the family". Throughout the 1880s orders averaged around 5,300 a year; they subsequently declined slightly as wives began to exercise their right to seek maintenance orders against their husbands under the Acts of 1886 and 1895[2]. However they proceeded, deserted wives faced insuperable difficulties in enforcing orders and they continued to form a significant group among the workhouse population.

Section 5 of the Poor Law Amendment Act 1850 was the first express statutory power to enable the cost of maintaining a wife out of the rates to be recoverable from her husband, but it applied only in the case of a lunatic. The Poor Law Amendment Act 1868 "impliedly recognized the common law liability by section 33, which laid down that 'when a married woman requires relief without her husband' the guardians of the Union or the overseers of the parish to which she became chargeable might apply to the justices to require the husband to show cause why an order should not be made upon him to maintain his wife ... "[3] Under the Married Women's Property Act 1870, a wife with separate property became liable to the poor law authorities for the maintenance of her husband. The law was consolidated by the Poor Law Act 1927, which provided that

> it shall be the duty of the father, grandfather, mother, grandmother, husband or child of a poor, old, blind, lame and impotent person, or other person not able to work, if possessed of sufficient means, to relieve and maintain such a person[4].

Thus, husbands were added to the relatives listed in the Act of 1601. Further, the liability imposed in 1870 upon a wife with separate property to maintain her husband, was continued. Such were the statutory provisions which imposed maintenance obligations upon liable relatives, when the National Assistance Act 1948 decreed that "the existing Poor Law shall cease to have effect". That poor law, writes Professor R. M. Titmuss,

---

[1] Cd. 4499, 1909, *Minority Report*, Part I, p. 374.
[2] Part I, Police; Criminal Proceedings, Prison, Table 8.
[3] L. Neville Brown, *op. cit.*, pp. 115–16.   [4] Section 41(1).

inevitably involved personal discrimination. The stigmata of the poor law test, moral judgments by people about other people and their behaviour, were a condition of redistribution . . . (the poor law) . . . was theoretically a neat and orderly world of eligible and ineligible citizens; of approved and disapproved patterns of dependency; . . . From its operation for over a century Britain inherited in 1948 a whole set of administrative attitudes; values and rites; essentially middle-class in structure; and moralistic in application."[1]

It was therefore only to be expected that the 16,000 separated wives receiving assistance when the National Asistance Board was established in 1948 would more than double in number by the summer of 1949. As the Board explained in its *Report* for 1949, this "was no doubt due in the main to the fact that many people who were, or would have been, reluctant to apply to the Relieving Officer for outdoor relief are less reluctant to apply to the Board for National Assistance"[2].

The Act of 1948 reduced the range of relatives liable to contribute to each other's support, and reaffirmed the reciprocal obligations of husbands and wives; but, while emphasizing the duties of parents towards their children, it relieved children of any statutory requirement to support their parents. The Act imposed maintenance obligations equally on both spouses and made their performance independent both of the end of cohabitation and of proof of a matrimonial offence. These seemingly absolute terms were qualified by the direction to the court to "have regard to all the circumstances"[3] before deciding to make an order. In 1952 it was held in the case of *National Assistance Board v. Wilkinson*[4] that the statutory obligation is still subject to the old common law qualifications that a husband cannot be compelled to support a wife who is in desertion or adulterous.

Under the Ministry of Social Security Act 1966, the National Assistance Board was replaced by the Supplementary Benefits Commission. This Act made no change in the liability of husbands and wives to support each other and their dependant children. The Commission has explained that

when a woman claims supplementary benefit because she is not being maintained by her husband, the Commission's first duty is to meet her requirements. As soon as possible thereafter the husband is told of his liability under section 22. If the man is able but unwilling to meet his obligations and it seems likely that the wife could obtain a maintenance order, she is encouraged to take proceedings, for which purpose legal aid is usually available. The Commission reserve their own powers to seek an order for use if the wife is unable or unwilling to take her own proceedings and to enforce these orders as appropriate. If a separated

[1] *Commitment to Welfare* (1968), pp. 189–90. [2] Cmd. 8030, 1949, p. 21.
[3] Section 43(2).   [4] [1952] 2 Q.B. 648.

wife has obtained an order herself she is encouraged to enforce it rather than that the Commission should institute proceedings.[1]

One reason why the Supplementary Benefits Commission urge wives who are receiving benefit to obtain their own orders in their own names is that an order obtained by the Commission cannot be varied to enable payments to be made direct to the wife. Thus, a wife without her own order may lose both supplementary benefit and her maintenance from her husband if she ceases to be entitled to benefit as a result of going out to work.[2]

The Commission can enforce orders obtained in its own name either by invoking the civil procedure under section 23 or by instituting criminal proceedings under section 30 against persistent defaulters. In 1968, the Commission took 196 husbands to court under section 23 and obtained convictions in 97% of the cases. In the same year, it proceeded against 517 persons (mainly deserting husbands) under section 30 and achieved a high rate of convictions. Under section 23, the court can commit to prison for up to six weeks; under section 30, the period is up to three months.

The administration of supplementary benefit to unsupported wives

The recurring references which have appeared in the Annual *Reports* of the National Assistance Board and of the Supplementary Benefits Commission to the difficulties in dealing with deserting husbands, suggest a feeling of frustration and despair among officials. The Board's second *Report* in 1949 said that

> in nearly half the cases the relative cannot be traced, and there are others where the relative has been traced but the courts would not consider it right to enforce the liability. Even where the relative can be brought to book, he may not be in a position to contribute, and where a contribution can reasonably be expected constant vigilance is often necessary to secure regular payment.[3]

Four years later the Board reflected sadly that "extracting money from husbands to support wives from whom they are separated is at best an uncertain business . . ."[4]. In 1966 the Supplementary Benefits Commission, in its first annual *Report*, recorded that

> although the number of cases of separated wives, mothers of illegitimate

---

[1] *Ministry of Social Security Annual Report, 1967*, Cmnd. 3693. p. 30.
[2] *Ministry of Social Security Annual Report, 1966*, Cmnd. 3338, p. 62.
[3] Cmnd. 8030, 1949, p. 22.   [4] Cmd. 9210, 1953, p. 19.

children and divorced women with legitimate children is only a small proportion—approximately 7 per cent—of the total number of cases in which supplementary benefit is being paid, the work necessary to persuade the man to meet his liability often involves disproportionate time and effort[1].

The court records on which this book is based tell nothing of the grievances or opinions of wives who applied for financial assistance. They showed that 24% of the wives who had obtained maintenance orders on the ground of their husbands' desertion were receiving assistance. But we know that court records do not contain adequate or reliable information (some contain no information) about wives' dependence on assistance. We had hoped to check for a sample of our court orders with the local offices of the National Assistance Board in order to discover what proportion of the wives were being helped. Regrettably, the Board declined to give us either this information or access to their files. Our only knowledge in this area was derived from the *News of the World* survey reported in Chapter 8. Of the wife respondents who completed the questionnaire, 87% (237) had applied for assistance since being separated from their husbands. Almost half these applicants to the National Assistance Board said that they had found the Board's officers to be positively helpful; rather more than one-third said that the officers did "not care and only helped when they had to"; and only 12% said that they found the officers unpleasant. As many of these wives must have been emotionally distraught when they approached the Board, we think that the small proportion who made a positive complaint is surprising, and very creditable to the Board's officers.

These wives made two main complaints about the administration of benefit: they resented what many described as "being forced into court as a condition of assistance"; and they disliked the inquisitorial procedures adopted, or alleged to be adopted, by the Board to ensure that they were not cohabiting with a man whilst receiving assistance.

Mrs. Pauline Morris's survey of *Prisoners and their Families,* published in 1965, records that many wives of husbands imprisoned for non-payment of maintenance, complained that they had been compelled to proceed against their husbands. Mrs. Morris's conclusion was that

we feel that most deserted wives are quite willing to take out orders against their husbands so long as there is no question of this involving his imprisonment, but they are very reluctant to do so if there is any likelihood of imprisonment resulting. It is quite possible that some element of misunderstanding arises between the wives and the N.A.B. officers, in so far as the latter try to persuade wives to take out orders for their own good, but the wives, who usually have some difficulty in understanding

[1] *Ministry of Social Security Annual Report,* 1966, Cmnd. 3338, p. 62.

the legal aspects of the situation, interpret this pressure as being a form of blackmail—if you do not take out an order we will not give you any more assistance. If our interpretation of the situation is correct, we nevertheless think it vital that the position should be made quite clear to the wife and that no pressure of this kind should ever appear to be exerted.[1]

Mr. Dennis Marsden has more recently reported a similar finding.

Mothers who were still emotionally attached to the children's father felt that the N.A.B. were inclined to ignore the fact that the relationship between mother and father might be in a delicate state of suspension. Many would have refused to take a court action had they not felt that as dependants on assistance they must do as the Board wished.[2]

The Social Security authority has always denied emphatically that any pressure is put on applicants for assistance to complain for orders. On the other hand, it has a duty to inform applicants that it is in their interest to obtain an order in their own names. Moreover, it has to give advice to people who are very likely to distrust the law and to fear the courts. Some of them will no doubt misunderstand what they are told, and others may use the Board as a scapegoat for their personal misery, anxiety and guilt. The root of this trouble lies in the criminal atmosphere of the magistrates' court and in the possibility that wives may be the means of sending their husbands to prison. The abolition of imprisonment for maintenance defaulters would go some way to removing this obstacle to the establishment of good relations between the Supplementary Benefits Commission and those of its clients whose poverty is exacerbated by the collapse of their marriages.

The Supplementary Benefits Commission will stop payments to a woman who is held to be cohabiting with a man. What constitutes cohabitation has never been precisely defined. The Ministry of Social Security Act 1966 provides that

where a husband and wife are members of the same household their requirements and resources shall be aggregated and shall be treated as the husband's and similarly, unless there are exceptional circumstances, as regards two persons cohabiting as man and wife.[3]

Officers of the Commission must interpret this vague statement, and doubtless they apply their own moral judgments to the behaviour and presumed sexual activities of other people in accordance with what they regard as proper and equitable as between unsupported women and ordinary wives. One consequence of this largely administrative rule is that some women may be

---

[1] p. 269.   [2] *Mothers Alone* (1969), p. 152.
[3] Schedule 2. Part 1, s.3(1).

denied the chance to establish an enduring friendship with a man. As Mr.
Marsden points out

> these aims involve the N.A.B. in supporting a conventional morality,
> which is difficult to define in principle and virtually impossible to specify
> in a set of checking procedures whereby women's relationships can be
> policed. It seems likely that, in a pluralistic and changing society, there
> are occasional issues such as this which have no finally satisfactory
> solution, and certainly none within the terms of national assistance
> legislation: we are here involved with the roots of family law. Yet it must
> be stressed that mothers said the effect of N.A.B. practices was often to
> discourage and punish those relationships with men on which depended
> happiness and the possibility of remarriage[1].

These are genuine problems which involve conflicts between the rights of
citizens and the duties of governments: they do not admit of easy solutions,
as the revealing letter of a widow to *The Times*, which we quote at length,
illustrates:

> It was announced recently that undergraduates may be given a state
> allowance for their partners; either the husband or wife, or the man or
> woman with whom they cohabit. I have no objection to this policy,
> which appears to recognise that needs have nothing to do with morals.
> But I do wonder why the Government does not co-ordinate its thinking
> on matters of needs and morals.
>
> As a widow in receipt of a state pension I am told that if I cohabit
> with a man my pension may be withdrawn, although the rules are not
> very clear. Of course if I remarry I cease to be a widow and must expect
> the widow's pension to stop. But if I have a male boarder or paying guest
> to supplement my pension, am I cohabiting with him? If a man lives in
> my house and does not pay board, just rent, and buys his own food, am I
> cohabiting with him? I suspect that if he lives here rent free I am
> cohabiting, even if he cuts the lawn, mends the fuses and chases the
> burglars in return for his room and gas-ring, although he never touches
> me. The really odd thing is that provided my male friend maintains a
> separate residence—i.e. has a separate address—we can have intercourse
> nightly, and daily, and my widow's pension will remain unaffected.
>
> To complete the picture, I receive a rather small private pension from
> the ex-colonial government which employed my husband. This naturally
> ceases if I remarry. But I can cohabit with or without intercourse or have
> intercourse with or without cohabitation and this widow's pension
> remains unaffected. The ex-colonial government condones my living in
> sin. The home Government places restrictions on where I may sin; it

[1] *Op. cit.*, p. 208.

would penalize me if my lover lives with me, but evidently not if he goes home occasionally. It's a pity I am too old to become an undergraduate's mistress; life would be much less complicated, and I could sin anywhere I liked, and draw an allowance for it.[1]

It is time to abandon administrative rules which give effect to *a priori* definitions of approved and disapproved sexual relationships. There must be a strong suspicion that the operation of the rules and the absurdities inherent in them inflict discrimination upon the poor.

By far the most important and beneficial change in the administrative procedures of the social security authorities was the adoption throughout the country in 1965 of an arrangement whereby wives, with maintenance orders within scale rates, who qualify for assistance, receive an order book which they can cash at the post office. In return, they sign a certificate authorizing the transfer to the Commission of any payments received by the court collecting office from the husband. Thus, assistance in such cases is calculated as though there were no maintenance order, and the wife receives regularly her full entitlement regardless of whether the order is paid regularly, intermittently, or never. This reform has relieved many women of the harassing anxiety of irregular payments and of the humiliating inconvenience of fruitless visits to the court collecting office.

The social characteristics of applicants for assistance

The annual *Reports* of the National Assistance Board and the Supplementary Benefits Commission have contained very little information about the social and demographic characteristics of the unsupported wives and mothers who receive assistance. The material that has been published is too scattered and unsystematic to permit a composite picture of one-parent families to be drawn. In 1966 the Ministry of Social Security undertook an enquiry, published under the title of *Circumstances of Families*, "to show the number of families whose resources were less than their requirements on the basic national assistance standards and the extent to which their needs could not be met by national assistance allowances"[2]. Special circumstances limited the enquiry to families with more than one child. Although the findings of the main enquiry were based on a sample of some 2,700 families, these included only 102 fatherless families of whom ninety-six gave satisfactory co-operation to the investigators[3]. On this rather narrow basis, the enquiry estimated that

there were 150,000 such families with two or more children, of which 40,000 were the families of widows and over 100,000 the families of

[1] From Mrs. J. C. Grey, 3rd April 1970. [2] P. iii. [3] *Ibid*, P. 67.

women who were divorced or, more frequently, separated from their husbands. The sample suggests that those whose initial resources, before assistance was paid, were less than their requirements, assessed by reference to the supplementary benefit rates, numbered about 75,000 of which only a small proportion were the families of widows[1].

Circumstances of Families reinforced the conclusions reached by other investigations[2] that a disproportionately large number of mothers, who are the sole supporters of their families, go out to work. The *Report* of the Seebohm Committee on Local Authority and Allied Personal Social Services emphasized that the special needs of such mothers are not yet being met by the social services.

There are at present 450,000 working mothers with young children under 5, about half of whom work part-time. Some can choose whether to go out to work or not: others, who are unsupported by a husband or who have to augment a very low family income, have little alternative. We are particularly concerned about these latter, as we believe that no mother who would prefer to look after her young children at home should be obliged to work for lack of a reasonable minimum income. This is an issue which must be faced in the context of the arrangements for social security benefits.[3]

The cost of assistance to separated wives

Up to 1965, the Annual Reports of the National Assistance Board recorded the yearly amounts of benefit paid to separated wives; but they gave no indication of the amounts paid to wives or mothers with children still at school, or of the sums received from husbands as contributions.

During the period 1956–1960, the number of separated wives receiving assistance ran at some 73,900 a year; and they were paid an average weekly amount of £2 15s. Average payments went up to £4 2s. per week during 1961–1965, when a yearly average of 96,800 separated wives were granted benefit. In 1965, 104,000 separated wives received assistance to the total of £27,440,000, an average of £5 2s. per head per week.[4] In addition they received an average amount of ten shillings per week from their husbands. Table 105 shows the amount of assistance paid to separated wives in 1965.

[1] *Ibid*, p. 14.
[2] e.g. J. W. B. Douglas and J. M. Bloomfield, *Children Under Five* (1958), p. 114 and S. Yudkin and A. Holme, *Working Mothers and their Children* (2nd. ed. 1969). pp. 78–79.
[3] Cmnd. 3703, 1968, p. 59.
[4] These statistics are based on, or have been taken from, the N.A.B. and Ministry of Social Security Annual Reports which include Scotland as well as England and Wales. A rough estimate of the numbers involving England and Wales can be obtained by reducing the totals by 10%.

TABLE 105   National assistance paid to separated wives during 1965.

Number of separated wives in 1965 receiving assistance: 104,000	Yearly total	Average amount	
		Yearly	Weekly
1. Assistance expenditure by N.A.B.	£27,444,000	£263 18s.	£5 2s.
2. Payments received direct by wife from husband	£2,754,000	£26 10s.	10s.
3. Payments received by N.A.B. through Court Order[1]	£2,065,000	£19 17s.	8s.
4. Net assistance paid by N.A.B. (1–3) ..	£25,379,000	£244	£4 14s.
5. Net assistance received by wives (1 + 2)	£30,198,000	£290 8s.	£5 12s.
6. Contributions received from husband (2 + 3)	£4,819,000	£46 7s.	18s.
7. Average contribution by those 37,000 husbands making any court or out of court payment		£130 4s.	£2 10s.

Source: *Report of The Committee on Statutory Maintenance Limits,* 1968, Cmnd. 3587, Appendix D. p. 90–94.

The National Assistance Board recovered some two million pounds through court orders obtained by wives who had authorized the Board to collect the money from the court. These sums were recovered by the Board after assistance had been paid and they can therefore be deducted from the Board's annual expenditure to establish the net yearly rate of assistance paid. Line 3 of Table 105 shows that the Board recovered 8s. from husbands for every £5 2s. in assistance given to wives. Thus, for every £100 assistance to separated wives, the Board recovered £7 10s. from the husbands. By making direct payments to their wives, as shown by line 2 of Table 105, husbands relieved the Board of an average weekly amount of 10s. Allowing for payments made through court orders, husbands contributed only some 16% of wives' financial needs as assessed by the Board[2] and under 10%[3] of all assistance paid to wives.

Mrs. Lena Jeger presented similar calculations to the House of Commons during a debate on deserted wives in 1968:

The situation is that, whether the Ministry of Social Security want to

[1] Calculated on the basis that N.A.B. received £3,024,000 from 41,000 "regularly" or "irregularly" complied with court orders, consisting of 28,000 separated wives as well as 13,000 mothers of illegitimate children and divorced women with legitimate children.

$$\left(\frac{28}{41} \times \frac{3,024,000}{1} = £2,065,000\right)$$

[2] This percentage results from the net assistance received by the wife (£30,198,000: Line 5 of Table 105) divided into the husband's total contributions (£4,819,000: Line 6), i.e.

$$\frac{£4,819,000}{£30,198,000} \times 100 = 15.96\%.$$

[3] $\dfrac{£2,065,000}{£27,444,000} = 7.5\%$: $\dfrac{£3,024,000}{£27,444,000} = 11\%$; the latter proportion being the maximum possible, whilst 7% to 8% is the more probable proportion.

take on any extra work or not, in fact they are already doing a very large proportion of the maintenance work . . . the Ministry's funds are being used to keep these families.

Why is that ? One of the reasons lies in the simple economic fact of the situation that one wage packet does not divide into the maintenance of two families. Many magistrates know that when they make the order and they know that any attempt to increase the payments from the husband will lead only to the impoverishment of two families. . . . These figures (1965) suggest that the whole system is breaking down and that we are continuing an illusion in maintaining the machinery of court orders and attempting the disengagement of the Ministry of Social Security from the heart of the matter. I know that my right hon. friend does not wish to be regarded as running a Ministry which is mainly a debt collecting agency, but to a large extent that takes place already.[1]

In its annual report for 1951, the National Assistance Board commented on the small amount of money recovered from husbands as compared with expenditure from public funds:

It is regrettable that in so high a proportion of cases little or nothing can be accomplished and so little of the cost to public funds can be recovered. It is far from easy to trace a man who is designedly hiding himself from possible discovery and who has the whole country and a population of fifty million to hide himself in, or can go abroad . . . given the difficulties the Board believe their officers do very well.[2]

It would be wrong to assume that the husband's minimal contribution is due solely to his non-payment of court orders or of voluntary agreements, as Table 106 shows.

Section A of Table 106 shows that there has been a slight increase in the proportion of wives with court maintenance orders from 37% in 1957 to 41% in 1965. The trend over the three most recent years suggests that this proportion is unlikely to change.

Though 41% (41,000) of all wives receiving assistance in 1965 had maintenance orders against their husbands, regular compliance with the order occurred in under half (49%: 21,000) of these cases, whilst a further 16% (7,000) were paid irregularly[3]. The fact that 21,000 wives required additional financial help from the National Assistance Board shows that the amount of maintenance ordered by the court was insufficient for their basic needs. No

---

[1] Hansard, House of Commons, Vol. 746, 1968, col. 98.   [2] Cmd. 8632, pp. 18–19.
[3] This compares favourably with the situation twenty years ago. In a survey of all (57,700) separated women drawing assistance in September 1950, one third (19,000: 33%) had live maintenance orders. Some 6,000 (10%) of all the wives received regular court order payments. One third (32%) of the husbands obligated to pay maintenance orders did so regularly. (Cmnd. 9210, 1953, Appendix XI.)

TABLE 106 Separated wives receiving assistance during the years 1957 and 1963-1965*.

| | Year | | | |
| | 1957 | 1963 | 1964 | 1965 |
Total number of wives on assistance	66,000	102,000	103,000	104,000
	Percentage			
A. *Proportion of wives with:*				
(i) Court order	37	39	42	41
(ii) Out of court arrangement	9	11	11	11
(iii) Neither (i) or (ii)	54	50	47	48
B. *Regularity of payment from husband*				
1. Court order or out of court arrangement:				
(i) Complied with regularly	24	28	27	28
(ii) Irregularly complied with	9	8	8	8
2. Husband makes no payment	67	64	65	64
C. *Reasons for husband's non-payment*				
(i) Court order not complied with	12	13	15	14
(ii) Cannot be traced or insufficient means ..	46	35	35	33
(iii) Wife has forfeited rights to maintenance and has no children	5	8	9	10
(iv) Court action pending, etc.	4	8	6	7

* Source: These figures are based on (1) a 2½% sample for 1957 (Cmnd. 446, pp. 15–16)—that included separated wives with illegitimate children; and (2) a 1¼% sample for the three years 1963, 1964 and 1965 which were published as Appendix D (p. 90) of the *Report of the Committee on Statutory Maintenance Limits*, Cmnd. 3587, 1968.
This information is obtainable only for the above four years.

fault can be found with those husbands who had paid regularly nor with the justices' assessment that their wages could not provide a larger order.

Some 11% (11,000) of all wives had out of court arrangements in 1965, in which payments were regularly received in 73% (8,000), and irregularly received in 9% (1,000), of all such cases.

If wives with either a court order or an out of court arrangement are included in a group which should have been receiving payments from husbands, there is a proportional rise of 6% from 46% in 1957 to 52% in 1965.

Section B of Table 106 shows that though 52% (54,000) of all wives in 1965 expected some form of payment from their husbands, only 36% (37,000) of all husbands actually paid; 28% (29,000) contributing regularly and 8% (8,000) irregularly. Thus, just over half (54%) of the 54,000 husbands who were expected to make either court order (41,000) or out of court payments (11,000) in fact paid regularly.

Nearly two thirds (64%) of all wives on assistance in 1965 received nothing from their husbands. This was a lower proportion than in 1950 but a slight improvement on that for 1957. The reasons for the non-compliance are shown in section C.

Section C of Table 106 shows that the most common reason for husbands' non-payment of maintenance in 1965 was that his whereabouts were unknown or that he had left the country. The 22% of husbands coming into this category in 1965 compares very favourably with the 42% in 1950[1]. In 14% of all cases the court order was totally disregarded by the husband[2].

In 1965, a further 10% of husbands were not in a position to pay anything, while another 2% did not or could not pay. In 10% of the cases the wife had forfeited her right to maintenance and had no children. In addition, there was a miscellaneous category accounting for 7% of the cases, which included cases where court action was pending. These figures show that at least 27% (28,000) of all husbands could not reasonably or legally be expected to make payments.

The inability of many husbands to pay is highlighted by the *Report* for 1968 which shows that about 37,000 husbands were receiving supplementary benefit who were themselves married but living apart from their wives[3]. They formed nearly 6% of all married men (642,000) who received supplementary benefit.

Analysis of the 1965 figures shows that even under the best possible circumstances, the state would still be paying out well over twenty million pounds a year in assistance to separated wives. This argument depends on three premises: (i) that the 21,000 husbands of separated wives who pay their court orders regularly, contributed all the £3,024,000 recovered by the National Assistance Board in 1965; (ii) that the 28,000 husbands listed in section C could not be expected to pay; and (iii) that the remaining 55,000 husbands paid the same average amount as the 21,000 regular payers. Even in these circumstances (and they are the most favourable the Board could hope for) the gain in contributions which the Board could set against their gross expenditure on assistance, would amount to only eight million pounds. In other words, if all husbands obligated to pay maintenance were to pay it regularly the Board's assistance of some thirty million pounds to deserted wives would have been reduced by one quarter. Even if all the wives being assisted had received regular payments under their maintenance orders, they would still have needed financial help.

As the Joint Under-Secretary of State for the Home Department (Mr. C. M. Woodhouse) pointed out in 1964:

if the State were to underwrite a husband's maintenance obligations it would still in many cases be found that additional payment was needed for relief of the wife's hardship. In other words, the extent of the

[1] Cmnd. 9210, 1953.

[2] As the total population—100%, of separated wives equalled 104,000: the percentages shown can be approximately translated into thousands.

[3] Cmnd. 4100, 1969, p. 248.

About 150,000 separated wives and divorced women were receiving supplementary benefit in 1968 (p. 250). Applying the 1965 proportions to this figure, some 132,000 of these wives would be separated. If all the 37,000 husbands referred to were married to wives obtaining benefit, then 28% $\left(\dfrac{37}{132}\right)$ of all these 132,000 wives would be married to husbands also obtaining benefit.

husband's maintenance obligation does not provide an appropriate yardstick for determining the extent to which the State should assist . . .

There is no way of calculating the sum which the men should have paid under court orders but failed to do so, but I assure my hon. Friend that the figure, if it could be ascertained, would be substantially less than £20,117,000 (1961), which the taxpayer had to meet[1].

The real problem is not that husbands do not provide maintenance through regular court orders, but that their incomes are too low to provide adequately both for their lawful wives and for themselves, whether living singly or with other women.

[1] Hansard, House of Commons, 1964, Vol. 693, col. 736–8.

CHAPTER 11

Affiliation

Changes in legal and social attitudes to illegitimacy

In England, the status of legitimacy has been restricted to children born within monogamous marriage. It was for long strongly held that the maintenance of monogamous marriage requires that an inferior status be conferred on bastards. Accordingly, all attempts to improve their situation have resulted in conflict between those whose first concern was to treat blameless children justly and those who held that the greater good was to protect the integrity of marriage. When the *legitimatio per subsequens matrimonium* of Roman and canon law was proposed by the English canon lawyers to the Council of Merton in 1234 in order to enable a child born before the marriage of his parents to inherit his father's land, the Barons of England replied with the celebrated dictum which stood for more than half a millennium: *nolumus leges angliae mutare quae usitatae sint et approbatae.*

From the middle ages until 1926 when the concept of legitimation was first introduced to English law, the relationship between the inferior status of bastards and their treatment in society is puzzling and has not yet been studied systematically. Writing of early English experience, Pollock and Maitland observe that "bastardy cannot be called a status or condition. The bastard cannot inherit from his parents or from anyone else, but this seems to be the only temporal consequence of his illegitimate birth . . . In all other respects he is the equal of any other free and lawful man."[1] The medieval phrase *filius nullius* did not denote ignorance of a blood relationship but only the moral antipathy, inculcated by the Church, towards illicit sexual intercourse. In the view of Dr. Pinchbeck, the only historian who has examined changing social attitudes to illegitimacy, the concept developed into a sort of technical fiction from which have come most of the disabilities from which the illegitimate child has suffered.

As later statute law and equity developed with regard to the relation of parent and legitimate child, the judges applied the maxim with

[1] F. Pollock and F. W. Maitland, *The History of English Law*, (2nd ed. 1898) Vol. 2, p. 379.

remarkable consistency to exclude the illegitimate child from most of their benefits. By carrying this doctrine to its logical conclusion, the illegitimate became a stranger in law to father, mother and all other natural relatives, and at common law had no right to look to them for custody, maintenance or education. The canon law, on the contrary, while regarding the illegitimate child as unlawful, nevertheless maintained that he had the right to support and approved the doctrine of legitimation by subsequent marriage.

It was not until the sixteenth century that social stigma attached to illegitimacy in any marked degree, and even then only upon a class basis. The cause of this change would appear to be twofold: first, dependency caused by providing for illegitimate children through the Poor Law, and, secondly, the rise of Puritanism, which was largely responsible for the obsession with moral guilt which characterized the early bastardy law.

The great increase in poverty in the sixteenth century, which compelled the development of the Poor Law, led to the widespread abandonment of illegitimate children of the poorer classes, with the result that Parliament was compelled to legislate for them in a Poor Law Act of 1576. *Filius nullius*, the child of nobody, now became *filius populi*, the child of the community, and upon the parish accordingly devolved the duties of guardianship and maintenance.[1]

Tudor and early Stuart legislation was concerned less to secure the welfare of the children than to expose and punish those who brought them into the world. Their parents were treated as criminals and put in the House of Correction for a year; their mothers were whipped at the cart tail and ostracized, with the result that births were concealed, and desertion, abortion and infanticide increased. "It is significant", Dr. Pinchbeck notes, "that the preamble of an Act of 1623 (an Act to Prevent the Destroying and Murdering of Bastard Children) refers to the great increase in infanticide which followed this brutal legislation. . . ."[2] From this time to the early nineteenth century, the "State was only concerned with illegitimacy among the poor, and . . . the grounds of its concern were the economics of maintenance rather than the circumstances of conception . . . ."[3] Hence the history of public attitudes to illegitimacy among the poor became an account of the squalid history of the poor law.

In the early nineteenth century, the inherited penal provisions against the parents of bastards were reinforced by Malthusian arguments which treated the "old" poor law, the "Speenhamland" allowance system, as a bounty upon reckless breeding and illegitimacy[4]. The Commission which

[1] "Social Attitudes to Illegitimacy", *British Journal of Sociology*, Vol. 5, No. 4, 1954, p. 315.
[2] *Ibid.*, p. 316.
[3] Ivy Pinchbeck and Margaret Hewitt, *Children in English Society*, Vol. 1 (1969), p. 221.
[4] This delusion is exposed in detail by James P. Huzel, "Malthus, the Poor Law and Population in Early Nineteenth Century England", *Economic History Review*, Second Series, XXII, No. 3 (1969).

reported in 1834 urged that the law should treat a bastard in accordance with "what Providence appears to have ordained that it shall be, a burthen on its mother, and, where she cannot maintain it, on her parents. The shame of the offence will not be destroyed by its being the means of income and marriage, and we trust that as soon as it has become both burthensome and disgraceful, it will become . . . rare . . . In affirming the inefficiency of human legislation to enforce the restraints placed upon licentiousness, . . . (we believe) that all punishment of the supposed father is useless."[1] The "new" poor law of 1834 did not accept this stern doctrine. It repealed the penal provisions but gave the poor law guardians the right to obtain an order for maintenance of an illegitimate child against the putative father. The order lasted until the child reached the age of seven. There was no limit upon the amount of such an order but no part of the father's payment could be given to the mother or used for her maintenance. Under the original Act, proceedings had to be initiated at quarter sessions; petty sessions were substituted in 1839.

A major change occurred as a result of the Poor Law Amendment Act 1844 which made bastardy proceedings a civil matter between the parents. The guardians lost the power to obtain an order against the father and for the first time the mother acquired the right to obtain her own order against the putative father for a sum[2]

not exceeding ten shillings for the expenses of the midwife attending the birth;
not exceeding ten shillings for a funeral if the child had died; at a rate not exceeding five shillings per week for the maintenance of the child for six weeks after the birth, and at a rate not exceeding two shillings and sixpence a week thereafter.

These payments could continue until the child reached the age of thirteen.

The Poor Law Amendment Act 1868 restored to the parish the power to recover from the putative father the cost of maintenance of a bastard child chargeable to the parish by providing that, where a woman who had obtained an order against the father of her child became a charge on the parish, the justices might order the payments to be made to the Relieving Officer. The effect of this provision was to subject the extent of the parish's recovery to the same limits as applied to the mother's order. This position still obtains today, in contrast to the recovery of assistance paid to a legitimate family, which is subject to no limits.

The Bastardy Laws Amendment Act 1872 raised the limit on the amount that could be ordered to five shillings a week throughout the currency

---

[1] *Report from . . . Commissioners for Inquiring into . . . the Poor Laws,* (1834), p. 250.
[2] This account of legislation in the Victorian period follows the very useful history given in Appendix B to the *Report of the Committee on Statutory Maintenance Limits,* Cmnd. 3587, 1968.

of the order, removed the limit on the accounts that could be ordered in respect of expenses incidental to the birth or funeral expenses, and provided that, while the order was normally to continue until the child was thirteen, it might last until the age of sixteen.

There were flurries of proposals within and without parliament to improve the situation of illegitimate children and their mothers on the eve and in the aftermath of the Kaiser's war. More than any other event, the foundation of the National Council for the Unmarried Mother and her Child in 1918 reflected new attitudes at the beginning of "the children's century". The maximum payment under an affiliation order was raised to ten shillings in 1918 and to twenty shillings in 1925. But the chief innovation was the provision, under the Legitimacy Act 1926, for the legitimation of children whose parents married after their birth and were free to do so at the time of the birth. The Legitimacy Act 1959 simply extended to the offspring of adulterers what the earlier Act had conceded to the progeny of fornicators. Finally, the Family Law Reform Act 1969 enacted the main recommendation of the Committee on the Law of Succession in Relation to Illegitimate Persons (the Russell Committee)[1] and has established near equality of inheritance for all children. With these striking legal changes, attention has turned to the economic disadvantages suffered by illegitimate children and their mothers. Indeed, it is likely that much of the stigma which attached to illegitimacy in the nineteenth century resulted from the inevitable involvement of poor mothers and their children with the poor law which put its thumb-print of degradation on all who fell within its care.

A study of the many illegitimates who never knew the workhouse might serve as a corrective to a too ready acceptance of the inevitability of suffering for all those born out of wedlock. The sexual waywardness of the territorial aristocracy in the late eighteenth and early nineteenth centuries did not endanger the integrity or succession of their family properties, which were regulated by primogeniture and entail. Countless children of the mist played happily in Whig and Tory nurseries where they constituted no threat to the interests of heirs. "The historian grows quite giddy", remarks Lord David Cecil, "as he tries to disentangle the complications of heredity consequent on the free and easy habits of the English aristocracy. The Harley family, children to the Countess of Oxford, were known as the Harleian Miscellancy on account of the variety of fathers alleged to be responsible for their existence. The Duke of Devonshire had three children by the Duchess and two by Lady Elizabeth Foster, the Duchess one by Lord Grey; and most of them were brought up together in Devonshire House, each set of children with a surname of its own"[2]. But middle class families handled their accumulating industrial wealth within a system of partible inheritance which demanded a severer morality imposing higher standards on women than on men. As the Lord Chancellor explained during the parliamentary debates on the proposal to

[1] Cmnd. 3501 (1966).   [2] *The Young Melbourne*, (1939), p. 11.

set up a divorce court in 1857, a wife could not be damaged by her husbands' adultery and could forgive him "without any loss of caste" but "no one would venture to suggest" that he could condone her adultery because "it might be the means of palming spurious children upon him"[1]. In moneyed circles, such a wife would have been thought to undermine the foundations of her family by admitting a fraud to the succession of its property. Nevertheless, if partible inheritance restricted the freedom of middle class women, their menfolk suffered no such disability and their illegitimate offspring often no serious disadvantage. Instances from fact and fiction quickly come to mind. For example, Barbara Leigh Smith was fathered by a wealthy, radical member of parliament, a cousin of the Nightingales and Bonham Carters, upon a milliner's apprentice. She inherited a large fortune, married Dr. Bodichon and became a leading figure in the movement for women's rights[2]. Trollope did not hesitate to make Mary Thorne both poor and illegitimate, but these disadvantages did not prevent her becoming one of the best-loved heroines of his mid-Victorian readers. Thomas Gibson Bowles, founder of *Vanity Fair*, Member of Parliament and friend of General Gordon and Lord Randolph Churchill, was the illegitimate son of Thomas Milner-Gibson who became President of the Board of Trade in 1859. Milner-Gibson took the illegitimate child into the nursery to join his eight regular children. His wife used to tell the guests: "This is Tom Bowles. Be civil to him—or leave the house."[3] At the end of the century, Keir Hardie had made his way to the political leadership of the sternly respectable labour movement despite his illegitimate birth, nor did Horatio Bottomley's public revelation of Ramsay MacDonald's illegitimacy during the Kaiser's war damage the latter's political career. Most illegitimate children suffered cruel treatment and impoverishment of life; but illegitimate birth unaccompanied by poverty did not necessarily result in misery. The Victorians did not always act upon the maxim of Montesquieu: *Il a fallu flétrir le concubinage, il a fallu donc flétrir les enfants qui en étaient nés.* In our own century, we have begun to generalise the more compassionate Victorian practice among the well-to-do.

The survey of affiliation orders

We now examine the extent of illegitimacy today as the background for the main findings of our survey of affiliation orders.

Statistics of illegitimacy contain more mysteries than certainties, and some examples from the recent past will quickly suggest the need for caution in interpreting the present. In the 1890s Ireland with 2·6 had the lowest

[1] *Hansard*, 1857, Vol. 145, col. 496.
[2] Gordon S. Haight, *George Eliot*, (1968) p. 105. She was a close friend of Hilaire Belloc's mother, Elizabeth Rayner Parkes, and their lives are described by Mrs. Belloc Lowndes in her *I, Too, Have Lived in Arcadia* (1941).
[3] Leonard E. Naylor, *The Irrepressible Victorian* (1965) p. 11.

percentage of illegitimate to total births of any country in western Europe. For England and Wales the ratio was 4·1 per hundred and the highest ratio was in Portugal which had 12·1. The low Irish rate had been established long before the Famine and was accompanied by an equally low rate of infanticide and abortion. It is as difficult to explain why the Irish peasantry in the nineteenth century produced the chastest women in Europe as it is puzzling to note the statistically accurate observation of an Irish priest in 1905 that "Orangeism and illegitimacy go together; . . . bastards in Ireland are in proportion to the Orange lodges"[1]. An explanation of similar variations in the incidence of illegitimacy in different parts of England and Wales was attempted in 1892 by Albert Leffingwell in his *Illegitimacy and the Influence of the Seasons upon Conduct*. He quoted the explanation offered by the fourteenth annual *Report* of the Registrar General that "it may be inferred that generally the unmarried women in the counties south of the Thames comprising the descendants of the old Saxon population, have few illegitimate children; Wales stands next in the scale; the West Midland, the N.W., and the South Midland counties, covering the areas of ancient Mercia, present less favourable results; while in Yorkshire, the Northern counties and the North Midland counties covering the area of the ancient Danish population, the number of illegitimate children is excessively great. "This", Dr. Leffingwell concluded, "is undoubtedly a bold hypothesis."[2] But bold hypotheses have been singularly unhelpful as explanations of the experience of different countries and regions and periods. Table 107 shows the incidence of illegitimacy in some western countries since 1930.

TABLE 107   **Illegitimacy per 100 births in selected Western countries, 1930–1960.**

	1930[3]	1940[3]	1950[3]	1960[4]
United States	3	4	4	5
Federal Germany	12	10	10	6
England and Wales	5	4	5	5
Sweden	16	12	10	11
France	8	7	7	7
Italy	5	4	3	3

The variations in these official statistics result from factors as diverse as, for example, better data collection in recent decades; or the extent and social toleration of pre- and extra-marital sexual intercourse; or the relation between illicit conceptions and legitimate births; or the degree of urbanization in the

[1] The complexities of the social situation, and the difficulties in explaining them, are admirably brought out in the elegant essay of K. H. Connell, "Illegitimacy before the Famine", in his *Irish Peasant Society* (1968), from which these details have been extracted.
[2] P. 55.
[3] W. J. Goode, *World Revolution and Family Patterns* (1963), p. 38.
[4] V. V. Saario, *Study of Discrimination against Persons Born out of Wedlock* (United Nations, 1967), pp. 216–24.

FIGURE 2 **Illegitimate births as a percentage of all live births. England and Wales and Scotland, 1911–1967.**

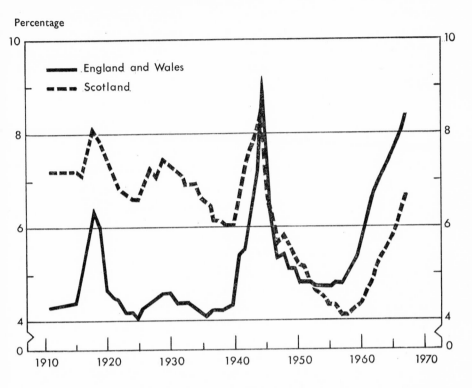

Percentage

several countries. Clearly, no single or simple explanation will suffice. Figure 2 compares the illegitimacy ratios of England and Wales and of Scotland since 1911.

No convincing explanation of the trends shown in Figure 2 has yet been offered, and Professor Illsley and Dr. Gill "cannot conceive of any interpretation based on genetics/racial origin/original sin" which would fit the facts[1].

In every generation too many moralists have been too easily attracted to the denunciation of other people's sexual behaviour. In their study of *Children in English Society*, Dr. Pinchbeck and Dr. Hewitt quote John Stretton writing in 1530 in terms which could be paralleled today from every newspaper[2]

> So many maidens with child
> And wilfully begylde. . . .
> So many women blamed
> And righteously defamed
> And so little ashamed,
> Sawe I never.

[1] in "New Fashions in Illegitimacy", *New Society*, 14th November 1968.
[2] p. 200.

We shall therefore not attempt to provide a moral commentary upon the only available national figures provided by the Registrar General.

Traditionally, it has been assumed that unmarried women aged 15–44 constitute the population at risk of bearing illegitimate babies but an investigation of 1961 census data by the Registrar General has shown that "nearly one illegitimate child in three may be born to a married woman, or, at least, to a woman who would describe herself as married in a census"[1]. Table 108 shows the figures adjusted to exclude illegitimate births to married women.

TABLE 108[2]   Illegitimacy rates for unmarried women in 1964, England and Wales.

Age	Number of illegitimate births to unmarried women	Population of unmarried women (thousands)	Illegitimacy rates per thousand population
Total	*46,429*	*3,368·5*	*13·78*
Under 20	16,444	1,687·0	9·7
20–24	16,533	648·3	25·5
25–29	6,860	234·5	29·3
30–39	5,493	339·4	16·2
40–49	1,099	459·3	2·4

The Registrar General comments that

> although more than a third of the illegitimate births to unmarried women are to teenage unmarried women, more than half of all the unmarried women aged 15-44 are teenagers, so that the illegitimacy rate (the probability of having an illegitimate child) is actually relatively low for unmarried teenagers and is three times as high for the 25–29 group.[3]

Further the Registrar General has produced Table 109 which adds the number of pre-marital conceptions (taken as births occurring to married women

TABLE 109[4]   Extra-marital conception rate for unmarried women in 1964, England and Wales.

Age	Illegitimate births to unmarried women	Pre-maritally conceived births to married women	Births conceived by unmarried women	Population of unmarried women (thousands)	Extra-marital conception rate for 1,000 unmarried women
Total	*46,429*	*67,933*	*114,362*	*3,368·5*	*34·0*
Under 20	16,444	33,340	49,784	1,687·0	29·5
20–24	16,533	27,494	44,027	648·3	67·9
25–29	6,860	4,985	11,845	234·5	50·5
30–39	5,493	1,987	7,480	339·4	22·0
40–49	1,099	127	1,226	459·3	0·3

[1] *Registrar General's Statistical Review . . . for 1964*, Part III, Commentary, p. 64.
[2] *Ibid.*, Table C52, p. 67.   [3] *Ibid*, p. 67.   [4] *Ibid*, p. 68.

within seven months of marriage) to the number of illegitimate births to unmarried women, and, by dividing the total by the number of unmarried women, provides an extra-marital conception rate for unmarried women.

The Registrar General points out that

it is only the fact that more than half of the unmarried women of child-bearing age are teenagers that produces the result that more than two-fifths of the births conceived extra-maritally by unmarried women were conceived by teenagers. It remains clear that extra-marital conception is not specifically a teenage problem; the probability that an unmarried woman will conceive in the course of a year is one in thirty-four if she is under 20, rises to a peak of one in fifteen if she is 20–24, falls to one in twenty if she is 25–29 and to one in forty-five if she is 30–39[1].

It is important to set the youthfulness of the mothers in our survey of affiliation orders in this context. In 1965, the Registrar General consolidated the illegitimacy rates for single, divorced and widowed women in the period 1955–1965 into a diagram, shown as Figure 3.

Figure 3 shows that the illegitimacy rate for unmarried women above the age of twenty turned downwards in the early 1960's, but, as the women under twenty constitute half the population of unmarried women, the continued increase in their illegitimacy rate must sustain the rate for the whole population.

The Registrar General has always provided information about the proportion of pre-maritally conceived maternities which have been legitimated by marriage before the birth. Figures for 1938 and 1967 are shown in Table 110.

TABLE 110[2] Illegitimate maternities and pre-maritally conceived legitimate maternities 1938 and 1967, England and Wales.

					1938	1967
Illegitimate maternities	..	..	..	..	27,440	70,456
Pre-maritally conceived	..	..	..	..	64,530	73,667
Total extra-marital conceptions	..	..	..	..	91,970	144,123
% of all maternities	..	..	..	..	14·4	17·3
% of extra-maritally conceived maternities legitimated by marriage before birth	..	..	..	..	70·2	51·1

A generation study of illegitimate children which the Registrar General published in 1965 has shown the extent to which different generations of children born illegitimate since 1926 have been legitimated under the Legitimacy Acts by the subsequent marriage of their natural parents or have been adopted. The results are set out in Table 111.

[1] *Ibid*, p. 67.
[2] *Registrar General's Statistical Review . . . for 1967*, Part II, Tables, Table VV.

FIGURE 3 Illegitimate births per 1,000 single, widowed and divorced women 1955–1965, England and Wales[1].

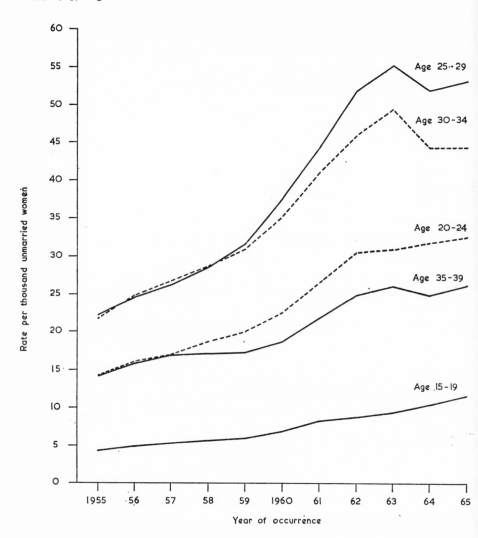

The table is confined to generations born since the passing in 1926 of the Legitimacy Act and of the Adoption of Children Act, and it demonstrates the result of this legislation. We quote at length the Registrar General's commentary on this illuminating table.

About 13 or 14 per cent of the generation born in 1927–1932 had become adopted or legitimated by their fourth birthday; legitimation was slightly more frequent for boys but there was little difference between adoption and legitimation for girls.

[1] *Registrar General's Statistical Review ... for 1965*, Part III, Commentary, p. 72.

TABLE III[1] **Proportion of children born illegitimate in England and Wales since 1926 who have been legitimated and adopted.**

| Generation born illegitimate in | Percentage of those surviving after 4 years who were: | | | | | | Average annual illegitimate births thousands |
| | Adopted | | Legitimated | | Still illegitimate | | |
	Boys	Girls	Boys	Girls	Boys	Girls	Total
1921–1926	0	0	0	0	100	100	36
1927–1932	5	7	8	7	87	86	29
1933–1939	10	14	9	8	81	78	26
1940–1945	20	14	6	6	74	80	43
1946–1949	22	23	5	5	73	73	45
1950–1954	21	22	6	6	73	72	33
1955–1959	23	23	8	8	69	69	35

Figures may not cast because of rounding.

Of the next generation examined—the illegitimate children born from 1933–1939—about 20 per cent had been adopted or legitimated by their fourth birthday and by then, 10 to 15 years after the passage of the two Acts, substantially more children were adopted than legitimated. It is interesting to note that a smaller proportion of boys than girls were adopted.

Because of all the social conditions of wartime the following generation of illegitimate children was very much larger; on average 43 thousand illegitimate births occurred each year between 1940 and 1945 compared with 26 thousand a year between 1933 and 1939. The number of re-registrations of births of legitimated persons did not increase, except for a temporary rise in 1939 and 1940, so that by their fourth birthday a smaller proportion of the generation of illegitimate children born from 1940–1945 had been re-registered as legitimated. A factor contributing to both the increase in the number of illegitimate births and the absence of an increase in the number of legitimations may have been that some of the children would have been born legitimate following the marriage of their parents, had it not been for wartime conditions which prevented either belated marriage before the birth of the child or marriage and legitimation after the birth.

On the other hand, during the war and immediate post-war years there was a very great increase in the number of adoption orders made. From 1931–1935 the annual average had been 4,500, whereas from 1946–1950 it was 17,600. It is very interesting to note that the proportion of illegitimate children still alive at their fourth birthday, who had been adopted, was more or less unchanged for girls. For boys, on the other hand, there was a material increase.

This change, from 10 per cent of the generation of boys born illegitimate in 1933–1939 having been adopted by their fourth birthday to 20

[1] *Registrar General's Statistical Review, ... for 1965*, Part III, Commentary, p. 84.

per cent of the generation of boys born illegitimate in 1940–1945 having been adopted by their fourth birthday is so striking that it is worth considering whether the increase consisted entirely of adoption by the boy's parent or by someone else.[1]

This is shown in Table 112.

TABLE 112[2] **Proportion of children born illegitimate in England and Wales 1933–1945, who were adopted by a parent or by another person.**

Generation born illegitimate in	Percentage of those surviving after 4 years who were adopted			
	By parent		By another person	
	Boys	Girls	Boys	Girls
1933–1939	0·9	0·9	9·2	12·6
1940–1945	3·8	3·2	15·9	10·6

The Registrar General's study was not carried beyond the generation born illegitimate in the period 1955–59 because the experience of the later generation was too limited to permit comparison with the earlier generations. The 1955–59 generation benefited from the Legitimacy Act 1959 and the proportion legitimated by their fourth birthdays was larger than in previous generations. But the full effect of the Act will not become apparent until the history of the post-1960 generation is known. Nevertheless, the rise in the number of re-registered births of legitimated persons from 6,506 in 1960, the first full year of the Act's operation, to 13,043 in 1967, is suggestive[3].

To the reduction of the population of illegitimate children which results from legitimation and adoption, there must be added an estimate of the numbers of dependant children under sixteen who, though bastards, are being brought up by their two unmarried parents in so-called stable illicit unions. In the course of attempting to estimate the likely effects of introducing irretrievable breakdown of marriage as a ground of divorce, the Law Commission calculated that "if the law were changed, about 180,000 living illegitimate children could be legitimated and that in each future year some 19,000 children who would otherwise be condemned to permanent illegitimacy might be born in wedlock or subsequently legitimated"[4]. The Law Commission's view that "there may be here a far more serious social problem than is generally realized"[5] is supported by Dr. Thompson's study of illegitimate births in Aberdeen in 1949–52. She found that only 49% were first births to single women. Of the remainder at least one-third were to women living in stable cohabitation with the father[6].

[1] *Ibid*, p. 85.   [2] *Ibid*.
[3] *Registrar General's Statistical Review . . . for 1967*, Part II, Tables, Table T3, p. 83.
[4] *Reform of the Grounds of Divorce: The Field of Choice*, Cmnd. 3123, 1966. The arithmetic and assumptions are explained in paras 34–36, pp. 18–19.   [5] *Ibid*.
[6] Barbara Thompson, "Social Study of Illegitimate Maternity", *British Journal of Preventive and Social Medicine*, Vol. 10, 1956.

Thus, "pure" illegitimacy exists quantitatively on a very much smaller scale than is suggested by the statistics of illegitimate births.

The Registrar General's figures leave many significant questions unanswered. Census data relate only to unmarried mothers who are heads of households and it is impossible to distinguish adequately between temporarily and permanently cohabiting couples. Some gaps in the national information were filled by earlier studies[1] promoted by, or drawing their material from such welfare agencies as the National Council for the Unmarried Mother and her child and the Church of England Moral Welfare Council. Although these organizations work on a national basis they deal exclusively with the self-selected group of mothers who use their facilities. In general, the small surveys, to which must be added the important work of Virginia Wimperis[2] in respect of such factors as the age and marital status have been confirmed by the Registrar General. All the studies pointed to a significant proportion of mothers living in stable unions with the fathers of their children. All, too, emphasized the likelihood that unsupported mothers and their children would experience severe poverty and that a high proportion would have to seek support from the National Assistance Board[3]. An affiliation order, on the other hand, provides maintenance for the child only and, until 1968, within a weekly maximum of fifty shillings.

The striking fact about affiliation has been the consistently small proportion, no more than 13%, of mothers who apply for a court order. The majority of applicants are successful but there are only some eight to nine thousand orders made annually. In our sample 55% of the orders were made by Petty Sessional Division Courts, 34% in the County Borough or Borough Courts and the remainder in Stipendiary Courts. All but 3% of the orders were being enforced in the court of their origin.

An application must be made within strict time limits. The woman may apply before the child is born; in our survey only 6% did so. She may come at any time during the twelve months after the child is born[4]. If she can prove—as 40% of all complainants did—that the father has paid money for the child's maintenance during those months, she may apply up to several years after the birth. 24% of all orders were made more than a year after the birth of the child. If the father was abroad at the time of the birth or

---

[1] These include: C. Joy, *Illegitimate Children and their Parents; a Survey of Casework for 1952*, (Moral Welfare, 1954); National Council for the Unmarried Mother and her Child, *Survey*, 1954; Church of England Moral Welfare Council, *Survey*, 1954; J. Spence, *A Thousand Families in Newcastle-upon-Tyne* (1954); C. Greenland, "Unmarried Parenthood: Ecological Aspects", *Lancet*, 19th January 1957.

[2] *The Unmarried Mother and her Child* (1960) which contains a survey of illegitimacy in "Midboro" carried out in 1949.

[3] The study of Professor Illsley and Dr. Gill emphasizes that the extension of illegitimate births to girls in the upper social class has been a new element in the rise of the rate in the 1960s.

[4] 76% of all orders were made within a year of birth. 72% of all orders were made within six weeks of the complaint. About four-fifths of all complaints were brought within a year of the birth.

during the following first year, the mother may apply during the twelve months after his return. Proof of the payment of maintenance has to be given in writing or on oath at the time of the application. The summons on the father must be made in the area where the mother is living. This calls upon him to appear at the hearing of the case but if he is known to have received the summons and does not appear, the case may still be heard but it will often be adjourned to enable him to attend. If it is thought that notification may prove impossible, the case will be heard in his absence. This occurred in 10% of all hearings for which information was known. A further 10% of defendants wrote to the court but did not appear at the hearing.

It is essential in every case that the mother give evidence which must be corroborated. The father himself can be called as a witness by the mother. Warrants may be issued to compel others to attend as witnesses. The necessity of corroboration cannot be dispensed with even when the father appears and admits paternity[1].

Table 113 shows the period between the making of the complaint and the court hearing by the date of the order.

TABLE 113   **Period between complaint and court hearing for affiliation orders live on 1st January 1966.**

Date of order	Under 6 weeks	6–8 weeks	8–12 weeks	Over 12 weeks
	cumulative percentages			
(a) England and Wales				
Pre-1960	81	90	95	100
1960–1963	72	84	95	100
1964–1965	62	72	85	100
(b) Northern England and Wales				
Pre-1960	85	93	98	100
1960–1963	68	84	94	100
1964–1965	74	83	93	100
(c) Southern England				
Pre-1960	79	88	94	100
1960–1963	75	84	85	100
1964–1965	51	62	79	100

The delay between the complaint and the hearing has increased for the most recent orders, and it is greater in the south than in the north of the country.

The majority of defendants were not represented. Only one per cent of them obtained legal aid. On the other hand, two-thirds of the complainants were legally represented and roughly one quarter had obtained legal aid.

The number of orders in our sample, the date they were made and their amounts are shown in Table 115.

---

[1] This was the case with three-quarters of the defendants in the sample.

TABLE 114 Representation of the parties at the hearing.

Defendant	Complainant			
	In person	Solicitor	Legally aided representation	Total
In person	131	94	54	279
Solicitor	11	64	26	101
Legally aided representation ..			5	5
No appearance	12	22	13	47
Letter only	19	18	13	50
Total	173	198	111	482

TABLE 115 Distribution of orders in the sample by date the order was first made and the amount of the order.

Date order first made		Amount ordered					Total	
		Less than 15s.	15s. but less than 25s.	25s. less than 35s.	35s. less than 50s.	50s.	No.	%
Before 1961 ..	No.	50	149	56	7	—	262	48
	C.T. %	19	76	97	100	100		
1961–1963 ..	No.	6	26	49	35	15	131	24
	C.T. %	5	24	62	89	100		
1964–1965 ..	No.	7	44	41	53	12	157	28
	C.T. %	4	32	59	92	100		
Total sample	No.	63	218	146	95	28	550	100
	C.T. %	11	51	78	95	100		

More than three-quarters of the orders made before 1961, constituting nearly half the sample, were for less than twenty-five shillings a week. In the case of orders made after 1961, the proportion of men paying less than twenty-five shillings fell to between a quarter and a third. As with the matrimonial orders, the statutory maximum which had been raised to fifty shillings in 1960 was hardly ever reached. Only one such order had been made before 1961 although 11% of the orders made from 1961 to 1963 and 8% of those made in 1964 and 1965 were for the maximum amount.

The putative father may also be made to pay the expenses incidental to the birth of the child. One quarter of the defendants in proceedings before 1961 were ordered to make such payments; for orders made after 1961 the proportion had halved. One third of the defendants had provided voluntary payments during the pregnancy.

One of the chief characteristics of the men required to pay under affiliation orders live on 1st January 1966, was their low earning power. 92% of them had earnings of less than £16 a week. In this respect, they were in the same situation as 87% of husbands under an obligation to pay maintenance to their

[1] See Chapter 5, Table 21.

TABLE 116   Earnings disclosed by putative fathers ordered to make payments for children in 1964 and 1965.

Earnings	Percentage of putative fathers
Less than £10.. ..	30
£10 but less than £14	50
£14 but less than £18	9
£18 and over	11

wives under magistrates' orders at the same date[1]. A detailed analysis of the earnings admitted to the court by the 157 defendants against whom orders were made in 1964 and 1965 is shown in Table 116.

Table 117 combines, for the ninety-four orders made in 1964 and 1965 for which the necessary information was available, the data shown in Tables 115 and 116.

TABLE 117   Relationship between amounts awarded on affiliation orders made in 1964 and 1965 and the income of the defendants.

Income of father per week	Under 5s.	5s. to 14s.	15s. to 24s.	25s. to 34s.	35s. to 44s.	45s. to 49s.	50s.	Total	C.T.	C.T. %
Under £5 ..	—	—	—	—	—	—	—	—	—	—
£5 but under £8 ..	1	1	3	3	2	2	—	12	12	13
£8 but under £10	—	—	8	4	3	1	—	16	28	30
£10 but under £12	—	—	4	9	12	1	—	26	54	57
£12 but under £14	—	—	4	5	6	—	3	18	72	80
£14 but under £16	—	2	2	3	4	—	—	11	83	88
£16 but under £18	—	—	1	—	—	—	—	1	84	89
£18 but under £20	—	—	—	—	2	—	1	3	87	93
£20 but under £25	—	—	—	1	1	2	3	7	94	100
Total	1	3	22	25	30	6	7	94		
C.T. %	1	4	28	54	86	93	100			

Rather more than half the orders made were for amounts of less than thirty-four shillings and were payable by men earning less than £12 a week, an income only two-thirds of the average earnings of manual workers in 1965.

The variation order procedure is as little used to adjust the amounts of affiliation as of matrimonial[1] orders. The experience of our sample orders is shown in Table 118.

Only 13% of the orders in the sample had been varied. 6% had been increased and 7% reduced in amount. 70% of the variations were for amounts of less than fifteen shillings. Ten (14%) of the seventy variation orders had been varied more than once.

[1] See Chapter 6, pp. 83–7.

TABLE 118 **Complaints for variation of affiliation orders live on 1st January 1966, by amount of variation and date of the original order.**

Date of order	Under 5s.	5s. to 14s.	15s. to 24s.	25s. to 34s.	35s. to 44s.	Orders varied	Orders not varied	Total	% varied
				Amount by which order was varied					
Pre-1955 ..	2	14	3	—	—	19	90	109	17
1955–59 ..	3	12	—	—	—	15	103	118	13
1960–61 ..	—	4	3	2	—	9	62	71	13
1962–63 ..	—	10	6	—	—	16	81	97	16
1964–65 ..	—	4	6	1	—	11	144	155	7
Total	5	44	18	2	—	70	480	550	13

The orders in the sample were examined to discover what proportion were being satisfied regularly in 1965. Irregular payment was defined as occurring if, on one occasion during 1965, payment lapsed for at least four weeks. The results are set out in Table 119.

Table 119 **Proportion of orders being paid irregularly during 1965.**

Regularity of payment	Under 5s.	5s. to 14s.	15s. to 24s.	25s. to 34s.	35s. to 44s.	45s. to 49s.	50s.	Total[2]	%
			Amount payable when order was made						
Orders made before 1961									
Regular ..	2	30	82	34	5	—	—	153	63
Irregular ..	0	14	57	18	1	—	—	90	37
Total	2	44	139	52	6	—	—	243	100
Orders made 1961–1965									
Regular ..	1	4	39	40	39	11	12	146	53
Irregular ..	1	6	29	46	30	5	14	131	47
Total	2	10	68	86	69	16	26	277	100

The incidence of irregular payments increased from rather more than a third of all orders made before 1961 to more than one half of those made after 1961. Nearly all the pre-1961 orders were for amounts of under thirty-five shillings but 40% of the 1961/65 orders were for more than that amount. Of these, 55% were paid regularly.

Table 120 shows that some 29% (157) of all orders live on 1st January, 1966, were in arrears for more than £20.

Table 121 shows that about one-third of all orders are in arrears irrespective of the amount of the order.

Table 122 shows the length of time between the making of the order and the first arrears hearing for an amount of more than £20 for the orders tabulated in Table 120[1].

---

[1] The necessary information was available only for 146 of the 157 orders shown in Table 120.
[2] Of the 262 orders made before 1961, the necessary information was available for only 243; similarly, of the 288 orders made from 1961 to 1965, only 277 appear in this table.

TABLE 120   Live affiliation orders in arrears for more than £20 on 1st January 1966.

Amount of arrears	Number of orders for			
	Less than 25s.	25s. to 34s.	35s. to 44s.	45s. to 50s.
Less than £40	22	7	3	3
£40 but less than £100	29	24	12	6
£100 but less than £150	3	2	3	0
£150 but less than £200	22	6	2	4
£200 to £500	3	5	—	1
Total	79	44	20	14

TABLE 121 Proportion of orders for different amounts in arrears on 1st January 1966.

Amount of order	in arrears
Less than 25s.	27
25s. but less than 35s.	30
35s. but less than 45s.	26
45s. to 50s.	37

The table shows a remarkable change in the speed at which payments under orders fall into arrears. In the case of orders made before 1961, some two-thirds of first arrears hearings took place more than two years after the orders had been made. For orders made after 1961, that situation has been reversed and nearly three-quarters of the arrears hearings occur before the orders are two years old. In order to test the possibility that there might be significant differences between single and married defendants in respect of the rate at which arrears accumulate, the data in Table 122 are analysed in Table 123 in accordance with the marital status of the 125 defendants for whom the necessary information was available.

TABLE 122   Length of time between the making of the order and the first arrears hearing for an amount of more than £20, all orders live on 1st January 1966 and in arrears, by date of hearing.

Date of hearing	Length of time between making the order and the first arrears hearing							
	Under 6 months	6 months but under 1 year	1 year but under 2 years	2 years but under 3 years	3 years but under 5 years	5 years but under 9 years	Over 9 years	Total
Before 1961								
Orders ..	4	7	14	9	13	19	11	77
C.T. % ..	5	14	33	44	61	86	100	
1961–1965								
Orders ..	19	14	17	12	7	—	—	69
C.T. % ..	28	48	73	90	100			

TABLE 123 Length of time between the making of the order and the first arrears hearing for an amount of more than £20, by marital status of defendants, all orders live on 1st January 1966 and in arrears.

Defendants		Total Number	Under 6 months	6 months but under 1 year	1 year but under 2 years	2 years but under 3 years	3 years but under 5 years	5 years but under 9 years	over 9 years
Single	..	78							
C.T. %	..		15	30	51	68	80	92	100
Married	..	47							
C.T. %	..		21	28	49	66	85	96	100

Clearly, the status of the defendant does not influence the rate at which arrears accumulate. Further, a detailed analysis of the amounts of arrears disclosed no tendency for married defendants to be owing larger debts than single defendants.

Arrears had been remitted in 22% of the orders in arrears. For two-fifths of the orders the amount remitted was less than £40, and for four-fifths of the orders it was less than £100.

Attachment of earnings orders[1] had been made in respect of 10% of the orders in the sample, and one-fifth of these were still in force on 1st January 1966. Only one quarter of the attachment orders were successful in clearing the arrears. The attachment orders were short-lived; 4% of them lasted for more than two years, 22% lasted for more than one year, rather more than one-third lasted longer than six months, and about one half survived for six months. In one case, the attachment order was discharged because the defendant was sacked from his job. With this single exception, every other order was discharged because the man had left his employment.

The number of committal orders increased during the early 1960s. Suspended committal orders were issued before 1959 for 12% of the orders, after 1959 the proportion had dropped slightly to 10%. According to the court records, only 3% of the defendants in the sample actually went to prison.

Court records provided limited information about the age and status of parties to affiliation proceedings. They stated the age of both complainant and defendant in only 18% of the instances. Table 124 compares their ages for this small proportion of the sample. There are no grounds, though, for thinking that these data are unrepresentative.

The age distribution of the complainants is in line with the Registrar General's figures. Twenty per cent had not reached their eighteenth birthday, nearly half are under twenty and 81% are under twenty-five. The corresponding proportions for the defendants show that they tend to be significantly older than their consorts. 11% had not reached their eighteenth birthday,

[1] Affiliation orders were included in the special study of attachment of earnings orders reported in Chapter 7, p. 102.

TABLE 124 Age of complainants and defendants when the order was made.

Age of defendant at the time of the order	Under 16	16 18	18 20	20 25	25 but under 30	30 35	35 40	40 and over	Total	C.T. %
16 but under 18	5	6	—	—	—	—	—	—	11	11
18 but under 20	—	5	12	2	—	—	—	—	19	30
20 but under 25	—	3	7	20	1	2	—	—	33	62
25 but under 30	—	—	4	14	2	—	—	—	20	82
30 but under 35	—	1	1	1	3	2	—	—	8	90
35 but under 40	—	—	—	—	—	1	2	—	3	93
40 and over ..	—	—	1	—	4	—	—	2	7	100
Total	5	15	25	37	10	5	2	2	101	
C.T. %	5	20	45	81	91	96	98	100		

Age of complainant at the time of the order spans the columns from "16 18" through "40 and over".

30% were under twenty and 62% were under twenty-five. There were more than twice as many men as women over twenty-five.

Table 125 shows the place of residence of complainants at the time when they applied to the court.

The majority of complainants were living at home at the time when the affiliation order was made as Table 125 shows.

TABLE 125 Place of residence of complainant at time of making the affiliation order.

Place of residence	Complainants No.	%
Parental home	250	63
Hostel	3	1
Private accommodation	114	29
With another man	7	2
Elsewhere	22	5
Total	396[1]	100

We do not know how many of the large number of complainants who were living at home when they applied to the court had been living elsewhere but had returned when they became pregnant. But the table suggests that parental pressure may result in an application for an affiliation order. Even so, one-third of the applicants were living away from home when they obtained their orders.

Information showing where more than half the complainants had their babies is set out in Table 126.

When applying for an order the mother must prove that she was a "single woman" at the time of her child's birth. All unmarried women, spinsters or widows or divorcees, fall within this category. To these groups must be added married women who are living apart from their husbands and have

[1] The total number in the sample for whom this information was available.

TABLE 126 Place of birth of complainants' babies.

Confinement	No. of babies	%
N.H. Hospital	246	77
Private Hospital	6	2
Hostel or Unmarried Mothers' Home	17	5
Maternal parents' home	29	9
Elsewhere	20	7
Total	318	100

forfeited their right to be maintained by them. Table 127 shows the status of complainants and defendants when the order was made.

TABLE 127 Status of complainants and defendants when the order was made.

Defendant	Single	Complainant Separated	Divorced	Total	%
Single	232	25	13	270	64
Married	120	21	11	152	36
Total	352	46	24	452	
%	83	11	6		100

More than one-third of the defendants were married. Further information disclosed that these ninety-seven defendants had fathered 213 children upon their wives. The Registrar General found that nearly one-third of the mothers of illegitimate children were married. On our survey the proportion was 11%, significantly smaller than the national figure.

Under section 3 of the Legitimacy Act 1959, a father may apply for an order for custody and access under the Guardianship of Infants Acts. In the whole of our sample, only one such application had been made and it was successful.

There was information to show that around one-fifth of the couples had cohabited before the application for an order. The differing periods are set out in Table 128. 4% of all complainants had an order for more than one child.

This table is drawn from court records and must therefore provide a minimum measure of the amount of cohabitation even allowing for the likelihood that casual affairs might have been interpreted as "cohabitation" in the period under six months. That nearly half the cohabitations had survived for more than three years is in line with the findings of other surveys. The collapse of those of longer durations must be reckoned as *de facto* family breakdowns. As is to be expected, only 1% of the couples who had been through the court in the course of affiliation proceedings had actually married each other by 1st January 1966. But in 11% of the instances the complainant had married another man, and in a quarter the defendant had married a different woman.

TABLE 128 Period of cohabitation of complainant and defendant before the application for an affiliation order.

Under 3 months	5
3 months but under 6 months	9
6 months but under 1 year..	15
1 year but under 2 years	16
2 years but under 3 years	11
3 years but under 4 years	12
4 years but under 6 years	11
6 years but under 8 years	7
8 years but under 12 years	15
12 years and over	4
Total orders	105

In 2% of the cases in the sample, the National Assistance Board exercised its right under section 44(2) of the National Assistance Act 1948, to recover payments from the putative father. Table 129 shows the proportion of mothers who were receiving national assistance when their orders were made.

TABLE 129 Proportion of mothers receiving national assistance at the time of applying for an affiliation order.

Orders made	Percentage of complainants receiving national assistance
Before 1960 ..	27
1960–1963 ..	43
1964–1965 ..	50

One quarter of the complainants in 1965 had authorized payments to be made direct to the National Assistance Board from which they were receiving regular assistance.

Table 130 shows that all but a handful of mothers had kept their babies.

There have been persistent criticisms of the affiliation procedure in recent years and its defects have often been cited as a part explanation of the small proportion of mothers who seek orders from the courts. The Chairman of the Law Commission, Sir Leslie Scarman, has observed that

It is a pity that affiliation proceedings carry with them the atmosphere of crime and the criminal courts. The sooner they take their place within a family court jurisdiction the better[1].

The 13% of mothers who come to the magistrates' courts may seem a very small proportion of the total number of women bearing illegitimate children. But the population at risk of complaining to the courts is smaller than the total of such mothers because it is necessary to deduct those living in stable illicit unions, those whose children are legitimated or adopted and those with

[1] Address to the Annual Conference of the National Council for the Unmarried Mother and her Child, November 1968, p. 7–8.

TABLE 130 **Parties having custody of children in respect of whom affiliation orders had been made, all orders live on 1st January 1966.**

Parties having custody of children	No. of children	%
Complainant	481	93
Adopted by mother	8	2
Adopted by another person	5	1
Local authority	16	3
Maternal grandmother	6	1
Total	516	100

private agreements. Those using the courts probably constitute between one-fifth and one-quarter of the actual population at risk. In 1965 the National Assistance Board was supporting some 36,000 mothers of illegitimate children. Of these, 9,000 or one quarter, had court orders and a further 7,000 had out-of-court arrangements. This left the majority of 20,000 mothers with neither a court order nor a private arrangement.[1] It seems reasonable to hazard the explanation that these mothers either cannot or will not complain to the court. From their point of view they will receive the same assistance whether or not they establish a legal claim against the father. It is hard for a wife to resist the suggestion of the social security authorities that she seek a maintenance order against the husband who has deserted her but the mother of an illegitimate child is in a stronger position. If she has been promiscuous, she may be unable to establish a claim. On the other hand, if she dislikes the prospect of subjecting herself and her lover to unpleasant proceedings in a criminal atmosphere, she can easily decline to complain. It is all the more likely that she will act in this way if she hopes to establish a permanent relationship with the father of her child.

[1] Information supplied by the Department of Health and Social Security to the Graham Hall Committee on Statutory Maintenance Limits and printed in its Report (Cmnd. 3587, 1968), Table 17(*a*), p. 92.

CHAPTER 12

Towards a Family Court

Conclusions from the research

COURT RECORDS

Good records are important in the administration of justice, and particularly so in this jurisdiction when the parties may resort to the court on several occasions. We found that in a few courts the records were excellent; but in many, they were defective. Court records vary in type and quality from court to court in a manner not compatible with the proper administration of justice. One example will suffice. Chapter 5[1] showed that the proportion of court records which contained no information about defendants' incomes ranged from one-third in the case of Married Women and Children orders to 45% in the case of Married Women Only orders. This matrimonial jurisdiction requires justices to make maintenance orders which may subsequently be varied by another court or by the same court with different justices sitting on the Bench. Clearly, the court cannot perform its duties unless it can rely upon receiving both accurate information about the resources and responsibilities of complainants and defendants and a reliable record of the financial evidence upon which previous decisions were made. The Magistrates' Association holds that

> lay justices are good at assessing the amount that a person can reasonably be required to pay. Justices commonly have a much greater knowledge of wage rates, overtime and so on and of rent and other outgoings than are possessed by, say, a county court judge[2].

Even if we were to agree that magistrates are good at making such an assessment based on the knowledge of earnings for particular trades, their local knowledge provides no more than a background against which to assess a particular defendant's earnings and capacity to pay maintenance. Some, but

[1] p. 69.
[2] *Annual Report*, 1968–69, p. 50.

not all, magistrates insist that the defendant produce certified returns of recent earnings. The Graham Hall Committee thought that

> the defect of the existing system is that the parties are not put sufficiently on notice before the hearing as to the matters about which the court will need to be informed. This could readily be remedied by sending each party, when the summons is issued, a questionnaire about their resources and liabilities. This might either be in a form which could be completed by them and handed to the court, or it could require them to have available evidence of the matters specified insofar as they were applicable. In either case the information on which the court bases its decision would be much more reliable than that provided at present. Much of the evidence we received from individual women suggested that defendants did not disclose all their earnings or sources of income. We were also informed that the courts were often forced to rely on their knowledge of the average wages of a particular trade in the locality. When evidence was produced it might relate to only one week's earnings which would often not be a typical amount. The defendant might have transferred property to a mistress or be being helped by her separate earnings. . . . We are of the opinion that a standard questionnaire could readily be devised on these lines and we accordingly recommend that such a questionnaire should be prepared and that its issue to both parties in domestic proceedings should be prescribed. We envisage that there will be some cases where the defendant may be deliberately seeking to misrepresent his resources. . . .
>
> Much of the value of the procedure we have recommended in the preceding paragraph would be lost if the information obtained by it were not preserved in a readily accessible way for reference in subsequent proceedings . . . and we recommend that, at the very least, it should be mandatory that the information obtained about the resources and liabilities of the parties should be clearly recorded in a standard form and kept with the order together with any other relevant information such as the entering by the defendant of an undertaking to make some payment[1].

Clearly, the introduction of some such procedure, as was recommended by the Graham Hall Committee, is one indispensable basis for the proper administration of the summary matrimonial jurisdiction. It is very encouraging that the Magistrates' Association noted the Committee's recommendation that "full information be established about the parties' resources and commitments and that this should be recorded in a standard form and be available for any subsequent hearings", and said that "we think this is an excellent recommendation and hope that it will be carried out"[2]. The Payne Committee

[1] Cmnd. 3587 (1968), paras 222 and 223.   [2] *Supra.*

made the same recommendation of "a prescribed form of questionnaire to ensure consistent and thorough examination of means in all magistrates' courts whenever it is necessary to enquire into a defaulter's resources, whatever the nature of his debts . . . "[1] Some courts have devised and use admirably constructed questionnaires. We have included one example as Appendix D. The way now seems open for the adoption of a standardized and systematic method of securing and recording reliable information about the resources of complainants and defendants. We also draw attention to the related recommendation of the Graham Hall Committee that magistrates should add to this information a brief statement of the reasons which led them to fix the amount of maintenance in order to assist any later determination affecting the amount to be paid by the defendant.

The advantages of good record-keeping, as we have indicated, go far beyond a better informed determination of maintenance. We quote at length the reasons advanced by the Justices' Clerk at Leicester to justify his use of the detailed questionnaire which we have printed as Appendix D. They explain why the time spent by court staff in completing it may result in advantage to the parties, in a better administration of justice and in a more economical use of the court's time. The original of the present form was produced "with the following ideas in mind".

(*a*) It would enable the magistrates, to whom the application for the summons was to be made, quickly to see from the particular allegations made by the complainant, when supplemented by questions, the chance of reconciliation.

(*b*) At the time the form was originated there was no Legal Aid available to the parties, and in the majority of cases one of the parties was not represented, and in many others neither. The Clerk, who had the duty under section 6 of the above Act [Summary Procedure (Domestic Proceedings) Act 1937, now section 61, Magistrates' Courts Act 1952] to assist the parties, had a basis upon which to elucidate, in questioning the parties, their case.

(*c*) The preliminary interviews also elicit the material facts of the marriage (and it is surprising how many do not know accurately the date of the marriage) and the names and the precise dates of birth of the children, and if there is uncertainty it can be clarified by requests for certificates to be produced at the hearing. The existence of this part of the record simplifies note-taking and saves time in court.

Nowadays when the parties are represented, the Clerk taking notes uses the form only for the purpose of checking the names and dates. When the form contains the other information as to occupation, employer and so on it is useful when the parties in court do not so

[1] Cmnd. 3909 (1969) para 1273.

easily remember these details, and gives a standard means enquiry by the court.

The form, it is true, takes the time of a senior clerk to prepare, but as will be seen below, a very considerable amount of court time is saved, and, more importantly, attempts at reconciliation are made at the earliest and best point. When agreed to by the complainant, the Probation Service attempts to effect this.

The procedure in detail is:

(a) The applicant calls at the office (even when a solicitor has been instructed it is unusual for the applicant to be accompanied by anyone from his office). Then an appointment is made for sometime on an afternoon during that week for the particulars to be taken on a form by a senior clerk.

(b) Each afternoon with the exception of Monday, there are three or four such appointments. On completion of the particulars the complainant is asked to attend before the magistrate sitting at 2.30 p.m. on the following Monday in the Magistrates' Room. The magistrate is attended by the Clerk or the Deputy Clerk and a Probation Officer.

(c) The Clerk with the assistance of the form which has been completed elicits from the applicant her grievances. The magistrate then, knowing the age of the parties, the length of the marriage and their family circumstances discusses with the applicant the question of reconciliation. If the applicant is willing the matter is referred to the Probation Service and the applicant is asked to wait and is interviewed later by the Probation Officer to set on foot arrangements for reconciliation. If the applicant insists on proceeding and the magistrate is satisfied that there are grounds on which to issue a summons a summons is issued either in the terms requested by a Solicitor, if one has been instructed, or upon grounds which appear to be open to the complainant. A date is fixed for the hearing and a summons is issued.

The hearings at the Domestic Proceedings Court also consider the question of reconciliation where there appears to be a reasonable chance of it. There is a Probation Officer present at each such court for the purpose of speaking to such parties if they wish for immediate advice or on an adjournment making arrangements for meetings to be held between the parties and the Probation Officer.

In all attempts at reconciliation by the Probation Service a Probation Officer is supplied with a copy of the form which is attached, containing the particulars relating to the case and has thus a good idea before dealing with it of the difficulties between the parties and the family background.

The system is not inflexible and from time to time there are cases where the issue of a summons is a matter of urgency. The circumstances are considered by the Clerk and if for any reason, such as the intention of the proposed defendant to go away without leaving an address or the safety of the wife appears to require it particulars are taken forthwith and the application placed before a magistrate the next morning for the immediate issue of a summons.

The main advantage of the system and one of the reasons for its adoption is the prospect of early intervention by a Probation Officer to make an attempt at reconciliation. This can be done before the husband has been affronted by the receipt of a summons and without disturbing further the relationship between husband and wife as happens after allegations have been made in open court. The advantages which flow from the formality imposed on the application for a summons are that wives who have hastily rushed to the Magistrates' Clerks' Office for a summons have time to reflect before attending at the appointment and a number of these are not heard of again. After attending at the appointment a further few do not attend to make application to the magistrate. The result of this is that the summonses which are issued almost all relate to intractable matrimonial disputes and thus the list is not cluttered up with insubstantial cases or with cases where the wife having issued a summons in hot blood feels she is bound to go on with it because her husband has had a summons.

In 1966 because of staff shortages and heavily rising court work it was decided to ask Solicitors, who in almost every case represented the complainant on Legal Aid, to complete the form for the Court. Apart from the fact that this was bitterly received and very poorly performed when done it had an interesting effect on the figures (of reconciliations). Although there were not less applications in 1966 . . . (fewer were) referred to the Probation Service for reconciliation and that the willingness of complainants to attempt reconciliation appeared to have decreased, there was further a sharp rise in the number of summonses issued and the completion of the form was again undertaken by a senior clerk in the Clerk's Office. The loss of correct information in court was badly felt. The Justices feel that the system is of great value to them in carrying out their duties and the staff agrees that the time spent in the office is adequately compensated by the saving of time in Domestic proceedings Courts. It is felt though that it is the real benefit to the parties which is the main object of the exercise.

We think that the experiences of this court provide compelling reasons for the mandatory introduction of standardized questionnaires and records, and we do not believe that there are any acceptable grounds for relieving small courts of the obligation. It is true that more than 80% of Justices'

Clerks have fewer than ten assistants, and many have several courts sitting every day. Nevertheless, courts ought to be given staff in the numbers necessary to carry out an essential feature of the due administration of justice.

NATIONAL STATISTICS

Good court records will also make possible the publication of meaningful, national statistics. In Chapter 2, we explained how the only statistical data relating to the matrimonial jurisdiction of magistrates' courts are obtained, and are published by the Home Office as Table VI of the annual *Criminal Statistics*. We also gave our reasons for thinking that even these limited statistics are unreliable and misleading; indeed it is not overstating the case to say that they cannot be relied upon save as a rough index of the annual volume of work. The Adams Committee gave detailed attention to methods of improving the present statistics, and concluded that

> the only real solution which will lead to detailed, useful and accurate statistics becoming available is standardisation of procedure and forms of application and orders, and inauguration, where they do not exist, of systems, by way of record cards or otherwise, of recording the information required for statistics, which although probably available among the case papers, is not at present formally recorded[1].

We have printed the Adams Committee's recommendation about the form and content of improved statistics of summary matrimonial proceedings as Appendix C, and we think that their implementation would meet all reasonable criticisms of the present statistics. The Adams Committee also followed the Perks Committee in recommending that publication of this material should be transferred from the *Criminal Statistics* to the *Civil Judicial Statistics*. If this were done, the police could be relieved of burdensome involvement in the collection of these statistics, which could be compiled centrally, in the same way as the divorce statistics are handled by the County Courts Branch of the Lord Chancellor's Department.

The Adams Committee drew attention to the demand for better statistics from "those concerned in welfare and sociological work"[2]. The provision of better statistics will promote a further, though perhaps related object. Justice will be better administered if magistrates sitting to hear matrimonial cases are aware both of the results of their decisions and of the characteristics of the parties who appear before them. In criminal procedure, it is now firmly established that sentencers must be supplied with "more information and information of a new type" because "sentencing is, in a sense, an emergent

[1] Cmnd. 3684 (1968), para 98.
[2] *Ibid*, para 100.

branch of the law . . . "[1] There is a similar need to provide magistrates in "domestic courts" with an understanding of the social setting and implications of their familial jurisdiction.

Ignorance of the working and effects of this (or of any) jurisdiction is damaging if only because a democratic society should keep its legal institutions under constant scrutiny. Responsible scrutiny requires full information, and it is not creditable that the ways in which family law bears upon many citizens should be unknown. Moreover, such ignorance may mislead lawyers and those responsible for the administration of justice. One striking though relatively minor example may be cited. We showed in Chapter 4[2] that all commentators, from the Law Commission to writers of text-books on family law, have readily assumed that magistrates' courts observe the rulings of the High Court, stretching now over seventy years, that non-cohabitation clauses (separation orders) should rarely be ordered. Our research demonstrates the falsity of the assumption. In no fewer than 40% of cases in 1964 and 1965, where orders for maintenance were awarded, a non-cohabitation clause was added.

SEPARATION ORDERS

The Magistrates' Association recently recommended that the power to make a non-cohabitation order should be abolished. It did so on the ground that the order "has come to be an embarrassment, for it has the effect of making it more difficult for parties who want to become reconciled, and it prevents a desertion from running which may be unfortunate if a divorce [on the grounds of desertion] is sought at a later date"[3].

We agree, but for very different reasons. We think that the point about a separation order preventing desertion from running will be of little importance after 1st January 1971 when the Divorce Reform Act 1969 comes into force and separation itself will then provide a presumption that the marriage has irretrievably broken down and so result in divorce[4]. So far as reconciliation is concerned, we do not believe that parties who have gone through the forensic mill are likely to become reconciled, but if that is their wish, the order of the court is hardly likely to provide a stumbling block.

The raison d'etre for the separation order has long since disappeared. An order that the spouses should live separate and apart is in most cases superfluous: the wife applies for maintenance firstly because she has become

---

[1] *Report of the Interdepartmental Committee on the Business of the Criminal Courts* (the Streatfeild Committee), Cmnd. 1289 (1961) paras 295 and 299. The social enquiry report has almost become the order of the day, and in cases where loss of liberty is involved almost a statutory requirement: see section 57, Criminal Justice Act 1967.

[2] pp. 59 *et seq.* See also Colin Gibson, "The Separation Order: a study in textbook law and court practice", *Modern Law Review*, Vol. 33, p. 63.

[3] Annual Report, 1968–1969, p. 48.

[4] In any event, we think that most separation orders are made inadvertently and this can be expunged from the record on application.

separated from her husband. In rare cases she may have reason to fear moles-
tation from her husband. The Magistrates' Association propose that these
cases can be adequately dealt with by binding the man over to keep the peace.
We are disposed to think that if a wife needs protection, she should go either
to the County Court or to the High Court for an injunction, breach of which
can be enforced, if necessary, by the civic process of committal. It would be
a retrograde step to apply a sanction of the criminal law to matrimonial
disputes when every proposal for reform is designed to detach the matrimonial jurisdiction from its criminal law encapsulation.

AFFILIATION

One of the major criticisms of the jurisdiction of magistrates' courts to award
maintenance to a mother of her illegitimate child against the putative father
is its lingering association with its origin in the criminal law. Affiliation
proceedings are treated by magistrates in much the same manner as they
handle maintenance applications. Since paternity is a crucial issue in affiliation, there is some value in the higher burden of proof in criminal cases, but
there is surely no point in continuing to insist on corroboration of an admis-
sion of paternity by the respondent.

As part of the attempt to mitigate the stigma of bastardy, it is desirable to
equate the maintenance of legitimate with illegitimate children. Every child
born out of wedlock should be regarded as potentially fatherless and treated
by the law on the same footing as children who become fatherless as a result
of the separation of their parents. Parental irresponsibility (if such it be),
whether it is displayed in or out of marriage, should carry no different legal
consequences for blameless children. Fatherless families have difficulties
enough without the addition of legal burdens.

The most noticeable imprint of the criminal law on affiliation is in the
appellate process. Appeals from magistrates' courts lie to Quarter Sessions
and thereafter to the Divisional Court of the Queen's Bench Division,
which can receive appeals direct from magistrates only on points of law by
way of case stated. The right to appeal, which includes a re-hearing before
Quarter Sessions, replicates the appeal process for criminal cases heard by
magistrates. Paradoxically, this system has one advantage over the matrimonial jurisdiction. Since the hearing before Quarter Sessions involves a
recital of the evidence, the existence of only a partial record of the proceedings
before the magistrates (usually a note by the Justices' Clerk) is unimportant.
Thus, justice can be more perfectly administered to the parties. While we wish
to see the end of appeals in affiliation proceedings to the higher criminal
courts, we do not want to lose the advantage of a more effective appellate
process. This points to a revision of the system of appeals in matrimonial
cases from magistrates' courts.

APPEALS FROM MAGISTRATES IN MATRIMONIAL CASES

We have not conducted an investigation of the appeals which come from magistrates to the Divisional Court of the Probate, Divorce and Admiralty Division. But we have been aware of the unsatisfactory nature of the appellate procedure. We were fortified in our impressionistic view by a vigorous plea for reform in this area by Sir Jocelyn Simon, the President of the Divorce Division of the High Court, in a recent public lecture[1].

Much of the problem stems from inadequate transcription of the evidence given before the magistrates. The judges of the Divisional Court find the recorded evidence in the form of a handwritten note by the Justices' Clerk so deficient that the appellate process is constantly frustrated. The Civil Judicial Statistics show that only a tiny proportion of the appeals are successful and a high proportion of them are ordered to be re-tried by the magistrates. In the result, a wealth of juristic learning is fashioned on appeals[2] that cry out simply for a review of the magistrates' findings of fact. The appeal court thus takes on an air of unreality that finds no parallel in any other jurisdiction.

In the absence of an improvement in court records within the foreseeable future, we would urge an appeal by way of re-hearing to a County Court judge sitting with two assessors[3], with an appeal on a point of law to the Divisional Court of the newly created Family Division of the High Court. Even if magistrates' courts were ever to be in a position to provide a transcript of the evidence given before the justices, there would be good reason to retain the appeal to the County Court judge with two lay assessors although it would be unnecessary to provide that the appeal should be by way of a re-hearing of the evidence.

VARIATION OF ORDERS

The Money Payments (Justices' Procedure) Act 1935 gave magistrates the power to vary amounts of maintenance awarded. Yet, as we showed in Chapter 6, this power has been very little used. With continuous inflation during the last quarter of a century, it was to be expected that applications would frequently be made by complainants and defendants to have their maintenance orders varied from time to time. In fact, only 32% of matrimonial orders were varied during their first five years, and the proportion had risen to only 39% after nine years[4]. Only 13% of affiliation orders had been

---

[1] The Riddell Lecture, 1970, on "Recent Developments in the Matrimonial Law".

[2] The doctrine of constructive desertion developed in the 1940s and 1950s was largely constructed out of appeals from magistrates' courts.

[3] There is a precedent in section 19(7), of the Race Relations Act 1968 which provides for two lay assessors with "special knowledge and experience of problems connected with race and community relations" to assist the County Court judge.

[4] Chapter 6, p. 83.

varied over their whole lifetime. Clearly, variation has not worked in the way intended by the Fischer Williams Committee. But some such procedure must be an integral part of the present system if a just allocation of resources between husband and wife is to be maintained in the face of their changing circumstances and responsibilities over a large number of years.

Although the courts take pains to explain verbally to the parties how variation works, the information is frequently not understood. A court hearing, when husbands and wives are emotionally distressed, is not conducive to the communication or assimilation of difficult and unfamiliar ideas, particularly if the parties are being exhorted to repeat an unhappy experience. For this reason, the Graham Hall Committee urged "the preparation of a series of simply worded explanatory leaflets similar to those issued in the social security field which, without relying on statutory wording in any way, make clear to the parties their position"[1]. We agree that this should be done, and think that a short account of the whole procedure should be given to the wife at the time of the complaint and to the husband with the summons. But we put less faith than the Graham Hall Committee in the written leaflet as a means of conveying knowledge. We hope that if the local legal centres, now being discussed[2], are established, they will experiment with various methods of educating parties to what is involved in matrimonial proceedings.

Table 85 in Chapter 8 demonstrates the confusion and uncertainty of defendants about the proper course of action when unemployment or illness makes it difficult or impossible for them to keep up their maintenance payments. More than one half of the men either continued to pay or, being unable to pay, took no action to apply for variation. In practice, but without statutory authority, some clerks, by a stroke of their pen, remit arrears which accumulate for these reasons, and avoid taking enforcement proceedings. At present the clerk can in effect write off arrears if the wife agrees that she does not wish to proceed to secure them. We think that it would facilitate the supervision of payments and save the time of the courts if clerks were given powers themselves to deal with such contingencies and to remit small amounts of arrears, at least with the consent of both parties. There would have to be both a limit to the amount which the clerk could deal with and an appeal to the court if a complainant or defendant were aggrieved by the clerk's decision.

We found great variation in the policies of courts towards enforcement. In some cases, arrears are allowed to accumulate undisturbed and, in others, automatic remittal is the rule when arrears reach a certain level. We think that all arrears should be scrutinized every twelve months. One anomaly should be removed from the procedure. When enforcement proceedings are heard, the court has no power to vary the order whatever the evidence

[1] Cmnd. 3587 (1968) para. 210.

[2] As in the report of the Society of Labour Lawyers, *Justice For All* (Fabian Society, 1968) and in the *Report of the Advisory Committee on the Better Provision of Legal Advice and Assistance*, Cmnd. 4249 (1970).

it receives about the resources of the parties, unless and until an application to vary is before the court. Similarly, if the court is hearing a complaint for variation to reduce or to increase an order, it must either accept or reject the complaint. Whatever the evidence, it cannot increase an order which it has been asked to reduce, or reduce an order which it has been asked to increase. We think that the need to issue fresh summonses in these situations is time-wasting, and that the court should have unfettered power to review the amount of any order whether the issue is raised by the complainant or by the defendant.

If the court exercised more frequently its power to vary orders, some of the problems of the enforcement of maintenance orders would disappear. A constant reappraisal of the capacity of husbands to pay maintenance would surely reduce the incidence of default. But the magistrates' court will always be faced with the problem of how to allocate inadequate resources so as to ensure financial support for separated wives and their dependant children and at the same time to leave husbands with sufficient to maintain members of the illicit unions which many of them establish. In so far as the order in favour of his legal wife makes it difficult for a husband to maintain his new family, there must be a constant struggle to enforce the legal obligation. English courts have not applied rigorously the principle that the resources of a "guilty" husband should be devoted preferentially to an "innocent" first wife. They have adopted a more realistic approach which recognizes that a husband, ordered to pay maintenance beyond his means, is likely to become a defaulter. Thus, the courts have helped to reinforce the moral obligation upon a man to support the paramour (or wife) and her children with whom he is living[1].

Much of our study has concentrated on this insoluble problem of husbands on average or below average incomes struggling to support two families. Their impossible financial situation raises two major issues in the enforcement of maintenance: attachment of earnings and the imprisonment of maintenance defaulters: We consider these separately.

ATTACHMENT OF EARNINGS ORDERS

The introduction of a procedure for attaching the earnings of maintenance defaulters in 1958 has not fulfilled the chief hopes of its sponsors. In 1959 and 1960 the effect of attachment could be measured by a halving in the number of maintenance defaulters sent to prison; but the statistics of committals since 1961[2] seem to suggest a return in the long run to the situation before 1958. Between 1961 and 1967, the number of defaulters imprisoned rose from some 2,800 to 3,500. Our survey of attachment of earnings orders showed that around three-quarters of them failed to achieve their object

[1] *Roberts v. Roberts* [1970] P. 1.
[2] But there were 153 fewer committals in 1967 than in 1966.

whilst fewer than one-quarter were successful. There is no doubt that many Justices' clerks are sceptical of their usefulness, and that some magistrates have reversed the intention of the Act of 1958 by using attachment as an enforcement method of last resort after imprisonment has failed to produce any money. Nevertheless, the procedure was extended to unpaid fines by the Criminal Justice Act 1967 and is proposed for the whole field of civil debt by the Administration of Justice Act 1970. Whether the provisions of this Act will overcome the disadvantages of the 1958 procedure in so far as maintenance is concerned, is a matter for conjecture. There are three main reasons for doubting the efficiency of the new procedure as applied to maintenance, in addition to the disappointing performance of the 1958 Act. First, an attachment procedure may work very efficiently in countries which have a complete system of national registration and of reporting changes of address and occupation to the police. This degree of control over the citizen is not compatible with British notions of liberty. Second, it is sometimes further observed that attachment of earnings has worked well in Scotland (where the procedure is known as arrestment) for many generations, and hence it should be made to work as well south of the Border. But the Scots system is more often praised than understood in England. It is a principle of Scots law that it is not for the court but for the successful litigant to secure obedience to an order of the court. Arrestment is therefore akin to the English system of garnishee. In the case of decrees for aliment (maintenance orders), the system has worked so badly that the Committee on Diligence (the McKechnie Committee) recommended in 1958 that court collecting offices on the English model should be established in Scotland[1]. Third, it is more difficult to secure the regular payment of maintenance (sometimes stretching over a large number of years) than to enforce the fixed amount of a fine or a civil debt. For these reasons we are sceptical of any significant improvement in the enforcement of maintenance orders by means of attachment of earnings.

THE VALUE AND UTILITY OF IMPRISONMENT AS A SANCTION AGAINST MAINTENANCE DEFAULTERS

We have already explained in Chapter 7[2] that we regard the retention or abolition of imprisonment of defaulters as a method of enforcing maintenance as an ethical question which in the final analysis cannot be settled by reference to empirical data. There are factual components to this ethical decision. There is knowledge both of the characteristics of the defaulters who go to prison and of the numbers committed by magistrates' courts and by the High Court in England and Wales and by the Sheriff Courts in Scotland. The Payne Committee examined the arguments on both sides as well as the factual

---

[1] Cmnd. 456 (1958) paras 258–98.   [2] p. 117.

material, and failed to agree; we have therefore focused our discussion on its Report.

In 1873, the Report of the Committee on Imprisonment for Debt (the Walpole Committee) recommended unanimously that "imprisonment for debt, as now exercised by the county court judges, should be abolished"[1]. The Report of the Committee on the Enforcement of Judgment Debts (the Payne Committee) made the same recommendation in 1969 and added "the hope that our recommendations will be more productive"[2]. That hope has been realized by the Administration of Justice Act 1970 which will relieve most civil debtors of the threat or experience of prison. It will also leave maintenance defaulters as the last large group of civil prisoners. The Payne Committee was unanimous about debtors, but divided over maintenance defaulters, and its Report sets out the views of proponents and opponents of the abolition of imprisonment for maintenance defaulters.

Of the twelve members of the Committee, six, including the two members of parliament, concluded that "the imprisonment of maintenance defaulters ... is morally capricious, economically wasteful, socially harmful, administratively burdensome and juridically wrong. We wish it abolished forthwith"[3]. Three members, including the Chairman, did not "shrink from the thought of imprisoning a defaulter who is guilty of culpable neglect of his family or defiance of the court"[4]. Two members agreed in substance with the arguments of those who wished to abolish the imprisonment of maintenance defaulters, and preferred them to the arguments of the three who urged retention of imprisonment, but on balance, held "that imprisonment should not be abolished for maintenance defaulters until either the State makes better provision for the deserted wife and child, or the new system for enforcement of civil debts has been in operation for some years and has been found to work efficiently"[5]. The remaining member of the Committee took a similar view and urged delay in abolishing imprisonment because "defaulting deserting husbands have not a good public image. They must not be surprised if some of us do not include them in the same Charter as civil debtors"[6].

All members of the Payne Committee rejected the view that "the imprisonment of civil debtors helps to inculcate or to maintain among the community the social and moral obligation to repay debts freely contracted"[7]. They found no evidence that "the vast structure of credit trading can depend on the threat of imprisonment or the ultimate sanction of imprisonment which results in a few thousand people being sent to prison even if it were abundantly clear that those in prison were all deliberate defaulters or dishonest..."[8] Similarly, no member of the Committee asserted that the family and the institution of marriage depend on the knowledge among husbands that they

---

[1] C-348, p. ix.   [2] Cmnd. 3909 (1969) para 1006.
[3] *Ibid.*, para 1099.   [4] *Ibid.*, para 1039.   [5] *Ibid.*, para 1104.
[6] *Ibid.*, para 1108.   [7] *Ibid.*, para 1091.   [8] *Ibid.*, para 960.

may land in prison if they wilfully fail to maintain their wives and children. The six members who wished to abolish imprisonment held that

> the family is a universal institution and remains, in a variety of forms of which monogamy is the commonest the world over, the basic social unit in all societies. It would, indeed, be astonishing if the existence of this institution in England depended on the maintenance of one particular method of enforcing a municipal legal rule. A vast body of sociological knowledge supports the view of Edward Westermarck that "the existence of marriage does not depend upon laws . . . if marriage is not an artificial creation but an institution, based upon deep rooted sentiments, conjugal and parental, it will last as long as these sentiments last"[1].

Thus, the whole Committee dismissed the theory of general deterrence as a justification for imprisoning civil debtors or maintenance defaulters. But two other considerations were stressed. First, an argument from the characteristics of debtors and defaulters; secondly, an argument from the administration of justice and the liberty of the citizen.

In deciding to recommend the abolition of imprisonment for civil debtors, the Committee was strongly influenced by evidence from the study by Pauline Morris of *Prisoners and their Families* (1965), from those engaged in welfare and social services and from the Governors of prisons which receive debtors. All presented a picture of civil debtors as feckless and socially inadequate people incapable of managing their own affairs and unable to appreciate how or why they had landed in prison. The Committee acknowledged that "the discovery of the type of man who goes to prison" was "one of the main arguments"[2] for abolishing imprisonment for civil debt. Accordingly, it is important to establish if characteristics of maintenance defaulters are significantly different from those of debtors. This point was examined by the six members who recommended the abolition of imprisonment.

> The comments of Prison Governors on civil prisoners suggest no clear distinction between debtors and defaulters. The Governor of a large prison which receives many civil prisoners emphasised their social incompetence and added that "the same inadequacy appears a salient factor in matrimonial maintenance cases . . ." Mrs. Morris's data were a sample of civil prisoners containing twice as many defaulters as civil debtors. She recorded that the main difference between the two groups was not so much in their social competence as in their attitude to debts, although maintenance defaulters were less often found among the incompetents. Mrs. Morris stressed "the low level of intelligence and social functioning which we believe to exist particularly among the debtors, though perhaps

---

[1] *Iibd.*, para 1091. The quotation is from *A Short History of Marriage* (1926), p. 308.
[2] *Ibid.*, para 1001.

less often amongst the maintenance defaulters"[1]. She explained the difference in attitude to debt in the context that "civil prisoners appeared to be truly social inadequates, needing almost permanent support if they were to survive in the community. The characteristics of those in for non-payment of maintenance were frequently quite similar but their attitude to the debt was very different. They often claimed that their default was a matter of principle, although most of them rationalised the situation and said it was because their wives were living with other men, or the children they were asked to support were not theirs. In fact, they simply hated their wives and were stubbornly prepared to undergo an infinite number of prison sentences rather than pay a penny"[2]. These observations suggest the likelihood that many maintenance defaulters are just as inadequate and socially incompetent as civil debtors although their inability to cope with reality takes a different form. We think that the evidence upon which the Committee relies . . . for its social profile of civil debtors does not permit a sharp distinction to be formed between debtors and defaulters. Indeed, it points rather to similarities than to differences[3].

Imprisonment is punishment by deprivation of liberty and is the most severe penalty which can be inflicted upon a citizen. The administration of justice requires that a civil offender should not be sent to prison without judicial consideration of the circumstances as scrupulous as that accorded to anyone accused of crime. For this reason, the Payne Committee reported unanimously that

> the present judgment summons procedure is not compatible with the administration of justice, especially in circumstances involving the liberty of the subject. The wide variation in the practice of county court judges and the sheer volume and pressure of work in these days make it impossible to distinguish in all cases between the recalcitrant and the inadequate debtor[4].

As the likelihood that civil debtors are being wrongly imprisoned by county court judges was given by the Committee as a reason for the abolition of their imprisonment, it is therefore of first importance to establish that such injustice cannot befall maintenance defaulters. The nine members of the Committee who considered this point were sharply divided.

Three members pointed to the formal requirements that magistrates must only hear a complaint for enforcement in the presence of a defendant unless he fails to appear after an adjournment, that they must inquire into the defendant's means and circumstances and that they must not issue a warrant

---

[1] *Prisoners and their Families* (1965), p. 245.   [2] *Ibid.*, 234–35.
[3] Cmnd. 3909, *op. cit.*, para 1092.   [4] *Ibid.*, para 961.

of commitment unless they are satisfied that the default resulted from wilful refusal or culpable neglect. Further, magistrates have the power to postpone the committal order so long as the defaulter pays up, as well as to remit arrears. The three members recognized fully that these present safeguards work imperfectly.

> One of the objections in the past to the use of committal as a final sanction in the magistrates' courts has been the difficulty of obtaining adequate evidence of the means of a maintenance defaulter before committing him to prison, and undoubtedly some magistrates have felt uneasy about the unreliability of some of the evidence and, in busy courts, about the limited time they have been able to devote to the necessary individual enquiry[1].

But they urged that several recommendations[2] of the main *Report* would improve the information available to the court about defendants' means although these must wait upon the acceptance[3] of the Committee's recommendation of an Enforcement Office and ancillary services. With such changes in mind, the three members were "satisfied that imprisonment as a final sanction should be retained . . . "[4]

Six members of the Committee did not share their three colleagues' confidence in the present or future ability of magistrates' courts to apply the crucial distinction between inability and refusal to pay. The courts

> have to draw a fine distinction in respect of allocation of income by the poorest and most inadequate husbands in the married community, many of whom have acquired not only a maintenance order but also an illicit family or paramour[5].

These members went on to contrast the results of enforcement proceedings in the High Court in England, in the Sheriff Courts in Scotland and in the English Magistrates' Courts, by examining the number of committals under the three jurisdictions in the two countries. Although all share the same rule that no defaulter may be committed without proof of contumacy, there are remarkable differences in the statistics of imprisonment. In 1965, magistrates' courts in England and Wales made some 31,000 orders for the maintenance of married women and dependant children, including affiliation orders. In

---

[1] *Ibid.*, para 1047. The findings of the present research certainly justify this unease.

[2] They include (*a*) the use "throughout magistrates' courts of a prescribed form of questionnaire to ensure consistent and thorough examination of means" (para 1273); (*b*) the addition to the staff of justices' clerks' offices of "a suitably qualified person" who could (among other duties) "assist defaulters in the completion of the form" (para 1269); and the establishment of "a social work agency with trained staff to assist the debtor and the court" (para 1213).

[3] None of the proposals set out in fn. [2] above has found a place in the Administration of Justice Act 1970.

[4] Cmnd. 3909 (1969) *op. cit.*, para 1032.   [5] *Ibid.*, para 1093.

that year they committed some 3,500 men for wilful refusal or culpable neglect to pay maintenance. In the same year, the High Court granted some 39,000 decrees nisi, made some 7,500 maintenance orders (of which around one-third were registered for enforcement in magistrates' courts), and, applying the distinction between refusal and inability to pay, issued no more than thirty-two orders of committal which may have resulted in the imprisonment of a handful of maintenance defaulters[1]. There is no summary procedure in matrimonial cases in Scotland. In 1965, the Sheriff Courts heard 502 actions for aliment[2] (maintenance) but no husbands were sent to prison for failure to implement an alimentary decree. Indeed, no husband has been imprisoned on this ground in Scotland between 1960 and 1968, the latest year for which the figures are available. The six members thought that there was

some evidence to suggest that magistrates' courts in England and Wales too readily and too easily make a finding of wilful refusal or culpable neglect to pay maintenance . . . We find it hard to resist the inference that the High Court in England and the Scottish courts apply the test of wilful refusal as distinct from inability to pay maintenance much more strictly than it is applied by magistrates' courts in England. We conclude that there are grounds for thinking that the liberty of the subject, if he be a maintenance defaulter, is no better protected in the magistrates' courts than if he be a civil debtor appearing in the county court[3].

These considerations carried no weight with the government. On the second reading of the Administration of Justice Bill, the Lord Chancellor defended his decision to retain imprisonment for maintenance defaulters by quoting the minority opinion of the Chairman and two members of the Payne Committee that

the selfishness and irresponsibility by which he (a maintenance defaulter guilty of culpable neglect of his family or defiance of the court) is motivated are . . . no less morally reprehensible and socially damaging in their effects than many offences against the criminal law in respect of which the courts' power to pass a sentence of imprisonment is not questioned[4].

[1] The Civil Judicial Statistics for 1965 (Cmnd. 3029, 1966), Table 11, do not provide a detailed breakdown of the thirty-two writs of attachment or orders of committal actually issued. The President of the Probate, Divorce and Admiralty Division of the High Court told the Payne Committee that "I have myself never found it necessary to commit a husband, for non-payment of a maintenance order of the High Court. I have, however, on occasion found it expedient to make a suspended committal order." (para 1093). The President supported the retention of imprisonment.
[2] The Civil Judicial Statistics compiled by the Scottish Home and Health Department achieve a high standard of obscurity and do not distinguish the various methods of enforcing decrees for aliment.   [3] *Ibid.*, para. 1093.
[4] Hansard, House of Lords, 4th December 1969, col. 203. The quotation is from para 1039.

The Lord Chancellor's conclusion "that it follows that to be able to send to prison someone who is determined to avoid his obligations may be the only practicable way of enforcing the court's order"[1], leaves two questions unanswered. First, the Payne Committee recommendation that imprisonment of civil debtors be abolished stemmed from its desire

> to provide a more effective means of compelling a debtor to meet his obligations than has existed in the past. If a debtor has money, goods or property, it must not be conceded that it is beyond the power of the court ... to attach his wages or assets and realise the sum required to satisfy the debt. If he has no means or assets the threat of imprisonment is futile[2].

If "it must not be conceded that it is beyond the power of the court" to lay hold of a debtor's resources, why should it be conceded that it is beyond the court's power to lay hold of a maintenance defaulter's resources ? If a maintenance defaulter has the means to pay, the best method of ensuring that the court's order will not be flouted is to establish an effective machinery of extraction. If he lacks the means to pay, his failure cannot be contumacious.

The second question which the Lord Chancellor left unanswered relates to the selfishness and irresponsibility of defaulters. They can only be sent to prison for not paying maintenance; they cannot be punished for any other form of selfish and irresponsible behaviour towards their families. There seems no escape from the conclusion of half the members of the Payne Committee that

> strict observance of husbands' liability to maintain their wives and families could be enforced only by limiting the right to live apart or to petition for divorce to men able to guarantee in advance the maintenance of their ex-families. This would involve the impossible task of enforcing rigidly indissoluble marriage or different rules of sexual behaviour for different income groups[3].

We find it hard to regard the retention of imprisonment for maintenance defaulters as other than a continuing discrimination between the very poor and the remainder of the population in the law which regulates family life; and we agree with the abolitionist members of the Payne Committee that

> imprisonment has no contribution to make to the solution of these problems. It is expensive, it is likely to reduce the already poor earning power of the defaulter, it provides neither financial assistance nor safe-

[1] Hansard, House of Lords, 4th December 1969, cols. 203 and 204.
[2] Cmnd. 3909 (1969) para 999.   [3] *Ibid.*, para 1097.

guards for wives or children and it damages marriage by destroying finally any hope of reconciling the estranged spouses or encouraging continuing relationships between fathers and their children[1].

We do not think that the policeman and the prison officer are appropriate agents for the regulation of family life, because they bring penal sanctions into a social area where compensation is the only relevant aim, and moral censure the only proper method of expressing disapproval. Citizens in 1970 do not think of failure to discharge matrimonial obligations as criminal behaviour, and to treat it as such by imprisoning offenders in the absence of supporting public sentiment damages the law, degrades marriage and perpetuates the criminal atmosphere of magistrates' matrimonial jurisdiction.

THE ATMOSPHERE OF THE COURT: JUDICIAL OR SOCIAL SERVICE?

We are conscious that some of the most disturbing findings in our research come from the opinions of wives and husbands who have been through the courts. Making full allowance for the unrepresentativeness of our samples of *The News of the World* readers who had experienced the matrimonial jurisdiction of magistrates' courts, we think that the findings in Chapter 8 are nonetheless disturbing. It is perhaps fair to insist at the outset that many magistrates share our misgivings about the defects of the present jurisdiction. Their feelings are prompted by the dilemma which they perceive from the Bench, whether their function is to conduct a judicial hearing (as in their criminal jurisdiction) or to try to serve as welfare workers within the limitations imposed by sitting on the Bench. The possibility of reconciliation, the statutory injunction to assist unrepresented parties by probing the facts themselves, and the use of probation officers and others to provide reports in custody and access cases, all prompt magistrates to remove their judicial garb and assume the social worker's habit. This unresolved dilemma partly explains the unsatisfactory state of this jurisdiction. But much consumer dissatisfaction also stems from the fact that many magistrates still regard the jurisdiction as the cinderella of their work.

One unhappy consequence of public and professional ignorance of the working and results of the jurisdiction has been a toleration of conditions and attitudes in the courts in which the criminal atmosphere is still redolent in the magistrates' matrimonial work. The Magistrates' Courts Act 1952 expresses the pious hope that the business of magistrates' courts shall be arranged in such a way as to separate matrimonial proceedings from other business[2]. That hope is all too readily unfulfilled. We have shown in Chapter 8 that fewer than one-third of the courts set aside a special time for hearing

---

[1] *Ibid.*

[2] The first expression of the hope came in the Summary Procedure (Domestic Proceedings) Act 1937.

matrimonial cases, let alone provide a separate courtroom. In a memorandum submitted to the Law Commission, the Magistrates' Association say that

> there is much to be said for a Domestic Court sitting at a place separate from the ordinary Magistrates' Court, or if that is not possible sitting on a day when the ordinary court is not in session. Either arrangement avoids the necessity of the parties having to wait together with persons who are appearing on criminal charges which is a point that sometimes causes distress. A separate place with a room that has no specific court furnishings may make it easy for the proceedings to have a less forbidding atmosphere. It must, however, be recognized that problems of accommodation, staffing and availability of justices may make special arrangements virtually impossible[1].

We have no doubt that the failure to make special arrangements is in part an explanation of the strong dislike for the procedure, the attitudes of the Bench and of officials, voiced by many of the husbands and wives using the courts. The material which we have presented in Chapter 8 suggests that magistrates' courts do not possess the confidence of the clients who seek its intervention in their marriages. We recognize fully that complainants and defendants come before the court at a time when they are in conflict with their spouses, emotionally distraught and all too ready to blame their misery on others. Nevertheless, we have found compelling the weight of evidence that the working class couples who go to the magistrates with their matrimonial troubles feel that they are treated like criminals in a court which is predominantly concerned with petty crime. Most significant was the fact that many wives who obtained orders felt dissatisfied with the manner in which the court found in their favour. Only by special arrangements and sittings can magistrates' courts hope to transform themselves into family tribunals. At present, their jurisdiction generates resentment. A court which deals with collapsing or with broken marriages must aim to mitigate pain and misery by enabling the spouses and their children to escape from their afflictions with justice and dignity. A major emphasis of this research has been the demonstration that magistrates' courts deal with the broken marriages of the poorest members of the community who are the least able to cope with economic difficulties. But the feelings and convenience of these litigants is not a first priority in the organization of the courts. They sit at times when defendants must lose wages if they attend the hearings, and, as we have shown in Chapter 8[2], when the parties subsequently come into contact with the court to pay or to receive their maintenance they are still subjected to inconveniences if not indignities. The opening hours of court collecting offices are ill-suited to the needs of those who must use them, and collecting methods sometimes are unhelpful. We think that the hours of opening should be

[1] Annual Report, 1968–9, *op. cit.*　　　[2] pp. 121–2.

arranged to suit the needs of husbands and wives. Nor do crowded waiting rooms without adequate seating and long delays in the court building before the hearing, promote the dignity of the proceedings. If magistrates' courts are ever to serve as respected family tribunals, they must be given the staff and facilities to enable them to create a new atmosphere. We think that special attention should be paid to matrimonial proceedings in the Lord Chancellor's training programme for newly-appointed magistrates who, unless tutored to regard this as a special jurisdiction, will bring the habits and manners of the criminal court to this work. Some magistrates positively decline to sit on matrimonial cases; we deplore this practice of selection of judicial work: it springs from the attitude that it is work unworthy of magisterial attention. If this jurisdiction is to survive, it will need a fresh approach from the magistracy.

We have pondered over the remedy for the legitimate and widespread complaint made by the wives and husbands who do not think that justice is being administered evenly or fairly. We were particularly struck by the fact that over 70% of the complainants (66% of husbands and 77% of wives) gave as their two main reasons for thinking that the court was unfair, that it failed to examine the other party fully or accepted "untruthful" evidence from the other party[1]. It would be instructive to know in what proportion of cases the parties were unrepresented, in which case there must have been a failure of the magistrates to exert their statutory duty under section 61, Magistrates' Courts Act 1952 to examine or cross-examine witnesses where it cannot effectively be done by the parties. Since those interviewed had recently experienced the matrimonial procedure (that is, since May 1961 when legal aid was applied to magistrates' courts) the duty under section 61 would not have applied so often, since the court would have been bound to leave the matter to the legal representatives[2].

The inability of magistrates on their own motion to elicit facts from the parties where they are legally represented raises the question whether lawyers assist or detract from the due administration of justice in this area of family law.

We think that this raises a fundamental issue about the nature of the jurisdiction which goes outside the conclusions of the research. We have already alluded to changes in the procedure and substantive law. But records, meaningful national statistics, the duration of separation orders, the merger of affiliation into maintenance proceedings, the system of appeals, the effective means of adjusting speedily the arrears payable under orders to reflect altered circumstances or numbers of dependants, the revised methods of enforcement involved as a result of the abolition of imprisonment of defaulters, and the transformation of the court atmosphere—all these, we conceive, are essential reforms if the magistrates' courts are to administer justice in matrimonial cases in accordance with the intentions of Parliament and within the

[1] Chapter 7, Table 80.   [2] *Ratcliffe v. Ratcliffe* [1964] 1 W.L.R. 1098.

spirit of existing legislation. All these reforms could be made within the present legislative framework of the jurisdiction.

Our research findings have pointed to some, if not all, of the changes proposed above. Throughout the study, however, we have been aware that many of our findings prompt consideration whether the jurisdiction should be retained at all, or if retained should be radically revised. Our findings on the way in which the wives and husbands perceive the court provide the major possibility of revision. We, therefore, pass on to those aspects, not strictly arising from our study, which indicate a field of choice for administrators and legislators who are concerned with the future direction of this area of family law.

Conclusions on the matrimonial jurisdiction of magistrates' courts

ACCUSATION OR INQUISITION ?

The overwhelming verdict of the users of the matrimonial jurisdiction of magistrates' courts that magistrates do not elicit the truth about the matrimonial offence or the financial state of the parties prompts the question whether our adversary system of administering justice is well-suited to this jurisdiction. Although the magistrates' court is statutorily empowered to effect reconciliation and to take an inquisitorial role where the parties are unrepresented, the procedure is still basically accusatorial in approach—that is to say, the eliciting of the facts (including the suppression of information unhelpful to a party's case) is left in the hands of the parties' legal advisers who carry over their gladiatorial combat from the criminal courts. The accusatorial nature of English legal procedure is evidently least satisfactory to the clients of the magistrates' court in matrimonial proceedings. A conscious adoption of the inquisitorial approach, in which the Bench would draw out all the relevant information, would more nearly approximate to the wishes of the parties.

Such a reform would have wide implications. If the Bench were given a roving commission to elicit the facts, would this make the legal representatives redundant; or if they were retained, would they readily accede to a change of role? And if lawyers were retained (and we see no prospect of the legal profession bowing out of this jurisdiction) would they happily fall into line with a judicial process utterly alien to their training and practice?

These questions will have to be answered generally if and when the structure of a family court is devised. Our only contribution is to proffer a view that an inquisitorial role for any family court is more likely to accord with what the users of such a court will expect from their legal system.

We pass on to two other choices facing law reformers, both of which are prompted in part by our findings and in part by social change and alterations in the law relating to social security and to divorce.

THE CURRENCY OF MAINTENANCE ORDERS

Some sixty years ago, the Gorell Commission expressed strong dislike of separation orders unlimited in time, on the simple ground that they inevitably resulted in illicit unions being formed without the prospect of those unions being legally regularized. Lord Gorell himself in *Dodd v. Dodd*[1] had expressed much the same judicial sentiment. The Commission recommended that such orders should not continue for longer than two years, after which the complainant should be required to apply for a decree of judicial separation. The Morton Commission revised the earlier proposal but did "not think that it would be right to set a limit to the duration of separation orders"[2]. Although the raison d'être for separation orders has long since disappeared (in spite of magistrates' courts including them in 30% of their orders) the reasoning of the Gorell Commission is as applicable today as it was at the beginning of the century. The continuous factual separation of spouses following the making of a maintenance order without the conversion of that separation into a divorce or judicial separation is equally undesirable, since the stable illicit unions lack the prospect of becoming licit.

The data in court records did not enable us to calculate the proportion of separation orders and/or maintenance orders which lapsed because the spouses were reconciled, but we were able to show in Table 25 of Chapter 5 the close similarity between the duration of marriages of those obtaining divorce decrees in the high courts and of wives obtaining orders for maintenance and separation from the magistrates' courts. Interpreted together with the fact that a high proportion of husbands cohabit with other women soon after the magistrates' courts' order is made against them, it is fair to assume that most existing orders of magistrates' courts represent irretrievably broken marriages.

Thus the matrimonial law administered in magistrates' courts satisfies neither of the Law Commission's two requirements for a good divorce law. The first is that "if the marriage is dead, the object of the law should be to afford it a decent burial"[3]. We showed in Chapter 9 that about half of the spouses coming before magistrates' courts do not go on to the divorce court to obtain a licence to marry again, and remain in a matrimonial limbo of being legally married but socially unmarried. The Law Commission's second requirement is that dead marriages should be buried with "the minimum of embarrassment and humiliation" to the parties[4].

If dead marriages are to be decently buried and if the numbers of illicit

[1] [1909] P. 189.   [2] Cmnd. 9678 (1956) para 1036.
[3] *Reform of the Grounds of Divorce: the Field of Choice*, Cmnd. 3123 (1966) para 17.
[4] *Ibid.*

unions and of illegitimate children are to be reduced, some method must be devised whereby the orders of magistrates' courts (or of any other preliminary procedure that may be adopted) cease to be a permanent alternative to the remedies available in the divorce court.

The proposal is not that the orders of magistrates' courts should be automatically reviewable after two years, although that is a procedural reform worthy of consideration. This is what the Magistrates' Association had in mind in a recent memorandum to the Law Commission where it stated

> that there would be some advantage in providing that matrimonial orders should have a limited validity of, say, one year. After this the complainant (husband or wife) would have to apply for it to be continued either indefinitely or for a fixed period, say for example, until the children have reached 16 years of age or finished full-time education. The details of this "temporary" and "final" order procedure would have to be worked out[1].

The Association does not explain how it reconciles this proposal, which would double the number of matrimonial hearings, with its earlier statement in the same memorandum "that problems of accommodation, staffing, and availability of justices" may make special arrangements to separate matrimonial proceedings from the original work of the courts "virtually impossible"[2]. Granted that an intermingling of the criminal and matrimonial jurisdiction would result from a great increase in the volume of work, many courts could not in any case cope with the additional burden of work.

Our proposal, on the contrary, is deliberately to convert the magistrates' courts' jurisdiction into a stepping-stone of short duration to the higher court. If the complainant wishes to be in receipt of maintenance under a court order —private maintenance agreements would be left untouched—he or she would be required to seek either a divorce or a judicial separation from the higher court within two years of the making of the maintenance order. In this way spouses would be forced to examine their matrimonial status after two years and plot the course of their lives. Thus a unified system of family law would serve as an active agent of social change, reducing the number of illicit unions and the incidence of illegitimacy. It would have the further beneficial effect of destroying the difference between the two jurisdictions, in which at present the limited legal remedies for matrimonial disaster available in magistrates' courts are used extensively for the poorest and least well-informed members of the community. A unified system would provide one law for rich and poor alike.

The major objection in principle to this proposal is that separated wives with two year maintenance orders will be forced, in effect, to have their broken marriages dissolved (it would be unrealistic to suppose that judicial

---

[1] *Annual Report*, 1968–69, *op. cit.*, pp. 51 and 52.   [2] *Ibid.*

separation would suddenly become a fashionable remedy) without their having committed any matrimonial offence. Whatever force that objection had in the past, it is untenable in the light of the changes wrought by the Divorce Reform Act 1969. It will be possible, after 1st January 1971, for a divorce to be granted after five years' separation even though one spouse declines to agree to a divorce, so long as the dissenting spouse is adequately provided for in financial terms[1]. In any event it is reasonable to assume that many wives with two-year maintenance orders and separated for two years will assent to a divorce under the other provision allowing a divorce after two years' separation when the respondent to the divorce petition consents to a divorce being granted[2]. Private and public morality alike require a development in our matrimonial proceedings whereby *all* marriages which have ceased to exist in social reality should be legally interred.

There are some serious practical implications in this proposal. First, there is the additional cost of proceedings in the High Court after the lapse of the maintenance order within two years. Since the beneficiaries of maintenance orders are the poorest in the community, the whole burden is likely to be borne by the legal aid scheme. If half the wives with orders from magistrates' courts who do not currently go on to the divorce court, wanted to continue their maintenance orders against their husbands, the additional cost to legal aid will hardly be less than £100,000 per annum. This may be reckoned a fair price for regularizing illicit unions and substantially reducing the numbers of illegitimate children.

Second, there is the prospect that if separated wives do not take the requisite action within two years of obtaining their maintenance orders, the Supplementary Benefits Commission which at present provides social security for a third of such wives, will have to press its clients into proceedings in the High Court. At present the Supplementary Benefits Commission, as a matter of policy, urges supported wives and unmarried mothers to apply to the magistrates' court for maintenance against the husbands and fathers. The exhortation to wives to apply to the High Court after two years would differ only in that the Supplementary Benefits Commission would be acting in the unfamiliar role of encouraging dissolution of the marriage. This may be unwelcome to that body, but if it is public policy, as reflected in the new divorce law, that dead marriages should be legally buried then there is nothing untoward in a Department of State promoting that policy.

Third, the failure of separated wives to obtain a divorce and maintenance after two years would mean that the Supplementary Benefits Commission would be supporting such wives and their dependant children without any reimbursement from the husbands and fathers. To the extent that the maintenance orders lapse by default, the State's bill in terms of social security would rise. This could be counteracted by the Supplementary Benefits

[1] Sections 2(1)(*e*) and 6, Divorce Reform Act 1969.
[2] Section 2(1)(*d*), Divorce Reform Act 1969.

Commission using more freely its present statutory powers of recovering from husbands the costs of benefits paid to the wives and children[1].

The effect of such a proposal would be to raise the divorce rate to the point where divorce was most nearly an accurate index of broken marriages. Substantially, the separated wives of these broken marriages would retain their right to maintenance under the divorce law, applicable indiscriminately to all classes of the divorcing population. Thus no greater financial burden would fall upon the State.

An alternative proposal would abolish the jurisdiction in favour of administrative action. All separated wives and their dependant children would be entitled to receive a fatherless family allowance under social security which would have the right of reimbursement from those liable to maintain the wives and children. This would transform the nature of the obligation to maintain.

THE DUTY TO MAINTAIN

In Chapter 1 we traced the history of the husband's obligation to maintain his wife and family, we showed that an effective, enforceable right to maintenance was the creature of Victorian legislation and that it developed after the poor law authorities had been given power to extract from relatives the cost of keeping paupers. The chief innovation in the twentieth century has been that social policy has set new standards of maintenance and has endowed wives and children with the additional right to financial support without stigma in their capacity as citizens. Our findings demonstrate that defendants in matrimonial and in affiliation proceedings before magistrates are drawn from the poorest stratum of the working class who cannot maintain themselves and the families from whom they have parted because they earn too little. Men from this stratum of society, no less than their financial betters, quickly acquire paramours and father children upon them. At present, there is reluctance to draw out the consequences of our social and familial situation. Until recent years, an adulterous wife who failed to obtain a matrimonial order against her husband could find herself in a more eligible financial position than that of the wife who had established her legal right to maintenance. The adulterous wife without an order straightway became a client of the National Assistance Board which gave her a book of vouchers for her subsistence cashable at any post office. The wife with a court order had to collect her payments from the court collecting office and suffer the hardship and inconvenience of irregular payments which could be mitigated but not avoided by frequent applications to the National Assistance Board for temporary support. Since 1965, wives have ceased to be harassed by this cruel absurdity, and the Supplementary Benefits Commission now arranges for those wives who are entitled to supplementary benefits to be given an order

[1] Section 23, Ministry of Social Security Act 1966.

book, and any payments made on the court order are collected by the Commission. Nevertheless, this was merely a tardy administrative improvement. What is now required is the recognition that the husband's obligation to maintain is in many cases a fiction. Most wives go to the magistrates' court to obtain maintenance; in reality, many receive it in the form of supplementary benefit, and the courts simply duplicate work which the Commission is better equipped to undertake. The Graham Hall Committee reported a

> general trend of thought among some witnesses that the State should assume responsibilities for payment and recovery of maintenance. It has been suggested that all separated wives should be able to obtain through the Ministry of Social Security or through the Post Office a regular allowance payable in the same way as family allowances; and that the State through the Ministry, should recover from defendants whatever the courts decided they should pay. At first sight a "maintenance" allowance would seem to be a promising method of relieving the immediate financial anxieties of deserted wives. But difficult questions of scope would arise. Should such an allowance be only as large in the individual case as the amount of maintenance ordered by the court? Should it be payable as of right or on some test of hardship and need? If as of right, would any person in whose favour maintenance had been ordered by a court be eligible for such an allowance? If it were not equivalent to the amount ordered by a court would the allowance be constructed from standard scales for women and children? Would supplements be payable if the man concerned could afford to pay maintenance above that limit? If the allowance were based on need, how would it differ from the present provision of supplementary benefit? Questions of this kind could hardly be settled, in any event, without regard to the general framework of social security. Indeed, it may be that the needs of deserted wives for whom maintenance is ordered by a court are so similar to those of fatherless families generally that separate provision for the former would be unrealistic[1].

This will be a central issue for the recently appointed Committee on One Parent Families. Its very wide terms of reference will require it to take up the discussion where the Graham Hall Committee left it.

The present matrimonial jurisdiction of magistrates was established in the days when there was one law for the well-to-do family and another for the poor. It unhappily retains many of the characteristics of these origins. We think that the Magistrates' Association is mistaken in its view that

> the effect of the Maintenance Orders Act 1968 may well result in a considerable increase in the number of complaints initiated before

[1] Cmnd. 3587 (1968) *op. cit.*, para 235.

Magistrates' Courts and in the proportion of complaints made as a preliminary step before a petition for divorce is presented[1].

Quite apart from the fact that before 1968 the maximum amount was hardly ever awarded, the removal of the statutory limits is very unlikely to alter ingrained social habits whereby only the poorest members of society resort to the magistrates' courts.

We hope that whichever choice is made among the various proposals discussed in this chapter, priority will be given to destroying the sharp distinction made by the law in providing one jurisdiction for the very poor and another for the rest of the community. Family law should be uniformly designed to regulate the behaviour of every family in Britain and not to perpetuate social class differences. The simplest way of erasing this inherited distinction is to establish a single jurisdiction in the form of a family court[2].

[1] *Op. cit.*, p. 52, para 20.
[2] See the discussion and accompanying bibliography in the article of L. Neville Brown, "The Legal Background to the Family Court", *British Journal of Criminology*, April 1966.

APPENDIX A, PART 1

Grounds for complaint by married women or married men[1]

Section 1 (1) of The Matrimonial Proceedings (Magistrates' Courts) Act 1960

[Dates in brackets indicate the first occasion on which that ground was included in the list of grounds of complaint.]

Jurisdiction of magistrates' court in matrimonial proceedings—

(1) A married woman or a married man may apply by way of complaint to a magistrates' court for an order under this Act against the other party to the marriage on any of the following causes of complaint arising during the subsistence of the marriage, that is to say, that the defendant—

(*a*) has deserted the complainant (1895) ; or
(*b*) has been guilty of persistent cruelty to—

    (i)   the complainant (1895 : modified in 1925); or
    (ii) an infant child of the complainant (1925); or
    (iii) an infant child of the defendant who, at the time of the cruelty, was a child of the family (1960); or

(*c*) has been found guilty—

    (i)   on indictment, of any offence which involved an assault upon the complainant (1875)[2]; or
    (ii) by a magistrates' court, of an offence against the complainant under section twenty, forty-two, forty-three or forty-seven of the Offences against the Person Act 1861, being, in the case of the said section forty-two, an offence for which the defendant has been sentenced to imprisonment or any other form of detention for a term of not less than one month (1878); or

---

[1] The complainant is almost always the wife.
[2] There is now no requirement that a minimum penalty should have been imposed on indictment for the offence.

(iii) of, or of an attempt to commit, an offence under any of sections one to twenty-nine of the Sexual Offences Act 1956, or under section one of the Indecency with Children Act 1960, against an infant child of the complainant, or against an infant child of the defendant who, at the time of the commission of or attempt to commit the offence, was a child of the family (1960); or

(d) has committed adultery (1937); or

(e) while knowingly suffering from a venereal disease has insisted on, or has without the complainant being aware of the presence of that disease permitted, sexual intercourse between the complainant and the defendant (1925); or

(f) is for the time being an habitual drunkard (1902) or a drug addict (1925); or

(g) being the husband, has compelled the wife to submit herself to prostitution or has been guilty of such conduct as was likely to result and has resulted in the wife's submitting herself to prostitution (1925); or

(h) being the husband, has wilfully neglected to provide reasonable maintenance for the wife or for any child of the family who is, or would but for that neglect have been, a dependant (1886; modified in 1895 and 1925); or

(i) being the wife, has wilfully neglected to provide, or to make a proper contribution towards, reasonable maintenance for the husband or for any child of the family who is, or would but for that neglect have been, a dependant, in a case where, by reason of the impairment of the husband's earning capacity through age, illness, or disability of mind or body, and having regard to any resources of the husband and the wife respectively which are, or should properly be made, available for the purpose, it is reasonable in all the circumstances to expect the wife so to provide or contribute (1960).

APPENDIX A, PART 2

Dates and amounts of changes in the statutory maintenance limits 1844-1960[1]

Year	Affiliation Proceedings	Matrimonial Proceedings		Guardianship Proceedings
		Wives	Children	
1844	2. 6d.[2]	—	—	—
1872	5s.	—	—	—
1878	5s.	no limit	—	—
1886	5s.	£2	—	—
1918	10s.	£2	—	—
1920	10s.	£2	10s.	—
1925	20s.	£2	10s.	20s.
1949	20s.	£5	30s.	20s.
1951	20s.	£5	30s.	30s.
1952	30s.	£5	30s.	30s.
1960	50s.	£7 10s.	50s.	50s.

[1] This table has been taken from the Report of the Committee on Statutory Maintenance Limits; Cmnd. 3587 (1968) p. 88.
[2] 5s. a week for the first six weeks.

The limits were abolished by the Maintenance Orders Act 1968.

APPENDIX B, PART I

The construction of the sample

Determination of sample design and size

A main consideration in producing our sample of courts for participation in the project work was that the selected sample should stand up to the recognized statistical tests of random selection. Every court for which figures were available should therefore stand an equal chance of selection, and there should be no determining prerequisite for the courts selected. There was a considerable variation in the number of orders held in courts, which ranged from large urban Borough and County Borough courts with full-time Justices' Clerks to the small Petty Sessional court with a part-time Justices' Clerk and a very small number of orders.

Construction of the sample

A representative number of large County Borough and Borough courts were included by sampling them in proportion to their size. On the other hand, Petty Sessional Division courts were sampled in accordance with their geographical distribution in order to ensure that the smaller courts were adequately represented.

(a) *Sample One: County Borough and Borough sample.* This sample was defined as all County Borough and Borough Courts. In practice these were courts listed at the end of the Return of courts for each county as shown in the working paper of the Association of Municipal Corporations and the Central Council of Magistrates' Courts' Committees[1]. In addition, we included the small number of such courts listed elsewhere in the Return.

An analysis based on the Local Government Manual and Directory for 1966 showed 155 County Borough and Borough Courts in England and Wales in 1965. However, the Working Party Return recorded fifteen of these courts with no maintenance figures at the time the sample was produced.

[1] See Chapter 3, p. 46.

Eleven of these 15 courts were County Borough or Borough Courts, whilst the remaining four were linked on the Return, under the same Clerk, with Petty Sessional Divisions. This left 130 courts of which thirty-one were shown as being combined with a Petty Sessional Division or Divisions and thus only one inclusive figure for both such Petty Sessional Divisions and County Borough or Borough courts was given in the Working Party Return. Removing these thirty-one courts left ninety-nine for which the Return showed one maintenance and affiliation order total. These ninety-nine courts were then ranked by size according to the combined total of affiliation and matrimonial orders held.

In the Borough Courts' sample, the fifth court on the list was taken as the starting point and every eleventh subsequent court was selected producing a sample of nine courts for the surveys of matrimonial and affiliation orders.

The Working Party Return showed the distribution of attachment of earnings orders among these ninety-nine courts as a single total for each court. The same procedure was followed as for the surveys of matrimonial and affiliation orders. Every fifth court was selected and this accordingly produced nine courts for the attachment of earnings orders survey.

(b) *Sample Two: Petty Sessional Divisions.* The second stratified sample was then defined as the courts falling outside the previous definition. These were all Petty Sessional Divisions in England and Wales showing figures on the Return, together with the thirty-one County Borough and Borough courts which were linked with a Petty Sessional Division. There were some 730 Petty Sessional Divisions, and information was available from 570 (78%), some of which were joined together under one Clerk.

The Petty Sessional courts listed in the first alphabetic sections of each county in the Working Party Return were left in alphabetical order. The counties were then sorted in alphabetical order within the Registrar General's Standard Regions. The Regions were then listed from 1 (Northern) to 10 (Wales). As the sample of Petty Sessional Division courts was selected in proportion to geographic distribution, it served equally for the matrimonial, affiliation, and attachment studies. Each eleventh court on the list was sampled.

The sample of married women orders

We decided that an examination of some 1,200 orders would yield statistically reliable conclusions. A draft questionnaire was prepared and sent, with a covering letter from the Home Office explaining the purpose of the study, to the Clerks of the forty-five courts constituting the sample of selected courts. The Clerks were asked to help in three ways: (i) by reporting the number of live orders held in their courts on 1st January 1966; (ii) by completing a small number of pilot questionnaires and by commenting on the questions and the layout; and (iii) by encouraging members of their staffs to volunteer to complete the required number of questionnaires to be calculated after the total number of live orders held by their courts had been reported to the researchers. A fee was offered for each completed questionnaire. In the event, only two courts in the large court sample and eight in the small court sample failed to provide volunteers. In these courts and in the London Stipendiary Courts, the work was carried out by our own research staff.

Courts were asked to complete questionnaires in proportion to the number of live orders they had reported. Those with more than 100 orders were asked to fill in a questionnaire for every tenth order; those with between ten and ninety-nine were asked to take every fifth order; and those with less than ten were asked to complete questionnaires for all their orders. Completed questionnaires were double checked by research staff. The reliability of a sample of court officials' work in extracting the data from court records and completing the questionnaires was tactfully tested by visiting research staff. Complete returns were obtained from all courts in the sample.

One of the most important aims of the survey was to arrive at a national figure for the current number of maintenance orders in existence. Once such a figure was obtained, we were in a position to translate the survey findings into figures which related to all orders throughout England and Wales.

APPENDIX B, PART 2

Method of calculating the national total of matrimonial and affiliation orders live on 1st January 1966

It was necessary to update the known but outdated Working Party Return national figures in the light of the more recent survey figure results.

1. The first step was to total the borough and county borough court Working Party Return figures for the nine courts in the sample. The returns showed this total as 8,383 orders. The total of all matrimonial, guardianship and affiliation orders held in the same nine courts at the time of our survey was 8,376 orders. These figures show a very slight decrease in "current orders" (i.e. 8,376) over the Working Party Return total of 8,383, the decrease being in terms of $\dfrac{8376}{8386}$ (0·9992 orders for every original 1·00 Working Party Return Orders).

2. The second step split these current "live" orders into (*a*) matrimonial

and guardianship orders and (*b*) affiliation orders. 79·36% of all our survey orders from the nine courts in the sample came into the first category whilst 20·64% were affiliation orders. Comparison of these proportions and those of the Working Party Return, gave (*a*) (0·9992 × 79·36) = 79·29 matrimonial and guardianship orders, and (*b*) (0·9992 × 20·64) = 20·64 affiliation orders for every 100 Working Party Return orders shown. This procedure produced figures which do not equal 100 when totalled.

3. This procedure was repeated for the thirty-seven Petty Sessional Division courts falling into the second part of our survey sampling frame. This produced a resultant factor of (i) 79·04 for matrimonial and guardianship orders and (ii) 19·21 for affiliation orders, for every 100 orders shown on the Working Party Return.

4. The next step put all courts for which Working Party return figures were available into the two types of court for each county. Returns of orders held at courts which at the start of the survey were not available, formed 10% of the known orders for both matrimonial and affiliation orders. Courts throughout England and Wales, which for one reason or another did not provide information concerning the number of orders held at their court, carried fewer than 1% of all orders for all types of orders. An estimate was made for such courts by comparing figures available for courts situated in the same geographical region and having comparable populations, as shown in the 1961 Census. Allowance was made for any difference in their respective total populations.

The final results are shown in Table 131 in which some 165,000 (80%) matrimonial and 41,000 (20%) affiliation orders are shown currently being enforced throughout the summary courts. Some 54% of all orders are held in Borough and County Borough Courts. The 1961 census shows that 60% of the population live in County, Metropolitan and Municipal Boroughs.

TABLE 131   Live matrimonial and affiliation orders held in magistrates' courts on 1st January 1966; England and Wales.

Order	Married Women and Guardianship of Infants orders			Affiliation orders		
Court	Borough; County Boroughs	Petty Sessional Division	Total	Borough; County Boroughs	Petty Sessional Division	Total
Current orders ..	65,007	59,648	124,655	16,914	14,497	31,411
Late Returns ..	5,255	8,297	13,552	1,224	2,349	3,573
Estimated Current Orders	103	1,427	1,530	103	373	476
Survey Court Orders	6,647	6,364	13,011	1,729	1,547	3,276
London	12,700		12,700	1,900		1,900
Total	89,712	75,736	165,448	21,870	18,766	40,636

APPENDIX B, PART 3

List of sampled courts by the Registrar General's standard regions

AREA	COURT[1]	COUNTY
1. *Northern*	Blyth	Northumberland
	Darlington	Durham
	Kendal	Westmorland
	Longtown	Cumberland
2. *East and West Ridings*	Barnsley (Staincross)	West Riding
	Bridlington (Dickering, Buckrose)	East Riding
	Doncaster*	West Riding
	Halifax (Calder)	West Riding
	Leeds	West Riding
	York*	County of York
3. *North Western*	Barrow-in-Furness*	Lancashire
	Manchester (Manchester County)	Lancashire
	Nelson (Nelson Borough, Burnley and Colne)	Lancashire
	Southport*	Lancashire
4. *North Midland*	Ashby-de-la-Zouch	Leicestershire
	Barton-upon-Humber	Lincolnshire
	Kettering	Northamptonshire
	Leicester*	Leicestershire
5. *Midland*	Coleshill	Warwickshire
	Coventry*	Warwickshire
	Hereford (Abbeydore, Bredwardine, Hereford County)	Herefordshire
	Lichfield (Lichfield Borough, Aldridge and Rushall, Litchfield and Brownhills, Tamworth)	Staffordshire
	Newcastle under Lyme*	Staffordshire

* Courts selected for the attachment of earnings study only.

[1] Some of the courts had jurisdiction over petty sessional divisions geographically away from the siting of the court. In such cases, their petty sessional divisions have been listed in brackets after the name of the court. Certain courts, such as Usk, covered more than one petty sessional division. These are shown in brackets after the court name.

AREA	COURT	COUNTY
6. *Eastern*	Dunstable	Bedfordshire
	Great Yarmouth	Norfolk
	Harlow	Essex
	Hunstanton	Norfolk
	Orwell	Suffolk
	Southend	Essex
7. (*a*) *London*	Bow	
	Clerkenwell	
	Lambeth	
(*b*) *South Eastern*	Arundel	Sussex
	Canterbury	Kent
	Deal	Kent
	Kingston-upon-Thames	Surrey
	Maidstone (Bearsted)	Kent
	Richmond*	Surrey
	Tonbridge	Kent
	Uxbridge	Middlesex
	West Ham	Essex
8. *Southern*	Gosport	Hampshire
	High Wycombe	Buckinghamshire
	Maidenhead	Berkshire
9. *South Western*	Bridport	Dorset
	Launceston (Dunheved, Stratton)	Cornwall
	Plymouth	Devon
	Stow-on-the-Wold (Northleach)	Gloucestershire
	Trowbridge (Bradford-on-Avon) Devizes, Devizes Borough, Melksham, Trowbridge, Whorwellsdown)	Wiltshire
10. *Wales*	Aberdare (Miskin Higher, Caerphilly Higher)	Glamorgan
	Colwyn Bay (Colwyn Bay, Uwchdulas)	Denbighshire
	Usk (Caerleon, Chepstow, Monmouth, Newport, Skenfrith, Usk)	Monmouthshire

* Courts selected for the attachment of earnings study only.

APPENDIX B, PART 4

Matrimonial, affiliation and attachment of earnings orders questionnaires

(a) MATRIMONIAL

			Punched Card Column Numbers
	Name of: Complainant. Respondent.		
	Card Running Number	1	1
	Serial Number (leave box blank)		2-5
1.	Class of Magistrates Court where the Order is at present held: (Ring)		6
	Stipendiary.	1	
	County Borough or Borough.	2	
	Petty Sessional Division	3	
2.	Order made originally by: (Ring)		7
	(Present) Court.	1	
	(Present) Court but later transferred to another Court.	2	
	Transferred to (Present) Court, from another Magistrates Court in England & Wales.	3	
	Registered from a Court outside England or Wales.	4	
	High Court (1) On divorce of parties.	5	
	(2) Under Section 23 of M.C.A. 1950.	6	
3.	Type of Order originally made: (Ring) (a)		8
	Guardianship.	1	
	Matrimonial Order		
	1. Married Women only.	2	
	2. Married Women with Child(ren).	3	
	3. Child(ren) only.	4	
	F.F.E. (Matrimonial Order made under the Maintenance Orders (Facilities for Enforcement) Act 1920).	5	
	If an Interim Order was made, refer to Question 20, but ring the relevant final Order above.		
	(b) Did the above Matrimonial Order have a Separation Order attached.		9
	No	1	
	Yes	2	
4.	Date the above order made: M YEAR (month—Scale 1—and year)		10-12
5.	Length of Order from date the Order was made to 1st January, 1966: (Scale 2)		13
6.	Complainant's home at the time of the original Order: (Ring)		14
	Was applicant staying in:		
	Matrimonial home without Respondent's concurrence.	1	
	Matrimonial home, that was freehold property.	2	
	Matrimonial home, leasehold property.	3	
	Matrimonial home, council property.	4	
	Parents home.	5	
	Hostel.	6	
	Private accommodation.	7	
	Living with another man.	8	
	Elsewhere than above.	9	
	Not known.	0	

7. | AGE

(a) * Year of Birth (to be calculated from Court records).

Ex.

1920	2	0
1939	3	9
1896	9	6

Complainant [ ] 15-16

Respondent [ ] 17-18

(b) * Age at time of original Order.
(Scale 5)

Complainant [ ] 19

Respondent [ ] 20

(c) * Age at time of marriage.
(Scale 5)

Complainant [ ] 21

Respondent [ ] 22

* Place X in box if age is not known.

8. | Marriage of the Complainant and Respondent.

(a) Date of Marriage. [ ]

(In full)   year only [ ] 23-24

(b) Length of marriage at time of the Order being made.
(Scale 2)   [ ] 25

(c) Status at marriage of parties: (Ring)   26

1. Complainant

Single   1
Divorced   2
Widow   3
Not known   4

2. Respondent

Single   5
Divorced   6
Widower   7
Not known   8

9. | Respondent living with a woman other than his wife; i.e. an extra-marital relationship.
(Ring)   27

(a) Was the Respondent living with another woman:

1. When the original Order was made
No   1
Yes   2
2. At a later date
No   3
Yes   4
Not known   X

(b) If 'yes' give the number of children of this relationship:
1. When the original Order was made   [ ] 28

2. At a later date   [ ] 29

10. | Occupation and Income of Complainant and Respondent

Complete only the boxes below:

Complainant

(leave blank)

At Time Of	Occupation	Income *		
				30
Original Order				31
At most recent date known (give date)				32
				33

Respondent

				34
Original Order				35
At most recent date known (give date)				36
				37

* This should be the average weekly net wage: if the figure shown is not this, please note.

11. | NATIONAL ASSISTANCE

(a) Was the Complainant on National Assistance at the time of the original Order: (Ring)

No   1   38
Yes   2
Not known

(b) Has the Complainant given authority to the Court to transfer Order payments to the N.A.B. during the year 1965.

No   4
Yes   5

12. | CHILDREN

Number of children of the Complainant and Respondent only.
(If no children, put 0 in box)

(a) (1) Of the marriage.   39

 (2) Under 16 years of age, as shown on:
    (i) the original Order.   40

    (ii) the Order on the 1st January, 1966.   41

(b) Dates of Birth
 (1) Show the month (Scale 1) and year of birth of the first two children of the marriage (as recorded in (a)(1)).
 (2) For any remaining children of the marriage note years of birth only. (If there are more than 4 children note the birth of the youngest child as being the 4th).

M   YEAR

    (1) 1st child   42-44

        2   45-47

    (2) 3   48-49

        4   50-51

(If any child of the marriage was born within 9 months of the original Order being made, it should be included in the return.)

13.	**COURT HEARING**	

Grounds for:

(a) Complaint   (a) [   ] 52

(b) Shown on Court Order   (b) [   ] 53

(c) Dismissed by Court   (c) [   ] 54

Scale

Maintenance Order for Child(ren) of marriage only	1
Desertion	2
Wilful Neglect by the husband	3
Adultery	4
Persistant cruelty to:	
I Complainant	5
II Child of Complainant	6
III Child of Respondent	7
Guilty of assault:	
I On Complainant	
II Offence (1861) Act	8
III Sexual Offence against child of family *	
V. D.	9
Forced Prostitution	
Habitual Drunkard	0
Drug Addict	
Husband obtains order due to Wilful Neglect by the wife.	X

* Under S. 1-29 Sexual Offences Act, 1956, or S. 1.
Indecency with Children Act 1960.
(If any ground falls under 8, 9 or 0, underline the actual ground on the scale whilst still putting the number in the box.)

Multicode the answer if there is more than one ground shown, i.e. place side by side in box, i.e.   [2 6]

14.	If desertion is proved in Court:

(1) The date of the Respondent's desertion.   [   ]

(2) The period of time from the time of desertion to the actual Court Order being made.   55
     (Ring)

Under 1 month	1
1 month but under 3 months	2
3 months but under 6 months	3
6 months but under 1 year	4
1 year but under 2 years	5
2 years but under 3 years	6
3 years and over	7

15.	Costs and Court Fees payable by Respondent at time of Court Order. (Ring) 56

Under £1	1
£1 but under £5	2
£5 but under £10	3
£10 but under £15	4
£15 and over	5

16.	Representation of Parties at Court Hearing. (Ring) 57

(a) Complainant:

No appearance	1
Letter only	2
In person	3
Solicitor	4
Solicitor or Counsel through Legal Aid	5
Not known	6

(b) Respondent:

No appearance	7
Letter only	8
In person	9
Solicitor	0
Solicitor or Counsel through Legal Aid	X
Not known	Y

17.	Date of complaint being made for a Maintenance Order (as shown on the form of complaint.	
	Time taken from complaint to Court hearing: (Ring)	58
	(a) Under 6 weeks 1 6 weeks but under 8 weeks 2 8 weeks but under 12 weeks 3 12 weeks and over 4	
	(b) If (a) was more than 8 weeks, but there had been no Court hearing previous to the Order being made, was this delay due to the:	
	Non-service of Summons 5 Solicitors application for postponement of hearing 6 Either parties' application for postponement. 7	
18.	Has the Complainant previously applied to a Court for a Maintenance Order. (Ring)	59
	No 1 Yes: once 2 twice or more 3 Not known 4	
19.	Order: Amount payable. (Scale 3.) (Do not show an Interim Order amount, this should be shown in Qu. 20.)	
	(a) When the Order was first made to: (1) Wife	60
	* (2) Child(ren)	61
	(b) On the 1st January, 1966 (1) Wife	62
	* (2) Child(ren)	63
	* Cumulative total if more than 1 child on the above order.	

20.	If an Interim Order was made, for how much:
	
	          (To the nearest pound—
	          take £10 - 0
	          £11 - X
	          £12 - Y
		64

THE COURT ORDER

Card Running Number

| | 2 | 1 |

Serial Number (leave box blank)

| | 2-5 |

21. VARIATIONS IN AMOUNT

Variations in amount from original Order: (for reference only)

Variation

	*0.0.	1st	2nd	3rd	4th	5th
Date						
Amount to a. Wife						
b. Child						
Total						
Variation in amount from original order						

*0.0. Original Order.
(Put + or —: before figure shown in comparison with the original order made according to whether it is a larger or smaller amount than the original amount ordered).
Total number of variations:

| | 6 |

(If none—0, pass on to Question 23).

22. Variations
(from Qu. 21. If there are no variations, pass on to Qu. 23).

For each variation, show the:
(a) The length of time (years) between this variation and the original variation.
    (Scale 2).
(b) The difference in amount from the original Order.
    (Scale 3).
(c) Reason for revoke or variation of the previous Order.
    (Scale 4).

Variation
1.

a | | 7

b | | 8

c | | 9

2.

a | | 10

b | | 11

c | | 12

3.

a | | 13

b | | 14

c | | 15

4.

a | | 16

b | | 17

c | | 18

5.

a | | 19

b | | 20

(If there are more than 5 variations, record the last one made, i.e. the present amount payable as the 5th variation. Quote details of other variations not included above).

c | | 21

23.

ARREARS
Court proceedings (to note for reference only):

Date of Complaint	Date of Court Hearing	Amount Due	Order of Court

If on either date below, the Respondent is more than £20 in arrears, record the arrears outstanding on the:

(1) 1st January, 1965. _____ (Scale 6) _____ 22

(2) 1st January, 1966. _____ (Scale 6) _____ 23

24. Have the payments been: (Ring)
Regular   1
or Irregular   2

("Irregular" should be taken as having missed 4 or more weeks payments that were due during 1965). 24

25. Have at any time the Court remitted arrears that were due from the Respondent: (Ring)

(1) No   1
Yes   2

If "yes": (2) Date (year only)

(3) Amount
(Scale 6)

25

26-27

28

26. Date of 1st hearing involving arrears of over £20:

_____

Length of time after the Original Order was made: (Scale 2) _____ 29

SUSPENDED AND PRISON COMMITTAL ORDERS

27. Suspended Committal Orders

(a) Number issued:
  (1) Before 1st January, 1959. — 30

  (2) After 1st January, 1959.
  (If nil, put '0' in Box) — 31

(b) If any S.C.O.'s have been made, show the month
  (Scale 1) and year each one was made.

	M	YEAR	
1st S.C.O.			
2nd S.C.O.			
3rd S.C.O.			
4th S.C.O.			
5th S.C.O.			

(If there have been more than 5 S.C.O's issued, record the last one as the 5th).

(c) +Number of times 1st S.C.O. reviewed by a Magistrate. — 32

28. How many Warrants—no bail have been issued against the Respondent:

(1) Before 1st January, 1959. — 33

(2) After 1st January, 1959. — 34

Place in box:
  None—0
  1 to 8—Put actual number in box.
  Over 8 but under 12—9 in box (Actual No.)
  Over 12 but under 20—X in box (Actual No.)
  Over 20   —Y in box (Actual No.)

29. Prison Committals

(a) Number of committals (If none, put 0 in box)
  (If any, complete (b)).   (a) — 35

(b) (1) Year committed   (b) 1st (1) — 36-37

  (2) Length served (days)   (2) — 38-39

  +(3) Number of times reviewed by a magistrate.   (3) — 40

          2nd (1) — 41-42

          (2) — 43-44

          (3) — 45

          3rd (1) — 46-47

          (2) — 48-49

          (3) — 50

+Reviewed by a magistrate under S. 18 of the Maintenance Orders Act, 1950.
(If there have been more than 3 committals to prison, record the last one as the 3rd).

	ATTACHMENT ORDERS		
30.	Number of Attachment Orders made. (if nil put 0, the rest of this page can be ignored).		51
31.	For the 1st Attachment Order made: The date made (in full) year only		52–53
32.	(a) Is the original Attachment Order still in force on the 1st January, 1966: (Ring) Yes 1 No 2		54
	(b) Have all the arrears been cleared by the use of an Attachment Order, either on the 1st January, 1966, or before being discharged: Yes 3 No 4		

	(c) If (a) no, was the Attachment Order discharged by:
	Respondent leaving work and employer consequently
	    obtaining discharge of A.O. 5
	Respondent dismissed from work and employer consequently
	    obtaining discharge of A.O. 6
	Maintenance Order revoked/discharged. 7
	On Respondent's application, having cleared arrears. 8
	Any other reason, give details. 9		

33.	If Qu. 32(a) is 'no', date A.O. discharged
	
	Length of time A.O. lasted before being discharged, or has been
	    in existence.
	    (Scale A below)
			55

SCALE A

Order never enforced	1	9 months but under 1 year	7
Under 6 weeks	2	1 year but under 1½ years	8
6 weeks but under 12 weeks	3	1½ years but under 2 years	9
12 weeks but under 20 weeks	4	2 years but under 3 years	0
20 weeks but under 28 weeks	5	3 years but under 5 years	X
28 weeks but under 36 weeks	6	5 years and over	Y

34.	Have any further Attachment Orders been made on the same Maintenance Order. (Ring) Yes 1 No 2 Not known 3		56

	If yes, show:
	(a) The length of time (Scale A above) between the date the first A.O. was discharged and
	    consequently remade by the Court.
	    2nd (a)
			57

	(b) the length of time (Scale A above) the new A.O. lasted, or has been in existence. (b)		58
	3rd (a)		59
	(b)		60
35.	Show the arrears due at the time of the original A.O. being made by the Court (£'s) (Scale 6)		61

(*b*) AFFILIATION

Court case Number

Name of: Complainant.
Respondent.

	Punched Card Column Numbers
Card Running Number 1	1
Serial Number (leave box blank)	2-5

1. Class of Magistrates Court where the Order is held:
   (Ring)

        Stipendiary.   1
        County Borough or Borough.   2
        Petty Sessional Division.   3

      6

2. Order made originally by: (Ring)

        (Present) Court.   1
        (Present) Court but later transferred to another Court.   2
        Transferred to (Present) Court, from another magistrates
            Court in England & Wales.   3
        Registered from a Court outside England or Wales.   4
        Order registered from the High Court   5

      7

3. (a) Date the above order made: M   YEAR
        (month (Scale 1) and year).

      8-10

   (b) Length of Order from (a) to the 1st January, 1966.
        (Scale 2)

      11

4. Date of birth of the child.

5. (a) Date the complaint for an Affiliation Order was made:

   (b) Was the complaint made before or after the birth.
          Before   1
          After   2

      12

   (c) How long a period of time was there between the birth of the child
        and the Order being made. (Scale 2)

      13

   (d) Time taken from the date the complaint was made to the Court hearing.
        (Ring)   Under 6 weeks   1
                    6 weeks but under 8 weeks   2
                    8 "   "   "   12   "   3
                    12 weeks and over.   4

      14

6. Was the Order made payable from the date of:
        (Ring)   Birth of the child   1
                    or Court hearing   2

      15

7. (a) Did the Court award an additional amount for expenses incidental to the
        birth of the child   No   1
                          Yes   2

      16

   (b) If (a) yes, what was the sum awarded.
        (to the nearest £)

      17-18

8. Age: (a) at time of original Order of:
        (Scale 5)   Complainant

      19

                 Respondent

      20

   (b) of complainant at time of her child's birth.
        (Scale 5)

      21

9. Complainant's and Respondents Occupation and Income

Complete only the boxes below:
Complainant

(Leave)
(blank)

At time of	Occupation	Income*
Original Order		
At most recent date known (give date)		

22

23

24

25

Respondent

Original Order		
At most recent date known (give date)		

26

27

* This should be the average weekly net wage:
if the figure shown is not this, please note

28

29

10. COURT HEARING

Representation of Parties at Court Hearing. (Ring)   30

        (a) Complainant:
            no appearance   1
            letter only   2
            in person   3
            Solicitor   4
            Solicitor or Counsel through Legal Aid   5
            Not known   6
        (b) Respondent:
            no appearance   7
            letter only   8
            in person   9
            Solicitor   0
            Solicitor or Counsel through Legal Aid   X
            Not known   Y

11. Legal and witness costs awarded against the Respondent at the time of
Court Order: (Ring)   31

        Under £1   1
        £1, but under £2   2
        £2, " " £3   3
        £3, " " £5   4
        £5, " " £7   5
        £7, " " £9   6
        £9, " " £11   7
        £11, " " £13   8
        £13, " " £15   9
        £15 and over   0

12. NATIONAL ASSISTANCE

(a) Was the Complainant on National Assistance at the time of the
original Order: 32
    (Ring)   No   1
                Yes   2
                Not known   3
(b) Has the Complainant given authority to the Court to transfer Order
payments to the N.A.B. during the year 1965;
                No   4
                Yes   5

13. Was the affiliation order originally given to the National Assistance Board or
Local Authority acting as the complainant but later transferred to the mother;   33
                No   1
                Yes   2

14.	Has at any time the National Assistance Board made complaint under Section 44(2) of the National Assistance Act, 1948; to recover payments from the putative father;		34
	No	1	
	Yes	2	

15.	Order. Amount payable;		
	(a) When the Order was first made. (Scale 3(a))		35
	(b) On the 1st January 1966. (Scale 3(a))		36

16. VARIATIONS IN AMOUNT

Variations in amount from original Order: (for reference only).

Variations	Original order	1st	2nd	3rd	4th
Date (ignore days)					
Amount payable					
Variation in amount from original order*					

*(Put + or —: before figure shown in comparison with the original order made being a larger or smaller amount.)

Total number of variations:

(If none, put 0 in box and pass on to Question 18.)   37

17. Variations

For each variation, show the:

(a) The length of time (years) between this variation and the original Order (Scale 2).

(b) The difference in amount from the original Order (Scale 3(a) and (b)).

Variation
1.   a   38
                      b   39

2.   a   40
                      b   41

3.   a   42
                      b   43

4.   a   44
                      b   45

18. **ARREARS**

Court proceedings (to note for reference only):

Date of Complaint	Date of Court Hearing	Amount Due	Order of Court

If on either date below, the Respondent is more than £20 in arrears, record the arrears outstanding on the:

    (1) 1st January 1965.   (Scale 4)   46

    (2) 1st January 1966.   (Scale 4)   47

19. During 1965, have the payments been: (Ring)

                     Regular   1   48
             or Irregular   2

("Irregular" should be taken as having missed 4 or more weeks payments that were due during 1965.)

20. Have at any time the Court remitted arrears that were due from the Respondent:

                 (1) No   1   49
                        Yes   2

If "Yes"

                 (2) Date (year only)   50-51

                 (3) Amount   (Scale 4)   52

21. Date of 1st hearing involving arrears of over £20:

Length of time after the Original Order was made:
                (Scale 2)   53

SUSPENDED AND PRISON COMMITTAL ORDERS

(Leave blank)		
Card Running Number	2	1
Serial Number		
		2-5

22. Suspended Committal Orders

(a) Number issued:

   (1) Before 1 January 1959.   **6**

   (2) After 1 January 1959.   **7**
   (If nil, put '0' in box)

(b) If any S.C.O.'s have been made, show the month
   (scale 1) and year each one was made.

	M	YEAR
1st S.C.O.		
2nd S.C.O.		
3rd S.C.O.		
4th S.C.O.		
5th S.C.O.		

   (If there have been more than 5 S.C.O.'s issued, record the last one as the 5th.)

(c) * Number of times reviewed by a Magistrate   **8**

23. How many Warrants—no bail have been issued against the Respondent:
   (If nil, put '0' in box)

   (1) Before 1 January 1959.   **9**

   (2) After 1 January 1959.   **10**

   Place in Box: None -0
                 1 to 8-Put actual number in box
                 Over 8 but under 12-9 in box (Actual No.)
                 " 12 "   "   20-X in box (Actual No.)
                 " 20   -Y in box (Actual No.)

24. Prison Committals

(a) Number of committals   (a)   **11**
   (If any, complete (b))

(b) (1) Year committed   (b) 1st (1)   **12-13**

     (2) Length served   (2)   **14-15**

   *(3) Number of times reviewed by a magistrate   (3)   **16**

* Reviewed by a magistrate under S. 18 of the Maintenance Orders
Act, 1950.   2nd (1)   **17-18**

(If there have been more than 3 committals to prison, record the
last one as the 3rd)   (2)   **19-20**

                                         (3)   **21**

                               3rd (1)   **22-23**

                                         (2)   **24-25**

                                         (3)   **26**

25.	**ATTACHMENT ORDERS**		
	Number of Attachment Orders made: (If nil put '0' in box and pass to Qu. 31)		27
26.	For the 1st Attachment Order made: The date made (in full) Year only.		28–29
27.	(a) Is the original Attachment Order still in force on the 1 January 1966: (Ring) Yes 1 No 2		30
	(b) Have all the arrears been cleared by the use of an Attachment Order, either on the 1 January, 1966, or before being discharged: Yes 3 No 4		
	(c) If (a) no, was the Attachment Order discharged by: Respondent leaving work and employer consequently obtaining discharge of A.O. 5 Respondent dismissed from work, and employer consequently obtaining discharge of A.O. 6 Maintenance Order revoked/discharged. 7 On Respondent's application, having cleared arrears. 8 Any other reason, give details. 9		
28.	If Qu. 27(a) is 'no', date A.O. discharged; (b) Length of time A.O. lasted before being discharged, or has been in existence. (Scale A. below)		31

SCALE A

Order never enforced	1	9 mths but under 1 yr	7	
Under 6 weeks	2	1 year " " 1½ yr	8	
6 wks but under 12 wks	3	1½ " " " 2 "	9	
12 " " " 20 "	4	2 " " " 3 "	0	
20 " " " 28 "	5	3 " " " 5 "	X	
28 " " " 36 "	6	5 years and over	Y	

29.	Have any further Attachment Orders been made on the same Maintenance Order; (Ring) Yes 1 No 2 Not Known 3 If yes, show: (a) the length of time (Scale A above) between the date the first A.O. was discharged and consequently remade by the Court.		32
	(b) the length of time (Scale A above) the new A.O. lasted, or has been in existence	2nd (a)	33
		(b)	34
		3rd (a)	35
		(b)	36
30.	Show the arrears due at the time of the original A.O. being made by the court (£'s) (Scale 4)		37

31.	Complainant's home at the time of the original Order.　　　　　(Ring) 　　Was the complainant staying in:	38
	Parents home　　　　　　　　　　　　　　　　　　　1 　　　　　Hostel　　　　　　　　　　　　　　　　　　　　　2 　　　　　Private accommodation　　　　　　　　　　　　　3 　　　　　Living with another man　　　　　　　　　　　　4 　　　　　Elsewhere than above　　　　　　　　　　　　　5 　　　　　Not known　　　　　　　　　　　　　　　　　　6	
32.	At the time of the Order was the:	39
	Complainant single　　　　　　　　　　　　　　　　1 　　　　　*Complainant married but separated from her husband　2 　　　　　*Complainant married but divorced from her husband　3 　　　　　Respondent single　　　　　　　　　　　　　　　4 　　　　　Respondent married　　　　　　　　　　　　　　5 　　　　　*(though single in meaning of Bastardy legislation)	
33.	Did they later marry?	40
	Marry each other　　　　　　　　　　　　　　　　1 　　　　　Both remain single　　　　　　　　　　　　　　　2 　　　　　Complainant marries another man, respondent remains single　3 　　　　　Complainant marries another man, respondent being already 　　　　　　married　　　　　　　　　　　　　　　　　　4 　　　　　Complainant remains single, respondent later marries　5 　　　　　Both marry other persons　　　　　　　　　　　6 　　　　　Complainant married; respondent later marries another woman　7 　　　　　Not known in case of complainant　　　　　　　8 　　　　　Not known in case of respondent　　　　　　　9 　　　　　Not known in either case of the complainant or respondent　0	
34.	If the Respondent is married at the time of the original Order being made, other than to the Complainant, number of children of this marriage.　　　［　　］	41
35.	Was child of the Order born in a: 　　　　　Hospital (under National Health Service)　　　　1 　　　　　Private Hospital　　　　　　　　　　　　　　　2 　　　　　Hostel or Unmarried Mothers' home　　　　　　3 　　　　　Maternal parents' home　　　　　　　　　　　4 　　　　　Elsewhere　　　　　　　　　　　　　　　　　5 　　　　　Not known　　　　　　　　　　　　　　　　　6	42
36.	Was the child of the Order later:　　　　　(Ring) 　　　　　Kept by Complainant　　　　　　　　　　　　　1 　　　　　Adopted by 3rd person　　　　　　　　　　　　2 　　　　　Adopted by natural mother　　　　　　　　　　3 　　　　　Put in care of Local Authority　　　　　　　　4	43
37.	If the child was put in the care of the Local Authority, were affiliation payments transferred to them instead of the mother? 　　　　　No　　　　　　　　　　　　　　　　　　　　5 　　　　　Yes　　　　　　　　　　　　　　　　　　　6	
38.	(a)　Has the Respondent made any application under S. 3 of the Legitimacy Act 1959, 　　　with regard to access to the child? 　　　　　No　　　　　　　　　　　　　　　　　　　　1 　　　　　Yes　　　　　　　　　　　　　　　　　　　2	44
	(b)　If yes, was the application successful? 　　　　　No　　　　　　　　　　　　　　　　　　　　3 　　　　　Yes　　　　　　　　　　　　　　　　　　　4 　　　　Application withdrawn before hearing　　　　　5	

39.	Has the Respondent made any attempt to provide maintenance within the year preceding the date the Order was made. (Ring)		45
	No 1		
	Yes 2		
	Not known 3		

(a) If Yes, was this a regular payment, i.e. every week (or equivalent)
    No   4
    Yes   5

(b) Did this voluntary payment, before the Order was made, last:
    Under 1 year   6
    1 year but under 2 years   7
    2 years but under 3 years   8
    Over 3 years   9
    Not known   0

40. Did Respondent admit paternity of the child at the Court Hearing.   (Ring)   46
    No   1
    Yes   2

41. (a) Did Respondent and Complainant live together before the complaint was made:
    (Ring)   47
    No   1
    Yes   2

(b) If Yes, for how long did this association last:
    Under 3 months   3
    3 months but under 6 months   4
    6 months but under 1 year   5
    1 year but under 2 years   6
    2 years but under 3 years   7
    3 years but under 4 years   8
    4 years but under 6 years   9
    6 years but under 8 years   0
    8 years but under 12 years   X
    12 years and over   Y

(c) ATTACHMENT OF EARNINGS

		Punch Card Numbers 1-4
Name of: Complainant	Respondent	
	Serial Number (leave blank)	

1. If this Attachment Order has been consequently discharged, have any further Attachment Orders been made before 1st January 1966, on the same Court Order

        No   **0**
        Yes (give number)

    5

2. Type of Attachment Order: (Ring)
        Affiliation   1
        Married Women   2
        Guardianship of Infants   3
        National Assistance   4
        Children and Young Persons Maintenance   5

    6

3. Category of Court where A.O. made:-
        County Borough/Borough   1
        Petty Sessional Division   2
        Stipendiary   3
        High   4

    7

4. Date Maintenance Order originally made   M YEAR
        (month—Scale 1—and year)

    8-10

5. Date Attachment Order was made   M YEAR
        (month—Scale 1—and year)

    11-13

6. Length of time between the Maintenance Order and the A.O. being made
        Scale 5

    14

7. Amount of maintenance payable per week at the time of A.O.
        Wife

    15

Scale 2
        Child(ren)

    16

8. At the time of the A.O. show (a) Normal Deduction Rate made

    17

        (b) Protected Earnings Rate made

    18

Scale 3

9. (a) At the time of the A.O. being made, did the Respondent have any other Court Maintenance Order(s)—other than the Maintenance Order in Qu. 4—made against him:-
        No   1
        Yes: Affiliation   2
        Married Women   3
        Guardianship of Infants   4
        N.A.B. or Childrens & Young Persons   5

    (b) If 'yes' for (a) did the above Order have an Attachment Order made before or at the same time as the present A.O.
        No   6
        Yes   7

    19

10. Did the Respondent have any other commitments when the A.O. was made:-
    (Ring)
        None   1
        Supporting another woman   2
        Supporting another woman & her (their) child(ren)   3
        Remarried after divorce from Complainant   4
        Supporting relatives   5
        Mortgage repayments on his own property   6
        Mortgate repayments on his wife's property   7
        Repayment of debt   8
        Any other commitments: (give details below)   9
        Not known   0

    20

		*Leave boxes blank	

11. Respondent's work: give details of

(1) Employment at time of A.O. being made   *   21

(2) *Income or salary   *   22

* This should be the average weekly net wage. If the figure shown is not this, please note.

12. (a) Does the Employer of the Respondent employ:
    (Ring)   under 10 persons   1
                over 10 persons   2   23

(b) Has the Employer complained to the court about 'extra work', etc. when the A.O. was placed on him?   Yes   3
                                  No   4

(c) For how long has the Respondent worked for the above employer before the A.O. was made: (Scale 4)   24

13. Did the Respondent attend the court hearing when the A.O. was made.   (Ring)   25

    (i) Voluntarily (including by summons)   1
    (ii) Under Bench Warrant (a) endorsed for bail   2
                            (b) not endorsed for bail   3
    (iii) Did not attend the court hearing   4
    (iv) Not known   5

Was the A.O. made as a result of:-

An application by complainant for A.O.   6
A Summons/Warrant for non payment of maintenance.   7
Respondent request the Court for an A.O. to be made   8

14. (a) Number of adjournments (if any), in the context of the A.O. hearing, made by the court before date of court hearing when the A.O. was made (if none, put 0; not known, put X)   26

(b) If (a) above was other than 0, was the first intended hearing adjourned due to: (Ring)   27

                        Non-service of summons on Respondent   1
                        Non-appearance at court of Respondent   2
                        Respondent unemployed   3
                        Respondent's ill-health   4
                        Giving Respondent chance to clear arrears   5
                        Further inquiries to be made   6
                        Any other reason than shown above   7
                        Not known   8
                        (if 6 applies, give brief details below)

15. If the reason for adjournment in Qu. 14(b) was 1 or 2; how many other consequent adjournments were due to the same reasons. (if none put 0; not known, put X)   28

16. (a) Is the above A.O. still in force on January 1st, 1966.
    (Ring)   Yes   1   29
                          No   2
                      (If yes, pass to question 17)

(b) If no: was the A.O. discharged by
Respondent leaving work and employer consequently obtaining discharge.   3
Respondent being dismissed from work and employer consequently obtaining discharge.   4
Maintenance Order revoked or discharged.   5
Maintenance Order varied.   6
On Respondent's application, having cleared arrears.   7
Court Order registered in Scotland or Northern Ireland.   8
Respondent never actually started work with employer named in A.O., having not yet joined employer when A.O. was made.   9
Employer unwilling to employ respondent because of A.O.   0
Any other reason: give details   X

17. If Question 16 (a) is yes:
for how long a period of time has the A.O. existed up to the 1st January, 1966.
               (Scale 4)   30

18.	If Question 16(b) is No, i.e. A.O. has been discharged, show date A.O. discharged:		
	(a) For how long a period of time did the A.O. last, if it was discharged before the 1st January, 1966. (Scale 4)		31
19.	(a) If Qu. 1 is other than 0—i.e. further A.O.'s have been made—give date of next A.O. being made.		
	(b) What was the length of time between the date that the A.O. was discharged and subsequently remade. (Scale 4)		32
20.	ARREARS. Show the amount outstanding at the time of the hearing when the A.O. was made (£). (Scale as per Qu. 28)		33
21.	(a) Have arrears been cleared by the A.O. (as first shown on the schedule) if still in force; (Ring) or before being discharged;		34
	No	1	
	Yes	2	
	(b) If (a) Yes: upon clearance of the arrears did:		
	(i) Respondent apply for and was granted discharge of the A.O.	3	
	(ii) Respondent apply for but was refused discharge of the A.O.	4	
	(iii) Upon the Collecting Officer's complaint the court reduced the N.D.R. to the normal weekly maintenance payment.	5	
	(iv) A.O. to remain same; as wife applied for, and was granted an increase to the same amount as the N.D.R.	6	
	(v) Any other action taken: give details below.	7	
22.	How many warrants 'no bail' have been issued before the A.O. was made. Place in box as follows:		35
	None	0	
	From 1 to 8—show actual number		
	Over 8 but under 12. (Actual number)	9	
	Over 12 but under 20. (Actual number)	X	
	Over 20. (Actual number)	Y	
23.	Have either Suspended or Prison Committal Proceedings been taken against the Respondent before the making of the A.O.		36
	No	1	
	Yes	2	
24.	If Qu. 19 is 'Yes'		
	(a) Number of Suspended Committal Orders made before A.O. was made.	a.	37
	(b) Number of times reviewed by the Court.	b.	38
	(c) Number of Suspended Committal Orders made after 1st January, 1959.	c.	39
25.	Date the first Suspended Committal Order was made. M YEAR		
	Date of last Suspended Committal Order before A.O. was made.		

26.   Prison Committals:

    (a) Number of Committals (if none, place 0 in box).   ☐   40

         If any:

    (b) Show (1) date of committal.
         and (2) length of time actually served in prison (days) for each committal.

	(1) Committal	M	YEAR
1st			
2nd			
3rd			

    Please give any other relevant details below.

	(2) Time	days	
1st		☐	41–42
2nd		☐	43–44
3rd		☐	45–46

    (If there have been more than 3 committals, take the last committal as the third; and note details below.)

27.   Remittance of Arrears

    (a) Has the Court at any time while the A.O. had (has) been in force, or at the time
         of the original hearing when the A.O. was made, remitted any of the outstanding arrears   47

         (Ring)   No   1
                   Yes   2

    (b) If yes; what was the length of time from when the A.O. was made.

         Remitted at time A.O. was made   3
         Less than 3 months   4
         3 months but under 6 months   5
         6 months but under 1 year   6
         1 year but under 2 years   7
         2 years but under 5 years   8
         Over 5 years   9

    (c) What was the amount remitted   ☐

                         (Scale as in Qu. 28 below).   ☐   48

28.   Show outstanding arrears from 1st January 1959 to 1st January 1966 (for the 1st January of each New Year).

1959 ☐	49
1960 ☐	50
1961 ☐	51
1962 ☐	52
1963 ☐	53
1964 ☐	54
1965 ☐	55
1966 ☐	56

Scale of arrears

		Under £10	1
£10 but under £20			2
£20	"	"	£40	3
£40	"	"	£60	4
£60	"	"	£80	5
£80	"	"	£100	6
£100	"	"	£120	7
£120	"	"	£150	8
£150	"	"	£200	9
£200	"	"	£300	0
£300	"	"	£500	X
£500 and over			Y

APPENDIX C

Recommendations of the Adams Committee on Civil Judicial Statistics for improvement of the statistics relating to matrimonial proceedings in magistrates' courts

DOMESTIC PROCEEDINGS

(A) *Matrimonial*

The number of applications and orders should be given showing:

- (*a*) Summonses
    - (i) not served
    - (ii) withdrawn
    - (iii) struck out
    - (iv) dismissed
    - (v) dismissed, but order made in respect of children.
    - (vi) otherwise disposed of.
- (*b*) Applications proved and orders made.
    The details under (*a*)(v) and (*b*) to include
- (*c*) The number of orders containing provisions for
    - (i) non-cohabitation
    - (ii) the maintenance of wife or husband and/or children
    - (iii) the custody of children
    - (iv) the care of children
    - (v) the supervision of children.
- (*d*) The tables of summonses and orders should show whether on the wife's or husband's complaint.
- (*e*) The following information concerning hearings resulting in an order should also be given.
    - (i) the length of the marriage
    - (ii) the number of dependant children
    - (iii) the ages of the children
    - (iv) the grounds on which the order was made.

(*f*) Original amounts ordered to be paid for maintenance should be shown in bands of ten shillings. The amounts for wives and children should be separately shown.

(B) *Guardianship*
  The number of applications and orders should be given showing:

(*a*) Summonses
  (i)   not served
  (ii) withdrawn
  (iii) struck out
  (iv) dismissed.
(*b*) Applications proved and order made
(*c*) Applications by fathers and by mothers should be shown separately.
(*d*) The following information should also be included:
  (i)   the number of children to which the proceedings relate
  (ii) ages of children
  (iii) original amount ordered to be paid for maintenance shown in bands of ten shillings.

(C) *Affiliation*
  The following should be given

(*a*) The number of applications and orders as in (B) (*a*) and (*b*) above.
(*b*) The amount ordered to be paid in bands of ten shillings.
(*c*) The number of appeals to Quarter Sessions.
(*d*) The results of such appeals.

(D) *Variation, Enforcement, etc.*
  Under each of the above headings (A), (B) and (C) the following should be shown:

(*a*) Variation. The following should be given:
  (i)   the number of applications
  (ii) the number of orders for variation of
    (*a*) maintenance
    (*b*) other matters.
(*b*) Revocation. The number of orders should be given
(*c*) Enforcement. The number of orders should be given for:
  (i)   attachment of earnings.
  (ii) committal
  (iii) remission of arrears
  (iv) other remedies

(E) *Proceedings under Maintenance Orders Acts*
    The numbers of orders should be given:
- (i)   registered under the Maintenance Order (Facilities for Enforcement) Act 1920
- (ii) confirmed or transmitted for registration under the above Act
- (iii) registered under the Maintenance Orders Act 1950.

(F) *Consent to Marry under Section 3 of the Marriage Act 1949*
    The following should be given:
- (*a*) the number of applications by
  - (i)   males
  - (ii) females
- (*b*) the results of such applications.

(G) *Collecting Office*
- (*a*) The number of orders live during the year, (i.e. on which payment has been made or enforcement proceedings taken) should be given.
- (*b*) The amount of money paid through the Court should be given, subdivided as to payments to:
  - (i)   wives, former wives, mothers, etc.
  - (ii) local authorities
  - (iii) Ministry of Social Security
  - (iv) Others.

APPENDIX D

Model court record form

DOMESTIC PROCEEDINGS

APPLICANT's full name..
Address..

SPOUSE's full name..
Address..

Date of marriage.. Place of marriage..............

Matrimonial home at...

Children of Family (to include dependants under 21).

(a) CHILDREN OF BOTH PARTIES.

Christian names.	Surname.	Date of Birth.	Sex.

(b) OTHER CHILDREN OF FAMILY.

Christian names.	Surname.	Date of birth.	Sex.	Status.

Parent of Child of Family (not a party).

Full name ....

Address ....

Relationship ....

Previous interviews ....

....

....Serial No. ....

Previous matrimonial proceedings (dates to be verified) ....

....

....

....

Previous proceedings before any Court in respect of any child of the family.

Name of Child.	Date of proceedings.	Nature of proceedings.	Result.

Solicitor for the Applicant ....

Solicitor for the Spouse ....

Occupation, employer and details of earnings of parties and particulars of out-of-pocket expenses, etc.

	APPLICANT.	SPOUSE.
Occupation		
Employer		
Net Wage		
Family allowance		
National assistance		
Unemployment benefit		
Pension		
Other income		
Travelling		
Clubs and H.P.		
County Court debt		
Nursery or child minder		
Other expenditure		

Rent of matrimonial home ....

Mortgage repayments ....

Rates ....

LEGAL AID.

	APPLICANT.	SPOUSE.
Date applied for		
Granted or refused		
Solicitor appointed		

APPLICANT'S ALLEGATIONS.

GROUND OF COMPLAINT (strike out those not applicable).

  (a) Desertion (from ....).

  (b) Persistent cruelty   (i) to complainant.
                                  (ii) to infant child of complainant.
                                  (iii) to infant child of defendant (child of family).

  (c) Found guilty of   (i) assault on indictment.
                                  (ii) assault. Section .... Offences Against the Person Act.
                                  (iii) Offence (or attempt) against infant child of complainant or defendant.
                                          Section .... of (Sexual Offences Act) or (Indecency with Children Act).
                         (Particulars of conviction to be supplied and entered hereunder).

  (d) Adultery (particulars to be supplied and entered hereunder).

  (e) Intercourse knowing suffering from venereal disease.

  (f) Habitual drunkard or drug addict.

  (g) Compelling wife to submit to prostitution.

  (h) Neglect to maintain wife or child of family.

  (i) Wife neglecting husband or child of family.

Particulars :

Justice hearing application ....

Date of application...

Decision—Summons to issue on ground(s) ....
....
....

Notice under Rule 3. ⎫
                         ⎬ *(Delete where not applicable).*
Notice under Rule 4. ⎭

Probation Officer to see parties.

Probation Officer appointed..

Date Probation Officer supplied with facts ....

Date Probation Officer's report received..

DATE OF HEARING...

Justices sitting ....

Result..

....

APPENDIX E

News of the World *sample questionnaires*

Enquiry into the Matrimonial Jurisdiction of Magistrates' Courts

(a) POSTAL EVIDENCE FROM HUSBANDS

1. What year did you and your wife separate? ....
2. How long had you been married? ....
3. (a) How many children were there at the time? ....
   (b) What were their ages? ....
4. Does your wife have custody of your children?

           No   Yes

                                       (Please tick)

   (If there are no children, please leave this question.)

   If 'Yes', are you able to see them as often as you would like to?

           No   Yes

                                       (Please tick)

   If 'No', why not? ....
   ....
   ....
   Do you have custody of any children? ....
5. (a) Did you leave your wife?
   (b) Did your wife leave you?

                                       (Please tick)
6. When your marriage broke down, did you go to anyone for help and advice? (Doctor, Clergyman, Citizens' Advice Bureau, Family Service Unit, Probation Officer, Solicitor, Magistrate, or Court Clerk, a relation or friend other than already mentioned. If anybody else, please name.)
   ....
   ....
7. (a) Did your wife take you to the Magistrates' Court?

           Yes   No

                                         (Please tick)

(*b*) If so, when ?...
....

8. How much notice were you given by the court of the court hearing ?
....
....

9. Were you represented at court by a solicitor or a barrister ?

    No   Yes

                                              (Please tick)

    (*b*) If 'No', would you have liked to be represented ?
    ....
    ....
    ....

10. (*a*) If the court hearing was after May 1961, did you obtain legal aid for this hearing ?

         Yes   No

                                              (Please tick)

    (*b*) If you did obtain legal aid, did you have to pay back some of the court costs ?
    ....
    ....
    ....

    (*c*) If (*a*) is 'No', did you know you might have been able to obtain legal aid ?
    ....
    ....

11. (*a*) Did the atmosphere of the court assist towards a fair hearing ?
    ....
    ....
    ....

    (*b*) Do you feel you had a fair hearing ?
    ....
    ....
    ....
    ....

    (*c*) If not, in what respect did it appear unfair to you ?
    ....
    ....
    ....

12. (*a*) Was your wife awarded a maintenance order against you ?

         Yes   No

                                              (Please tick)

    If so, how much ?
    (1) for your wife ....
    (2) for your children (if any) ....

(*b*) What were your work and earnings at the time of the hearing?

....

....

....

(*c*) Do you think the amount the magistrates asked you to pay was fair?

Yes   No

(Please tick)

If not, why not?   ....

....

....

....

....

....

13. Would you have preferred a private agreement to pay maintenance voluntarily instead of a court order?

....

....

....

14. (*a*) Have you been unemployed or sick since the maintenance order was made?

Yes   No

(Please tick)

(*b*) If "Yes", did you go on paying the order, or did you ask the court to reduce the amount?

....

....

....

....

15. Are the court officials generally helpful when you ask advice about the order against you?

....

....

16. In your dealings with the court, what do you:

(1) like best ....

....

(2) dislike most...

....

....

....

17. Do you have to keep any other persons who depend upon you?

Yes   No

(Please tick)

If so, please give details

....

....

....

18. Are there any other comments you would like to make ?

....

....

....

....

(*b*) POSTAL EVIDENCE FROM WIVES

Number
1. What year did you and your husband separate ? ....
2. How long had you been married ?   ....
3. How many children were there at the time ?   ....
   What were their ages ?   ....
4. (*a*)   Did you leave your husband ?
   (*b*)   Did your husband leave you ?

(Please tick)

5. When your marriage broke down, to whom did you first go for help and advice ? (Doctor, Clergyman, Citizens' Advice Bureau, Family Service Unit, Probation Officer, Solicitor, Magistrate or Court Clerk, a relation or friend other than already mentioned. If anybody else, please name.)

....

....

6. Who advised you to go to court, or did you know yourself that you could go there to obtain a maintenance order ? ....

....

....

7. What year did the court hearing take place ?   ....
8. If you did not take your husband to court, why was this ?
   Please tick:
   (*a*)   Too expensive
   (*b*)   Dislike of the court and the law
   (*c*)   Hope for his return
   (*d*)   Private maintenance agreement made between you and your husband
   (*e*)   Any other reason—please state:

....

....

9. (*a*) If you have a private agreement, why did you decide to have a private agreement?

....

....

....

   (*b*) Has the agreement worked well?

....

....

....

   (*c*) If it has not worked well, why not?

....

....

....

10. (*a*) Did the magistrates issue a summons against your husband immediately you applied to them?

....

   (*b*) If not, what reasons did they give for a delay, and how long after you applied did they issue a summons for your husband to appear in court?

....

....

....

11. (*a*) If the court hearing was after May 1961, did you obtain legal aid for this hearing?...

   (*b*) If "no", did you know you might have been able to obtain legal aid?

....

....

12. (*a*) Did the atmosphere of the court assist towards a fair hearing?

....

....

....

   (*b*) Do you feel you had a fair hearing?

....

....

....

....

   (*c*) If not, in what respect did it appear unfair to you?

....

....

....

13. What was your husband's work, and what were his earnings at the time of the hearing?

....

....

14. (*a*) What was the amount in maintenance awarded by the magistrates,
  (1) for you...
  (2) for your children (if any)   ....

  (*b*) Do you think this fair ?
  ....
  ....
  ....

  (*c*) Do you think your husband could have paid more ?
  ....
  ....
  ....

15. (*a*) Have you been short of money since your husband left ?
  ....
  ....

  (*b*) If so, please give details   ....
  ....
  ....
  ....

16. Do you have to get extra money by working ? ....
  If so, please tick: (1) Part-time
                        (2) Full-time

17. Have you applied for National Assistance since your husband left ?.........
  If so, did you find them: (Please tick)
          (1) Helpful to you and your children's needs ?
          (2) Not caring, and only helping when they had to ?
          (3) Unpleasant ?
  If (2) or (3) applies, please give your reasons:
  ....
  ....
  ....

18. (*a*) Have you ever been refused help by the N.A.B. ?   ....
        If so, please give details:
  ....
  ....
  ....
  ....

  (*b*) If your husband does not pay what he owes, what do you do ?
  ....
  ....
  ....

19. Are the court officials generally helpful in letting you know of the payment or non-payment of your maintenance orders ?
  ....
  ....

20. In your dealings with the court, what do you:
    (1) like best ....
    (2) dislike most...
....

21. Are there any other comments you would like to make?

....
....
....
....

(c) INTERVIEW INFORMATION FROM HUSBANDS AND WIVES

Instructions to interviewer

Explain the project's aims and purpose—that we wish to obtain an accurate picture of the problems faced by a married man when his marriage breaks up. Stress confidentiality.

Questions marked with an asterisk (*) are the important ones and should be completed if possible.

Questions to husbands
    MARRIAGE
*1. (a) When did you marry your wife? ....
    (b) How long did the marriage last before your wife obtained a maintenance order against you?

....

*2. Where did the marriage take place?
    (a) In a church: (1) Roman Catholic
                  (2) Protestant
                  (3) Jewish synagogue
                  (4) If of other religious belief, please state
    (b) In a Registry Office
3. How long had you known your wife before you were married?

....

4. Did you become engaged before you married?
            (1) No   (2) Yes
    If "yes", how long did the engagement last?
               (1) Under 3 months
               (2) 3 to 6 months
               (3) 6 to 9 months
               (4) 9 to 12 months
               (5) 1 to 2 years
               (6) Over 2 years

....

COURT HEARING AND PROCEDURE

*5. (*a*) How long did you have to wait in the Court waiting-room before the hearing began ?

....

   (*b*) Were there many other people waiting ? (i.e. for criminal cases or other domestic hearings.)

....

....

*6. How long did the Court hearing take ?

....

....

7. (*a*) Did you know beforehand what the Court procedure would be ? (Was the hearing as you expected it to be ?)

....

....

....

   (*b*) If so, who had advised you ? (Friend, Court Clerk, Probation Officer, etc.)

....

....

*8. If your wife could (how does he know ?) live reasonable on less maintenance, what action—if any—would you take ? (To find out if husband knows about variation procedure.)

....

....

....

....

*9. If you are sick or unemployed and are unable to pay, what do you do ? (i.e. contact Clerk, nothing, etc.)

....

....

....

....

....

*10. Have you been able to pay regularly ?

....

If not, is this because of financial reasons, or because you feel bitter about having to pay ?

....

....

....

*11. What aspects, if any, of the Court procedure would you like to see changed?

....

....

....

....

....

*12. How many times have you actually appeared before the Magistrates in connection with this order?

....

....

*13. Have you been threatened with imprisonment for non-payment

....

If so, how? ....

....

....

....

14. (*a*) Have you ever been to prison for non-payment? ....
If "yes", how did your going to prison affect your work and private life?

....

....

(*b*) If "yes", what were your experiences and impressions of prison?

....

....

15. Has an attachment order ever been made against you?
      (1) No   (2) Yes
If yes, did you welcome this? ....

WORK AND INCOME

16. What is your present occupation and income?

....

....

17. Has the existence of the order made any difference to your work? (i.e. change of job, over-time, had to give up job as cannot keep up the struggle?)

....

....

....

18. What is your net income per week? (Explain "net", i.e. after deductions.)
                    Under £10 per week
                    £10 to £15 per week
                    £15 to £20 per week

£20 to £25 per week
Over £25 per week

....
....

If over-time is worked, how much income ?

19. How does your wife's earnings compare with your own at the present time ?

....
....

*20. Did you give your wife any money before she obtained the Court Order against you ?

        (1) No   (2) Yes

....
....

21. Have you ever given your wife any money other than that ordered by the Court ?

        (1) No   (2) Yes

22. Have you ever given your wife and the children presents since you separated ?

        Wife
        Children

....
....

BREAKDOWN OF MARRIAGE

23. When the marriage showed signs of strain, were you given practical help and/or advice by anyone ?

    e.g. 1. Your relatives
          2. Your wife's relatives
          3. Friends
          4. A professional person whom you already knew (doctor, clergyman, etc.)
          5. Probation officer
          6. Marriage guidance counsellor
          7. Any other social worker

Please give details ....
....
....
....
....
....

*24. What do you think caused the marriage to break down ?

    e.g. 1. Financial difficulties
          2. Friction with relatives

3. Inadequate housing
4. Your ill-health
5. Wife's ill-health
6. Sexual incompatability
7. Wife's inability to face up to her responsibilities
8. Your inability to face up to your responsibilities
9. Wife's association with another man
10. Your association with another woman
11. Disagreements over the children
12. Lack of common interests

Please give details ....

....

....

....

....

*25. What do you feel are the main problems which you have to face as a husband living apart from his wife? (e.g. financial, loneliness, absence of children, etc.)

....

....

....

*26. (*a*) Have you since regretted the breakdown of your marriage?

      1. No   2. Yes

    Give reasons ....

    ....

(*b*) Would you have welcomed the chance for reconciliation before the Court hearing began?

      1. No   2. Yes

(*c*) Do you feel the Court hearing gave any encouragement to reconciliation?

      1. No   2. Yes

(*d*) Would you like you and your wife to come together again?

      1. No   2. Yes

27. Do you feel your health suffered as a result of this separation?

      1. No   2. Yes

*28. Has any friendship developed between you and another woman since you and your wife parted? (Probe gently! We really want to know if he is living with and supporting another woman.)

      1. No   2. Yes

If "Yes":

(*a*) Do you live with this woman?

      1. No   2. Yes

(*b*)   How long has this association lasted ?

....

....

(*c*)   Is the woman: (1) single, or (2) married ?
(*d*)   Was she the reason you left your wife ?
        1. No   2. Yes
(*e*)   Does she now work ?
        1. No   2. Yes
If "Yes", how much does she earn per week ?

....

....

....

(*f*)   Are there any children of which you and this lady are the parents ?
        1. No   2. Yes
If "Yes", how old are they ?

....

....

(*g*)   Do you support any children of which she is the mother ?

....

....

DIVORCE

*29.   Would you consider re-marrying if you were free to do so ?
        1. No   2. Yes
*30.   Have you ever thought of obtaining a divorce ?
        1. No   2. Yes
If "Yes", have you taken any legal advice, i.e. consulted a solicitor or the Citizen's Advice Bureau ?
        1. No   2. Yes
*31.   Do your religious views debar you from applying for a divorce ?
        1. No   2. Yes

....

....

*32.   If you would like to obtain a divorce, why have you not done so ?

....

....

33.   What sort of problems do you imagine you would have to face in connection with your responsibilities towards your present wife and children in the event of your remarrying ?

....

....

....

CHILDREN OF THE FAMILY (if any)

34. Do you feel that the maintenance you pay ought to be only for the children?

        1. No   2. Yes

....
....

35. How do you feel your children (of the marriage) have been affected by the breakdown of your marriage?
    1. They have suffered a great deal
    2. They have suffered a little
    3. I have not noticed any effect
    4. They are not affected at all
    5. They are better off than they were before

....
....
....

36. How often do you see your children?

....

37. If you do see them, does your wife welcome this?

        1. No   2. Yes

....

38. Do you feel that the maintenance order enforcement discourages you from visiting them?

        1. No   2. Yes

....
....

39. If your wife remarried, do you think the children would be:

        1. Better off, or   2. worse off?

....
....

HOUSE AND PROPERTY

40. What type of housing accommodation did you have after you were married?

....
....

41. Did you have to live with your parents?:   1

                        in-laws: 2

            Does not apply,

                    i.e. no: 3

    For how long a period of time was this?

....
....

*42. Have you stayed in the house your wife and you were living in ?

....
....
....

FINANCE

*43. Did you have expenses directly as a result of the breakdown of your marriage (e.g. moving house, etc.) Give details:

....
....

*44. Did you have to move into cheaper accommodation after your marriage broke down ?

....
....

*45. Have you turned to anybody for financial help ? (i.e. N.A.B. or any other welfare organization to whom he might have applied.)

....

46. If yes, to whom, and details of this contact. (Were they helpful ?)

....
....

47. Has it been more of a financial struggle for you to maintain your home and children since the breakdown ?

....
....

48. Do you have any other income other than from your work ?

....
....

49. Do you have any money left over to spend on luxuries ? (i.e. on entertainment, holidays, etc.)

....
....

50. Since your separation, have you had regular holidays ? (i.e. every year)

....
....

TAXATION

*51. Have you had any taxation problems with regard to your maintenance order ?

....

GENERAL

52. Are you in close touch with your family? (i.e. parents, brothers and sisters, other relatives)

....

....

53. Do you find this a friendly neighbourhood to live in?

....

54. (Does the husband appear to go out very much? Has he friends, contacts?)

....

*55. Do you find the welfare agencies in this area helpful? (Do not probe or help.)

....

....

56. (What is your—the interviewer's—impression of the condition of the home?)

....

....

....

GENERAL NOTES

(d) ADDITIONAL INFORMATION REQUESTED FROM WIVES

Question

No.

MARRIAGE

5. Were your parents happily married?

HUSBAND

6. (a) Was your husband in regular employment during your marriage?

(b) If not, why did he change his job?

7. (a) Did he give you enough housekeeping money?

(b) Did you receive the money regularly?

8. Was he willing to discuss money matters with you?

COURT PROCEDURE

16. What do you think the court should do if your husband does not pay?

WORK AND INCOME

46. What job were you doing when you married.

How much were you earning per week?

47.   Did you have a job after you married?

48.   Have you had a job since you and your husband parted? Details.

CHILDREN OF THE FAMILY

38.   Are there any children working?
       Are they living with you? Do they give you anything. If so, how much?

39.   Are there any children over 16 years of age still studying?

40.   Have any of the children been in care of the local authority?

41.   Who looks after the children if you work?

The following questions were asked only of husbands:
Question numbers 12, 13, 14, 15, 17, 19, 28, 34, 39, 48

APPENDIX F

Comparison of data in the News *of the* World
survey and the main magistrates' courts survey

We have been able to compare directly (i) the social class of husbands, (ii) the types of order made by magistrates, and (iii) the amounts awarded to children.

(i) Social class

Social Class	News of the World No.	%	Magistrates' Courts No.	%
I	0	0	5	1
II	30	7	41	5
III	216	53	422	50
IV	78	19	166	19
V	41	10	142	17
VI	43	11	65	8
Total	408	100	841	100
% not known		33		32

(ii) Type of maintenance order made

Type of order	News of the World No.	%	Magistrates' Courts No.	%
Wife only	141	26	355	39
Wife and child	323	60	627	51
Child only	78	14	248	20
Total	542	100	1,230	100

(iii) Amounts awarded to children

Amount payable	News of the World No.	%	Magistrates' Courts No.	%
Under 15s.	31	8	15	5
15s. but under £1 15s. ...	100	27	121	43
£1 15s. but under £2 15s.	97	26	87	30
£2 15s. but under £4 10s.	74	19	44	15
£4 10s. but under £6 10s.	60	16	18	6
£6 10s. and over ..	14	4	4	1
Total	376	100	289	100

APPENDIX G

Definitions of the different types of orders for the maintenance of women* and/or their dependant children used in this book

---

(*a*) MATRIMONIAL ORDERS

Matrimonial orders are strictly defined as orders made under section 2 of the Matrimonial Proceedings (Magistrates' Courts) Act 1960, which codified the earlier statutes giving magistrates power to make maintenance and separation orders. Matrimonial orders may include provision for the custody of and access to children as well as for the maintenance of the complainant and her dependant children. For the purposes of this book, matrimonial orders are more loosely defined as orders for the maintenance of wives and/or their dependant children.

(*b*) MARRIED WOMEN ORDERS

Married women orders is a phrase frequently used both in a general sense synonymous with matrimonial orders as defined in (*a*) above and in a narrower sense to denote orders directing payments to married women in respect of their maintenance alone.

(*c*) GUARDIANSHIP OF INFANTS AND CHILDREN ONLY ORDERS

The High Court, the county courts and magistrates' courts have power to order payments to wives in respect of their dependant children and irrespective of any matrimonial fault on their part. Maintenance can be ordered in the course of an application for custody. Before 1960, wives commonly applied to magistrates' courts under both the Summary Jurisdiction (Maintenance and Separation) Acts and the Guardianship of Infants Acts in order

---

* Wives may now be ordered on all relevant grounds to pay maintenance to their husbands. This rarely occurs. In practice, almost invariably applicants for maintenance are wives.

to obtain maintenance for their children under the latter if their applications failed under the former. Under the Matrimonial Proceedings (Magistrates' Courts) Act 1960, magistrates are bound to consider the welfare and maintenance of children upon wives' applications, and a separate guardianship application is no longer necessary. In such case the order is described as a Children Only order.

(*d*) AFFILIATION ORDERS

Under the Affiliation Proceedings Act 1957 orders can be made against fathers in respect of the maintenance of their illegitimate children.

(*e*) POOR LAW ORDERS

These were orders made under the Poor Law Acts before 1948 against relatives liable to reimburse the Poor Law authorities in respect of expenditure incurred in maintaining members of their families.

(*f*) NATIONAL ASSISTANCE AND SOCIAL SECURITY ORDERS

These are orders made under the National Assistance Act 1948 and its successor, the Ministry of Social Security Act 1966, which require husbands and wives to reimburse the social security authorities in respect of assistance or benefit provided for each other or for their children, legitimate or illegitimate.

(*g*) CHILDREN AND YOUNG PERSONS ORDERS

These are orders (often called contribution orders) for the payment of maintenance under the Children and Young Persons Act 1933 by parents to local authorities in respect of children committed to the care of a fit person or sent to approved schools, and for the payment to local authorities of sums due under affiliation orders. In practice, such applications are usually brought by local authorities against parents whose children have been taken into care.

(*h*) LIVE ORDERS

These are any of the above orders currently in force. For the purposes of this research, live orders were those in force on 1st January 1966, whatever the date on which they had been made.

INDEX